Understanding
JULIO CORTÁZAR

Understanding Modern
European and Latin American
Literature

James Hardin, *Series Editor*

volumes on

Ingeborg Bachmann
Samuel Beckett
Thomas Bernhard
Johannes Bobrowski
Heinrich Böll
Italo Calvino
Albert Camus
Elias Canetti
Camilo José Cela
Céline
Julio Cortázar
José Donoso
Friedrich Dürrenmatt
Rainer Werner Fassbinder
Max Frisch
Federico García Lorca
Gabriel García Márquez
Juan Goytisolo
Günter Grass

Gerhart Hauptmann
Christoph Hein
Hermann Hesse
Eugène Ionesco
Uwe Johnson
Milan Kundera
Primo Levi
Boris Pasternak
Octavio Paz
Luigi Pirandello
Graciliano Ramos
Erich Maria Remarque
Alain Robbe-Grillet
Jean-Paul Sartre
Claude Simon
Mario Vargas Llosa
Peter Weiss
Franz Werfel
Christa Wolf

UNDERSTANDING

JULIO
CORTÁZAR

PETER STANDISH

UNIVERSITY OF SOUTH CAROLINA PRESS

UNIVERSITY OF SOUTH CAROLINA *BICENTENNIAL*

© 2001 University of South Carolina

Published in Columbia, South Carolina, by the
University of South Carolina Press

Manufactured in the United States of America

05 04 03 02 01   5 4 3 2 1

Library of Congress Cataloging-in-Publication Data
Standish, Peter.
  Understanding Julio Cortázar / Peter Standish.
    p.   cm. — (Understanding modern European and Latin American literature)
  Includes bibliographical references and index.
  ISBN 1-57003-390-0
  1. Cortázar, Julio—Criticism and interpretation. I. Title. II. Series.
PQ7797.C7145 Z793   2001
863'.64—dc21   00-012030

. . . it was a matter of achieving the appropriate degree of correction in order to ensure that the subject was properly framed, without the photographer's shadow treading on his toes.

Julio Cortázar, "Los pasos en las huellas"

Contents

Editor's Preface

Understanding Modern European and Latin American Literature has been planned as a series of guides for undergraduate and graduate students and nonacademic readers. Like the volumes in its companion series *Understanding Contemporary American Literature,* these books provide introductions to the lives and writings of prominent modern authors and explicate their most important works.

Modern literature makes special demands, and this is particularly true of foreign literature, in which the reader must contend not only with unfamiliar, often arcane artistic conventions and philosophical concepts, but also with the handicap of reading the literature in translation. It is a truism that the nuances of one language can be rendered in another only imperfectly (and this problem is especially acute in fiction), but the fact that the works of European and Latin American writers are situated in a historical and cultural setting quite different from our own can be as great a hindrance to the understanding of these works as the linguistic barrier. For this reason the *UMELL* series emphasizes the sociological and historical background of the writers treated. The philosophical and cultural traditions peculiar to a given culture may be particularly important for an understanding of certain authors, and these are taken up in the introductory chapter and also in the discussion of those works to which this information is relevant. Beyond this, the books treat the specifically literary aspects of the author under discussion and attempt to explain the complexities of contemporary literature lucidly. The books are conceived as introductions to the authors covered, not as comprehensive analyses. They do not provide detailed summaries of plot because they are meant to be used in conjunction with the books they treat, not as a substitute for study of the original works. The purpose of the books is to provide information and judicious literary assessment of the major works in the most compact, readable form. It is our hope that the *UMELL* series will help increase knowledge and understanding of European and Latin American cultures and will serve to make the literature of those cultures more accessible.

J. H.

A Prelude

The Library of Congress lists in its catalog about two hundred books by or about Julio Cortázar (1914–1984). A major bibliography devoted to him and published in 1985 had 2619 entries; now the total would probably run close to 4000. Cortázar published thirty or forty books, several of which were widely translated, and he has been much analyzed, commented upon, and criticized ever since he first achieved recognition in the early fifties. Cortázar is significant for three reasons: the quality of much of his literary output, especially his short stories and one of his novels, the variety of that output, much of which cannot easily be described in terms of traditional literary genres, and the fact that comparatively late in his life he became politically involved and a prominent and controversial figure.

In a number of respects Cortázar was unusual. Although he was modest and private by nature, his personality, or, to be more exact, his inescapable *persona,* has become a major factor influencing the way in which his works have been read. One could say that unwittingly Cortázar has shown us how far the reading of any text is an activity that is colored by the reader's own cultural and ideological baggage.

Another element that must be allowed for in any consideration of Cortázar is the fact that he gave many published interviews, three of which were substantial enough to fill books. While Cortázar frequently said that whatever readers and critics saw in his works had its own legitimacy, his many comments about the processes of composition, about his attitude to his characters, and so forth, inevitably influence one's reading, even to the point of their seeming to constitute a "metatext." Although these interviews are enticing and revealing, they are in some ways prejudicial.

Cortázar was very much a man of his time, one who reflected its literary and historical imperatives. His popularity peaked in the sixties, and his most important novel, *Rayuela (Hopscotch),* published in 1963, is the focal point of his success. Yet nowadays, as one looks back to that period, at the feelings ranging from euphoria to outrage that arose as established institutions and mores were challenged, one realizes that a great deal of what at the time struck people as urgent, groundbreaking, and epochal has lost its immediacy, that what was controversial has become commonplace, that what once seemed vibrant and essential to so many who came of age in those years now seems passé to most. Now that nearly two decades have passed since the death of Cortázar, his works are taking on a new face. We can claim a certain distance from our subject, and we also read Cortázar in the light of a body of creative writing that has been amplified and modified, that has "moved on." Even reading *about* Cortázar is a changing experience, subject to critical fashions that come and go with what seems to be increasing rapidity.

These are the considerations that I have taken into account, while trying not simply to duplicate what has been said elsewhere. I have also kept firmly in mind that for many readers this book will be their introduction to Julio Cortázar and his work. Instead of attempting to discuss everything that Cortázar wrote, I have preferred a selective and illustrative approach, particularly as regards his many short stories. Quite a number of works by Cortázar were published posthumously; I have chosen to respect the chronology of publication, dealing with those in a separate chapter that follows the discussion of the main body of his work, even though most of the works that appeared posthumously were in fact composed early in Cortázar's literary career. They came into the public domain in the eighties and nineties, and so there is a sense in which the posthumous publications *are* late works. So far as the rest are concerned, thematic and formal considerations, as much as chronology, have determined my approach in this book.

Bearing in mind Cortázar's love of play (the "ludic") and of music, for my chapter titles I have preferred "prelude" to "preface" and "postlude" to "conclusion." Gentle and considerate as he was, one of Cortázar's more puzzling passions was for boxing; he wrote about boxing, set some stories in boxing environments, and titled one of his most important books *Último round* (The final round). That passion, combined with another, his love of games with words, explains why I have also played with boxing terminology:

"Sparring Session" presents a brief overview of Cortázar's life and work.

"The Weigh-In" deals with his early creative works.

"Winning by a Knockout" draws largely on the short-story collections in order to illustrate key thematic and stylistic features of his work.

"Break" briefly discusses Cortázar's poetics, especially his ideas about the short story, language, and genre. Cortázar spoke of stories winning by a knockout, and of novels having to win on points. Thus this chapter provides a bridge between the preceding and following chapters, which cover works in each of those two genres.

"Winning on Points" covers the first three novels that Cortázar published, dealing at greatest length with *Rayuela* (*Hopscotch*).

"The Brawl Outside" considers changes in Cortázar's political awareness, the resulting tensions between politics and aesthetics, the role of the Latin American intellectual, but above all Cortázar's "political literature."

"The Final Round (and Much More)" deals with the considerable body of miscellaneous creative works, including his poetry.

"Down, but Not Out" discusses the posthumous publications, including drama.

Throughout this book, unless otherwise indicated, page references to works by Cortázar refer to the editions published by Alfaguara. In keeping with the norms of the series, quotations in the original language have been kept to a minimum, confined to cases where the original words seem particularly illustrative. Translations are my own.

The selective bibliography lists all major works by Cortázar, as well as book-length translations of his works into English. Otherwise, once again in keeping with the norms of the series, it lists only works cited. In this connection, it should be borne in mind that in writing my account of Cortázar I have only sparingly called on the work of other critics. I have preferred not to attempt to provide a digest of the countless works of criticism on Cortázar. The results of such a digest would no doubt be stifling for all concerned, and in any case the reader has a right to expect something more than second-hand views. Most of this book, then, consists of my own analyses, rather than being the product of a systematic trawl through the writings of other critics. Nonetheless, it would be foolish and dishonest to imply that my ideas have not been affected by countless works of criticism written by others. More important, I believe that the greatest satisfaction (and perhaps the greatest hope of originality) is to be found in discovering things for oneself, or at least in the illusion that one is doing so. If this is true for me, then it applies no less to my readers; therefore I hope that they will find this study helpful, but that it will not sabotage their own opportunities for discovery.

Finally, a word of acknowledgment to my wife, who read the manuscript, pointed out places where I was woolly or pompous, and above all put up with all those times when I was "on the other side."

Chronology

1914	Julio Florencio Cortázar is born on 26 August in Brussels, of Argentine parents.
1918	His family returns to Argentina and lives in Banfield, a town on the outskirts of Buenos Aires. Shortly after, his father abandons the family.
1932	Cortázar qualifies as a primary school teacher.
1935	He qualifies as a secondary school teacher.
1936	He begins studies at the University of Buenos Aires but a year later abandons university and starts work as a teacher, first in Bolívar and then in Chivilcoy, two towns in the province of Buenos Aires.
1938	Cortázar publishes a book of poems (*Presencia*) under the pseudonym of Julio Denis.
1944	He is invited to teach literature at the new University of Cuyo (Mendoza, Argentina).
1946	Unhappy with political pressures in the university, Cortázar resigns and moves back to Buenos Aires, where he manages a publishers' association.
1947	He qualifies as an official translator.
1949	The first book to appear under his real name is published: the play *Los reyes*.
1951	Having been granted a scholarship by the French government, Cortázar goes to Paris. France will be his country of residence for the rest of his life. He publishes his first collection of stories (*Bestiario*) and a translation of *Little Women*.
1953	Cortázar spends some time in Italy, marries fellow Argentine Aurora Bernárdez, and begins work as a translator for UNESCO.
1956	His second collection of stories appears under the title *Final del juego*. He publishes a translation into Spanish of the complete prose works of Edgar Allan Poe.
1959	Cortázar publishes *Las armas secretas,* a collection of short stories.

1960	His first novel appears: *Los premios.* He travels to the United States for the first time.
1962	He publishes *Historias de cronopios y de famas.*
1963	*Rayuela,* Cortázar's most important novel, is published. He makes his first trip to Castro's Cuba.
1964	An amplified edition of *Final del juego* is published.
1966	The stories of *Todos los fuegos el fuego* appear. Antonioni's film *Blow-up* is released, based on an earlier Cortázar story.
1967	Cortázar's first "miscellany" appears: *La vuelta al día en ochenta mundos.*
1968	He publishes the novel *62: Modelo para armar.*
1969	The second major miscellany, *Último round,* appears.
1970	The texts of important political debates in which Cortázar was a participant are published in *Viaje alrededor de una mesa* and *Literatura en la revolución y revolución en la literatura.* Cortázar's short stories to date are gathered and reorganized into three (later augmented to four) volumes, under the title *Relatos.*
1971	Friends persuade Cortázar to publish his selected poetry; it appears under the title *Pameos y meopas.*
1972	*Prosa del observatorio* is published, inspired by a visit to India.
1973	*Libro de Manuel,* Cortázar's fourth and most controversial novel appears, angering people of both the right and the left.
1974	He publishes *Octaedro,* another collection of short stories. He is awarded the Prix Médicis for *Libro de Manuel* and gives the prize money to support the legal defense of political prisoners in South America. He begins his activities as a member of the Russell Tribunal on human rights.
1975	In an attempt to give greater publicity to the Russell Tribunal's deliberations, Cortázar publishes *Fantomas contra los vampiros multinacionales.*
1977	More short stories appear under the title *Alguien que anda por ahí,* in Mexico and Spain. The book is banned by the military regime in Argentina, and Cortázar's exile ceases to be voluntary.
1978	Cortázar publishes *Territorios,* one of the most important of his books relating to visual art.
1979	*Un tal Lucas* appears. Cortázar begins his intense involvement with Nicaragua, supporting the revolutionaries.
1980	He publishes his penultimate book of short stories: *Queremos tanto a Glenda.*
1981	Cortázar is granted French citizenship.

1982	His second wife, Carol Dunlop, dies of leukemia. Cortázar publishes his last collection of stories, *Deshoras*.
1983	He publishes *Los autonautas de la cosmopista* and *Nicaragua, tan violentamente dulce.*
1984	Julio Cortázar dies in Paris on 12 February and is buried there, in Montparnasse.

CHAPTER 1

Sparring Session

Cortázar's Life and Works

Julio Cortázar (1914–1984) was, as one critic put it, a writer of the stature of Borges but one who was able to bridge the gap between abstract intellectual activity and human sentiment.[1] He died after spending half his life in France, but by parentage he was Argentine, he was educated in Argentina, and he wrote his creative works almost always in a perfectly accessible, but distinctly Argentine, variety of Spanish. With the exception of Jorge Luis Borges, the doyen of twentieth-century Latin American letters, he is the one Argentine author who has had the widest influence on world literature. There are other reasons to link the name of Cortázar with that of Borges: the latter recognized the younger man's talent and afforded him a publishing outlet that helped bring him to readers' attention. The two were never close friends, and, as the years passed, a political gulf between them became visible; but Cortázar was quick to acknowledge the influence on him of Borges's short and highly disciplined fictions. Cortázar wrote a great deal, even from an early age, but chose not to publish much of it until he was well into his thirties, preferring to wait until he felt sure that he was producing work that met his own high standards.

That Cortázar began and ended his life in Europe is a matter of crucial importance if one is to understand his literature and the attitudes of some of his critics. At the time of his birth, his father was an economist attached to the Argentine embassy in Brussels. The year was 1914, the start of the First World War; Belgium was occupied by the Germans, so the family sought refuge first in Switzerland and then in Spain, before moving back to Argentina when Julio was about four. Though his father's family was Basque in origin, his mother's included French and German elements. In Europe, French had been the language the family used at home, with the result that the children arrived in Argentina not knowing Spanish. A year or two after their return to Argentina, the father abandoned his family. Julio would never see him again and rarely mention him. Even in Cortázar's creative writings, father figures are conspicuously absent.

His mother struggled to make ends meet, and they continued to live in Banfield, a suburb of Buenos Aires, where the boy began his schooling. In the eyes of their schoolmates, he and his sister, Ofelia, were figures of fun; Julio, in particular, spoke with uvular "r" sounds that were more like the French ones (a speech characteristic that he would never lose). His awareness of being different combined with a natural introversion to make Julio see his home and the garden in Banfield as a happy refuge. Cortázar attributed his early interest in literature to his mother, whom, he recalled as someone who read widely, albeit undiscriminatingly, and was very imaginative apart from speaking several languages. If not reading, he would often play alone. He was close to his sister and mother—he would write regularly to his mother throughout his life—but also reserved a private world that was his alone. The child Julio was sensitive, deeply affected by experiences that others of his age seemed to take in their stride; examples he would remember in later life involved the death of a pet cat and instances of what he saw as betrayal of his absolute trust in others. Nor was he comfortable with the fact that his physical development (he was thin, lanky, well over six feet tall, and in later years disheveled in appearance) made him quite literally stand out among his peers, as, figuratively, did his interests in things that most of them viewed as appropriate only for girls. Cortázar's sensitivity as a child, as he admitted in a number of interviews, was to be reflected in the children who populate his works.

With the father gone, the household now consisted of Julio and women: his mother, his maternal grandmother, an aunt, and Ofelia, who recalls him being lost in the world of Jules Verne even at the age of six, having to be forced to come out of his room to eat. As a reader he was largely self-taught and so precocious in his reading habits that they took him to the doctor to see if there was anything wrong. There was, although only indirectly related to his reading: he suffered from asthma and therefore had a less active childhood than most. In 1975, in an interview with Elena Poniatowska, Cortázar said that he thought that he had been a "tiny metaphysical animal" even at the age of six or seven, and the fact that he seemed so often to be in a world of his own, a world of fantasy detached from the world around him, had bothered the adults.[2] Introversion and perhaps a certain hypochondria in the household at large also encouraged his reading. In an interview published in 1980, Cortázar spoke of how as a child he had devoured works that were intended for older people, quoting the example of Montaigne's essays, which he had tackled when only twelve years old.[3] But Tarzan was in the picture, along with detective stories and much else besides. One of the writers who most impressed him was Edgar Allan Poe, whose complete stories he would later translate into Spanish.

Despite a fine school record, economic considerations would limit Cortázar's post-secondary education. He spent the requisite seven years to qualify at the Mariano Acosta teacher training college, a famous and highly respected institution, though Cortázar's memories of it were none too complimentary: he saw it as a factory of received ideas and prejudices. Late in his life, when interviewed by Omar Prego,[4] he spoke of the gratitude he had felt toward two of his teachers from his days at the Mariano Acosta school, Arturo Marasso (who taught Greek and Spanish literatures) and Vicente Fattone (who taught philosophy). Beyond that, Cortázar felt that the place was a sham, but it had given him the chance to make some lifelong friendships. That period of teacher training also saw the growth of several of the interests that would become visible in Cortázar's works, such as mythology, art, oriental philosophy, and boxing. Another key interest was music; there had been plenty of music at home and his aunt was a music teacher, but during the teacher training years he discovered jazz. Methodical and meticulous in such matters, Cortázar compiled a card index for Greek mythology and another for jazz.

He qualified as a teacher in 1932 and went to work in towns in the province of Buenos Aires: Bolívar and, more important, Chivilcoy, which at that time was a community of about nine thousand inhabitants and had the distinction of being the place where the paved road ended. There, Cortázar taught almost anything but literature.[5] Evidently he was liked and respected by his pupils and by fellow teachers, but is remembered as a solitary person who spent long hours reading, perfecting his knowledge of English and German (some of the latter having come to him via his mother) and writing. In the Chivilcoy of those days cultural activity was very limited, so Cortázar would sometimes return to Buenos Aires for the weekend.

He had written from his earliest days at school, but well into adulthood he remained highly critical of his own work and for that reason reluctant to publish prematurely. Cortázar had seen other budding Argentine writers rush into print and live to regret it, and he preferred to wait until he felt he had satisfied his own exacting standards. In one of his last publications, *Salvo el crepúsculo* (1984, 168; Save twilight), a collection of poetry with occasional interpolated prose passages, he expresses his regret at having burned both a study on Pindar that he had written while at college and a six-hundred-page novel. The novel in question was called *Soliloquio* (Soliloquy); in the seventies Cortázar said to Ernesto González Bermejo simply that he had thought it too digressive and sentimental;[6] in *Salvo el crepúsculo* he refers to it as "noticeably homosexual."

Cortázar's first publication turned out to be a slim volume of sonnets with a very limited print run. The title was *Presencia* (Presence), and it appeared in 1938 under the pseudonym Julio Denis. Cortázar deprecated those poems in later years, saying that they betrayed too much influence of Mallarmé. During the early forties he also published one or two stories, mostly under this same pseudonym; the story that was the most indicative of what was to come, which appeared under the name of Julio F. Cortázar, was titled "Bruja" (Witch); it was published in Buenos Aires in 1944 in *Correo literario.*[7]

That same year, an acquaintance from Cortázar's days at college who now had a position of responsibility was organizing the new Universidad de Cuyo (located in Mendoza, the main city in the wine-growing region to the west, close to the Andes) and invited him to teach English and French literature there. The invitation came at an opportune moment, for it allowed Cortázar to escape the hostility of some people in authority who had come to see him as a dangerous left-winger. However, once in Mendoza, he met with a new kind of suspicion from people who thought he was too far to the political right. In fact, the Cortázar of those days was not a political animal, yet, in a small but curious way, this experience of antagonism emanating from different ends of the political spectrum in some way portends the serious political controversies in which the mature Cortázar would become embroiled years later. At that time, in Mendoza, Cortázar's relationship with his students was good, but he was uncomfortable with the nationalistic tendencies of the administration.

This was the period during which Juan Domingo Perón was rising in power. Perón was president for two nonconsecutive periods, the first running from 1946 to 1955. The rise of Perón, a paradoxical man, who turned out to be an immensely important phenomenon in twentieth-century Argentine history, was based on a combination of support from the military and from the working and lower-middle classes. He was involved in a deliberate, if crude and somewhat self-serving, campaign to integrate the population, shift the powerbase, and bring about some social reforms. Many of those who so fervently supported Perón were not only poor but also recent immigrants; many were provincials, often they were mestizos, and they were flocking to the capital, Buenos Aires. Not surprisingly, the Creole establishment there saw Perón as a threat, not only as a threat to the economic and political status quo, but also as a threat to good taste. Here was a man who, together with his mistress—later his wife—"Evita," a woman of illegitimate birth, was encouraging the invasion of Buenos Aires by riffraff from the provinces. The term *cabecitas negras* entered the language, used at first in a pejorative way to refer to riffraff; literally it translates as "black heads," but it conveyed something like the English term "blue-collar workers" combined with an unhealthy dose of racial prejudice. The intelligentsia, who tended to be in thrall to French culture, if not quite threatened by the new wave of populism, at least felt marginalized by it. Cortázar was opposed to Perón, although his opposition was hardly energetic. Soon he resigned his post at the university, valuing his independence too much to allow himself to be subjected to pressure to conform with the prevailing ethos.

Probably dating from the time he taught classes in Mendoza, we have *Teoría del túnel* (The tunnel theory), a long essay expounding Cortázar's ideas on the situation of the modern novelist; finished in 1947—by which time he was back in Buenos Aires—it was, however, only published posthumously, as a volume of the *Obra crítica* (Critical works), in 1994.

In the Buenos Aires of the late forties the author worked as manager of a publisher's association, a part-time job that left him plenty of time to do two things: write literature and qualify as a certified translator. In the very last story of the last collection that Cortázar published, "Diario para un cuento" (*Deshoras,* 1982; *Unreasonable Hours*), he evokes that period in Buenos Aires by portraying a public translator whose work obliges him to deal with tedious documents such as immigration papers and patents. However, the fact is that translation is a skill that Cortázar valued highly; he viewed the practice of translation as ideal training for any creative writer, engaged in it professionally throughout his life, and thematized it more than once in his fiction. But in real life, such were the pressures and tensions, albeit self-inflicted, that Cortázar felt during the period when he was endeavoring to qualify as a translator that he began to become neurotic and experience nightmares. These nightmares and neuroses had their beneficial side in that writing literature proved to be a therapeutic way to exorcize them, and thus they provided the genesis of several of the stories that would later come together in his first collection, *Bestiario* (1951; Bestiary).[8]

Before that date, the first major work to be published under Cortázar's real name had already appeared, *Los reyes* (1949; The monarchs), a serious play based on the myth of the Minotaur, to which the author gives an unconventional twist. Although theater is not a genre that one readily associates with Cortázar, in later life he did write a little more, this time in an absurdist vein. As for *Los reyes,* it is not only serious but also wordy, a poetic drama whose style and message are somewhat ponderous, but a work that nevertheless does have moments of lyricism and evinces signs of what was to come. Above all, here Cortázar begins to deal with issues related to power and to repressed desires, both of which figure prominently in his later works. *Los reyes* was destined to pass almost unnoticed. However, one or two of the short stories that Cortázar published in the late forties did attract interest, especially after Jorge Luis Borges, who was as important as anyone on the contemporary Argentine literary scene, published Cortázar's "Casa tomada" (House taken over) in a journal of which he was the editor.

As we have seen, three years elapsed after the publication of *Los reyes* before Cortázar felt that he had a group of stories of sufficient quality to publish together as *Bestiario.* The appearance of this collection of stories coincides with

Cortázar's leaving Argentina, armed with few possessions and little money, for France. There he would live for the rest of his life, more than thirty years, at first in Paris and later in Saignon, a village in Provence. Evidently Cortázar had felt ill at ease with Argentina's political and social trends in the late forties, and its cultural life seemed to him to be ossified and restrictive. He left of his own free will, and for many years his "exile" was voluntary, though by no means did it go unnoticed by people at home; as the years passed and Cortázar's success and fame grew, he began to find himself under attack from fellow countrymen who saw him as disloyal, not only as an expatriate but an ex-patriot. One or two even argued that no writer who was living and working abroad could consider himself truly an Argentine writer. There is little doubt that ideology and personal envy were among the motivating forces behind the antagonism. Cortázar was by no means the only Latin American writer to have such charges leveled against him, though he probably suffered more attacks than did others. He responded that being away had allowed him to see the homeland in a new light and had heightened his awareness of it in a way that would not have been possible had he stayed at home. Moreover, he drew attention to the inescapable fact that many, if not most, of the writers who were making their mark internationally as part of the "Boom" in Latin American Literature were writing from abroad (and not a few of them from Paris). Indeed, there has been a long tradition of Latin American writers, and perhaps especially Argentine writers, working in Europe, a tradition stretching well back beyond the beginning of the twentieth century and continuing to this day. It is true that many of these writers lived abroad because their exile was not voluntary; nor, for that matter, would Cortázar's own exile always be voluntary. The move to Paris in the early fifties, as we shall see, represents a milestone on Cortázar's private path toward self-discovery and on his public one toward notoriety.

For a long time his life in Paris was insecure and money was in short supply. He took temporary jobs, such as one in which he spent his time making up parcels (apparently doing it very well), before he settled into contract work as a translator for a United Nations agency in Vienna, where Cortázar's first wife, Aurora Bernárdez, also found employment. She, too, was a translator. The couple had first met in Argentina in 1948 and were married in 1953. For a number of years after they moved to Europe they would divide their time between Vienna and Paris. Cortázar was also making his mark as a literary translator; the fifties, for example, saw the publication of his translations of *Little Women* and of the complete prose of Edgar Allan Poe; other authors whose works he translated at one time or another include G. K. Chesterton, Daniel Defoe, André Gide, and Marguerite Yourcenar.

Final del juego (End of the game) and *Las armas secretas* (Secret weapons) are two further short story collections that appeared in the fifties and consolidated Cortázar's reputation as a writer of short fiction. It had become characteristic of Cortázar to include fantastic, monstrous, and mythical elements in his stories; many of these stories were disturbing, even horrific, and they often began with ordinary people in ordinary situations who, on finding themselves faced with the extraordinary, somehow took it in their stride. However, in *Las armas secretas* (1959) there are two stories that herald an important shift of focus from the fantastic and horrific toward the exploration of deeper things: on the one hand human psychology (and, by extension, existence) and on the other the very processes of fiction. One of the stories in question is "El perseguidor" (The pursuer), a biographical study of sorts, based on the life of the famous jazz musician Charlie Parker (1920–1955); critics and author alike have regarded this story as evidence of Cortázar's growing interest in character, and they have seen in it a foretaste of the metaphysical concerns that would underly his major novel, *Rayuela* (1963; *Hopscotch*).

Other works from the early sixties are Cortázar's first published novel, *Los premios* (1960; *The Winners*), *Historias de cronopios y famas* (1962; *Cronopios and Famas*), and an amplified *Final del juego* (1964), containing ten additional stories. *Los premios,* for the most part an extremely readable and engaging novel, tells of a motley group of Argentines who have won the lottery; the prize is a cruise departing from Buenos Aires. Using the ship-of-fools motif, Cortázar explores the social dynamics of a group of people thrown together by chance, but *Los premios* also delves deeper: whereas the majority of the passengers is looking for a pleasant and undemanding time, for a few of them the experience of the cruise is a crucial personal adventure that leads to self-knowledge. Accessible though it generally is, *Los premios* also contains a series of cryptic, contemplative episodes that perhaps sit uncomfortably beside the rest but clearly portend the intellectual self-consciousness of *Rayuela*. As for *Historias de cronopios y famas,* it is anything but serious. Like several books that would come later, it resists categorization; it consists of brief prose passages grouped in bizarre categories, often under harmless-looking subtitles. This eccentric and amusing little book gave the Spanish language a new word, *cronopio,* which subsequently acquired some general currency. A *cronopio* is a spontaneous and unconventional being, like several of Cortázar's heroes and like the author himself, who is sometimes referred to as "the great *cronopio*" and so identified on the plaque that now graces the facade of the house in Brussels where he was born.

Little of what had gone before seemed to prepare Cortázar's readers for the onslaught in 1963 of *Rayuela,* which is the most significant of the three great novels of the early sixties around which the phenomenon of the "Boom" in Latin American literature centers (the others being Carlos Fuentes's *La muerte de Artemio Cruz* [*The Death of Artemio Cruz*] and Mario Vargas Llosa's *La ciudad y los perros* [*The Time of the Hero*]). Arguably, *Rayuela* is the greatest Latin American novel of the century. Cortázar, a writer known for his compact fictions, was now challenging his readers with a long, complicated book. Gone is the easy readability of *Los premios*. *Rayuela* begins with an invitation to read it in a number of ways, the most enticing of which is not chronological, and so the reader jumps about, to discover that not a great deal happens in terms of plot and that the unifying element is a protagonist who is engaged in a search, apparently for a lost lover, but that at bottom the search has to do with the nature of existence and with personal ethics. The reader passes through a collage of experiences ranging from the moving to the hilarious to the philosophical, and for much of the time (the) fiction itself is put under a microscope. Predictably, *Rayuela*'s surprises, its irreverence, and its demand that the reader be an "accomplice" rather than a passive consumer provoked mixed reactions. But it did not take long for the book to become emblematic of the new Latin American fiction, and of its times. Without question, *Rayuela* is the most successful of Cortázar's novels; its continuing interest was a source of great satisfaction for the aging Cortázar, who at the time of writing it had felt that he was baring his soul in a way that might strike a chord with contemporaries who were middle-aged like himself, but who found, even decades later, that his book was attracting much younger readers.

Just as the fifties had begun with a milestone in Cortázar's life—his translation to Europe—so, too, had they closed with another, the Cuban Revolution and Fidel Castro's takeover in 1959. During the sixties Cortázar made a number of visits to Cuba, and, like most other Latin American intellectuals, including Fuentes and Vargas Llosa, he was active in support of the new regime. He now became far more aware of the Latin American condition and of the role played in it by the United States; no longer would he keep his distance from sociopolitical realities. This politically conscious Cortázar, looking back on his early work and waxing somewhat self-critical, said that prior to the Cuban Revolution he had been an ivory-tower writer, motivated above all else by aesthetic considerations. It was true that he had opposed Perón, fascism, and the rise of Franco in Spain, but he had always done so from the comfort of an armchair. Still, as many critics have demonstrated, there are latent political issues in many early Cortázar works, and it is not difficult to interpret a good deal of his creative writing that dates from before 1966 as political allegory or allusion.

I have singled out the year 1966 because it marks the appearance of one of his best collections of short stories, *Todos los fuegos el fuego* (1966; *All the Fires the Fire and Other Stories*), and in that collection we find the first example of a piece of creative writing that is overtly inspired by political reality: the story "Reunión" (Meeting) is based on some passages written by the revolutionary leader Che Guevara, and thinly disguised as characters in Cortázar's story are Guevara himself and one or two other revolutionaries, including Fidel Castro. But if "Reunión" is the signpost indicating a new role for politics in Cortázar's work, it also seems to warn us, through the leitmotif of references to Mozart, that aesthetics are still demanding a hearing. It is conspicuous that elsewhere in *Todos los fuegos el fuego* one is hard-pressed to find any hint of politics, although one or two of its stories do deal with power struggles of one sort or another. Much the same may be said of the amplified edition of *Final del juego* and of the elaborate literary experiment that in 1968 followed *Rayuela* and arose from that novel's chapter 62; it was another novel, called *62: Modelo para armar* (*62: A Model Kit*).

In short, there now seemed to be two sides to Cortázar: on the one hand there was the literary artificer, interested in aesthetics and in human psychology, on the other the increasingly public figure who was speaking out in support of Cuba and rubbing shoulders with protesting students who were barely half his age, during the Paris riots of 1968. This was about the time when Cortázar became involved in controversy regarding what constituted the proper role for the Latin American intellectual. Attacked by those who found his works unacceptably elitist, Cortázar defended himself in what became a famous open letter to Roberto Fernández Retamar. Fernández Retamar was a Cuban intellectual who at the time held an important post in Casa de las Américas, a cultural institution that served the interests of the revolutionary regime. In that letter Cortázar speaks of the profound influence that the revolution had had on him, how it had sensitized him to sociopolitical problems in Latin America, and how as a consequence he would never be the same man, but instead would be making his own contribution to change, in his own way. He rejected the pressures of those critics who were demanding that he write propaganda for a particular version of socialism: "At the risk of disappointing catechists and advocates of art to serve the masses, I am still that same *cronopio* who writes for his own amusement or suffering, with absolutely no concession, with no pragmatic, a priori obligation to being "Latin-American" or "Socialist" (*Último round,* 2:277; The final round). His ideas about literature, he wrote, had changed: no longer could he view it as a purely aesthetic construct, nor would he ever write for any interest whether minority or majority; whatever repercussions his books might have for other people would be coincidental to the enterprise. Nonetheless he was aware that thenceforth he would be writing "in order that"; he explained that "hay una intencionalidad que apunta a esa esperanza de un lector en el que reside la semilla del hombre futuro" (278; there's an intentionality directed toward the hope that in the reader might be found the seeds of the mankind of the future).

No less public were two important debates that took place during the late sixties, once again on the role of the intellectual. The most well-known of these debates was carried out in the pages of a Uruguayan magazine called *Marcha,* though it was subsequently gathered in book form as *Literatura en la revolución y revolución en la literatura* (Literature in the revolution and revolution in literature).[9] The principals in that debate were Cortázar, Vargas Llosa, and a young Colombian called Oscar Collazos, who was toeing the standard revolutionary line. In the course of that debate Cortázar recognized that writers had a social responsibility but spoke in favor of a far more radical concept of literature than was current among revolutionaries. Literature, according to Cortázar, had to play a crucial part in carrying the revolutionary process beyond its initial stages, beyond its material aspects, and fostering "total revolution." Hence "revolutionary novels are not simply ones that have revolutionary 'content,' they are ones that seek to revolutionize the novel itself."[10]

The second debate, which again involved Vargas Llosa, took place in Paris with radical students in 1970, and it drew similar comments from the Argentine. He argued that the worst mistake that revolutionaries could make was to try to dictate that literature be tied to immediate reality; every author, he claimed, should be left to write as he wished. Personally, Cortázar asserted his right to continue his "solitaria vocación de cultura, [su] empecinada búsqueda ontológica . . . [sus] juegos de la imaginación" (lonely cultural vocation, his stubborn ontological quest . . . his games of the imagination); yet all this, he emphasized, was no longer taking place in an ivory tower. Cortázar's contribution to this second debate is recorded in *Viaje alrededor de una mesa* (1970; A trip around a table). It is interesting to note in passing how very different the subsequent evolution of the two writers would be: Cortázar would continue to be a supporter, albeit a critical one, of Cuba and other left-wing movements, whereas Vargas Llosa, who had began his career as a Marxist, would later veer dramatically to the right. Vargas Llosa's preface to the edition of Cortázar's complete stories (*Cuentos completos,* 1994; Complete stories), is also interesting in this context: Vargas Llosa writes that, for all the political distance that grew between them, he never lost his respect for Cortázar.

Numerous texts, such as a report in *Life* magazine[11] and a speech to a student gathering in Venezuela,[12] attest further to the changes in Cortázar and to his sincerity; in *La vuelta al día en ochenta mundos* (1967; Around the day in eighty worlds) he wrote, almost as if in desperation at the criticisms that were being leveled at him: "Everybody knows that I occupy the left, the red area" (2:193).[13]

It was at about this time that events in Cuba began to alienate many intellectuals. Late in the sixties, the distinguished Cuban writer Guillermo Cabrera Infante, a former supporter of the revolution and for a while one of the diplomats of the Castro regime in Europe, went into exile and spoke out against it. Then the governing body of the Cuban Writers' Union publicly disapproved of the decision of its own juries to award prizes to two writers, whose texts the union did publish, but with a prologue condemning them. This was followed by advice from the Cuban armed forces' magazine that writers stop complaining about compromised artistic freedom and devote themselves to more revolutionary topics. But the event that provoked outrage was the subsequent imprisonment for counterrevolutionary activities of one of the prize-winning authors, the poet Heberto Padilla. There was an international furor. Cortázar was among a group of over fifty intellectuals who addressed a letter to Castro, asking for an explanation; the aggressive tone of the letter's first draft had been mollified at Cortázar's behest, but for all the politeness of the final version it provoked a violent reaction from Cuba. Castro responded with a public declaration that pseudo leftist bourgeois liberals working in Europe had no right to make patronizing comments about real writers, real revolutionaries, and that none of these critics of the revolution were welcome in Cuba.[14] Shortly afterward, in scenes reminiscent of the mock trials of intellectuals in Soviet Russia, Padilla made a public confession of guilt. The protests from outside the island grew louder: a second letter, which Cortázar did not sign, was addressed to Castro and published in *Le Monde,* accusing him of following in Stalin's footsteps. While most of the critical intellectuals, a good number of whom had actively supported Cuba up to that time, had by now lost sympathy with it, Cortázar tried to bridge the gap and hold on to what had become his ideological base; but Cuba was now closed to him, and even his personal friends there became silent. Cortázar then made what seems in some respects to be a humiliating, fawning attempt to stay in Cuba's good books: he wrote a prose poem called "Policrítica a la hora de los chacales," in which he cautiously expressed a number of concerns but declared his continuing commitment to "my love . . . my wounded cayman," to the sugar that would be harvested in a time when there would no longer be any slaves or empires. Although the wounds of estrangement (he was, in effect, ostracized by Cuba for about seven years) would be somewhat healed in later years, it is perhaps significant that Cortázar's attention was henceforth largely centered on other areas of Latin America.

In his private life, too, significant changes had been taking place: by the late sixties Cortázar and Aurora Bernárdez had separated (though they remained close friends, and she was beside him at his deathbed years later). Julio Cortázar now had a relationship with Ugné Karvelis, a woman of Lithuanian origin, who at the time of postwar Soviet expansion had left for Germany and then France; she was on the editorial staff of the French publishing house Gallimard, which was publishing translations of a good number of Latin American writers. After a somewhat tempestuous relationship, Cortázar and Karvelis parted company in the late seventies. It was she who had helped foster Cortázar's awareness of Latin America and encouraged his new participatory role.

For many people, however, this politically active Cortázar remained a problem, and the controversy surrounding him continued unabated. At their most extreme, those on the Right accused him of betraying his bourgeois roots, while, as we have seen, those on the Left attacked his intellectualism and demanded that he write in the demotic. The attacks from "comrades" on the Left were the most painful for Cortázar; in response he insisted time and again that no one had the right to prescribe how or what an author should write, that any true revolutionary must conceive of literature in aesthetic, not only in doctrinaire terms, and that the frontiers of literature itself had to be pushed back too. In ensuing years Cortázar made a number of attempts at reconciling aesthetic and sociopolitical aims, with mixed success. One such attempt, *Vampiros multinacionales* (1975; Multinational vampires) used the pulp-fiction hero Fantomas and projected Cortázar and other writers into a comic strip, all in an attempt to draw attention to the way in which multinationals, and particularly U.S. companies, were exploiting underdeveloped countries and keeping corrupt people in power. The fourth novel he published, *Libro de Manuel* (1977; *A Manual for Manuel*), is in a number of ways radically different from *62: Modelo para armar* and was written under pressure. Cortázar was motivated to act quickly both by the hardening (the "chitinization," he would call it) of the revolutionary line in Cuba and by political developments in the Southern Cone. *Libro de Manuel* is based on the story of a revolutionary group that plans to kidnap a political figure and, by ransoming him, free some political prisoners. The political commitment of this book is undeniable, but so too are its playfulness, its metaphysical dimension, and the fact that it scrutinizes the revolutionaries themselves. *Libro de Manuel* did nothing to reduce the controversy in which its author was enmeshed.

The publication of another collection of stories, *Alguien que anda por ahí* (Someone walking around), also in 1977, marked the point at which Cortázar's "exile" ceased for some years to be voluntary. During the seventies he had befriended Salvador Allende, the democratically elected left-wing president of Chile, who was soon overthrown by General Pinochet's coup, with U.S. backing.

12

Then another military regime, that of General Videla, had come to power in Argentina. Thus had begun the repressive era that over the years sent hordes of people from the Southern Cone of South America into exile, if, that is, they escaped with their lives. It is an era that also gave the language a new transitive verb, "to disappear," meaning "to cause to disappear," a euphemism for "eliminate." Cortázar spoke out openly against these regimes. Apart from *Libro de Manuel* he had also written one or two stories that the Argentine authorities of the day found too near the political knuckle, with the result that their publication in Argentina was forbidden. One of the offending stories, "Segunda vez" (Second time around), seemed to anyone aware of what was happening in Argentina to refer to the "disappearances." Another was inspired by a visit Cortázar had made to Nicaragua and by his sympathies with the revolutionary Sandinista movement, which overthrew Somoza's dictatorship in that country. In his later years, Cortázar was to become increasingly involved with Nicaragua, to the extent of giving the royalties of some of his last books in support of the Sandinistas and publishing one titled *Nicaragua, tan violentamente dulce* (1983; Nicaragua, so violently sweet). Other works of significance in his later years include the eccentrically autobiographical *Un tal Lucas* (1979; *A Certain Lucas*) and the story collections *Queremos tanto a Glenda* (1980; *We Love Glenda So Much*) and *Deshoras* (1982; *Unreasonable Hours*).

In 1981 President Mitterand issued a decree granting Cortázar French citizenship, something Cortázar had wanted for a long time, although only on the understanding that he could have it without sacrificing his Argentine citizenship. One may wonder to what extent the desire for French citizenship took shape as a result of the personal hostility of some of Cortázar's compatriots, to what extent it stemmed from his generally prickly relationship with Argentina, whether he saw the conferral of French citizenship as a recognition of his affinity with the country in which he had lived so long and for whose culture he had always had such sympathy, or whether in some way it all represented a refuge. (During Cortázar's final visit to Argentina, in 1983, an Argentina that was now in the democratic hands of President Raúl Alfonsín, some of his friends had hoped that the president would formally receive Cortázar in a gesture of belated official recognition; but it was not to be.)

By the late seventies Cortázar had found the love of his life, the woman who was to be his companion in his final years and his second wife. Carol Dunlop was an American who had been active in political protests during the Vietnam era and had lived for some time in French Canada. She was also a writer and a photographer. With her, Cortázar, already in his mid-sixties, conceived a bizarre "voyage" down one of the French *autoroutes* in an aging Volkswagen camper, a voyage that they would chronicle in a parody of the chronicles of the great explorers. The result is *Los autonautas de la cosmopista* (The autonauts of the cosmoroute), published in 1983, about a year after the death of Carol Dunlop from leukemia. The moving postscript that Cortázar appended to this book provides ample evidence of their deep mutual devotion; her death, and his own illness with that same disease, brought about a rapid decline in him. The man who for so long had seemed to be twenty years younger than he actually was now looked old; she had, as he put it, become his raison d'être. He continued many of his activities, but without the same enthusiasm. He died in Paris on 12 February 1984.

Several works have been published since his death, including one or two that he had already prepared for publication. For example, a good deal of his poetry was gathered in *Salvo el crepúsculo* (1984; Save twilight); *Nada a Pehuajó* (Nothing to Pehuajó), an entertainingly absurd play dating from the seventies, came to light, as did a piece for radio, *Adiós, Róbinson* (Goodbye, Robinson); and one or two other brief theatrical works. Much was republished, as Alfaguara, one of the most important Hispanic imprints, attempted to bring everything together in one series, by a single publisher, Cortázar's works having previously been dispersed among several. The appearance of the complete collection of stories in 1994 made available a few that had escaped inclusion in the various collections published over the years. Three volumes of critical works appeared, as did an early book on John Keats and other little-known works from earlier years, some of them never before published. These include two novels, of which *El examen* (The examination) is especially important in retrospect. Thanks to the attentiveness of Aurora Bernárdez (bolstered, no doubt, by a certain degree of commercial opportunism on the part of the publishers), every work that Cortázar considered finished has become readily available, though among the newly available material there is possibly some that he would have been loath to publish in his lifetime.

In all, the creative *oeuvre* includes, among other things, more than eighty short stories, six novels, some poetry, a few plays, some miscellanies, and not a few texts (some of book length) that in some way relate to or accompany visual images. The number of major literary translations into Spanish done by Cortázar is also significant.[15]

Music and art persistently give tone and color to his works. Among the great number of writers who influenced him are Keats and Poe, the surrealists, Gide, Cocteau, Raymond Roussel, Alfred Jarry, Lewis Carroll, Shakespeare, and, among Spanish Americans, Borges, Leopoldo Marechal, Macedonio Fernández, Felisberto Hernández, and Roberto Arlt. Cortázar's culture was extensive, his reading wide but unsystematic. So far as European literatures were concerned, he was more at home with French, British, or German than he was with Spanish literature. He was in many respects a romantic, the prime source of his romanticism being English poetry of the nineteenth century; and yet he was heavily indebted to surrealism, more to its painters than its most eminent writers. He would have liked to be a painter, a philosopher, a musician, but felt that his talent did not lie in those fields. The literature he wrote instead is both cosmopolitan and quintessentially Argentine. It has a playfulness beneath which there lies a deep ontological concern. It is occasionally outrageous but always motivated by a strong sense of the ethical.

CHAPTER 2

The Weigh-In

Early Publications

There was a long silence of some ten years between Julio Denis's publication of the poems in *Presencia* and Julio Cortázar's first book, which appeared in his late thirties. In his interview with Ernesto González Bermejo[1] he explains that rigorous self-criticism was the reason for his silence: admitting that he was perhaps erring on the side of vanity at the time, he says that he had set himself a high standard and was not prepared to publish anything more until he felt that that standard had been met, in part, perhaps, as a reaction to the readiness of so many contemporaries in Argentina to publish indiscriminately. Cortázar even burned a six-hundred-page novel, an action he came to regret, if only because he would have liked to have kept it among his personal papers. Several other texts were held back at the time of completion, though some of these have appeared posthumously, proving, in one or two cases, that his critical instincts in those early years had served him well.

Los reyes (The monarchs), which appeared in 1949, was the first book that Cortázar published under his own name, and he did so "in a private, almost clandestine way." One cannot be quite sure whether this phrase of his is a reflection of his own uncertainty about the book's quality, or whether he is referring to the limited distribution and impression *Los reyes* made on the reading public: the fact is that it met with what Cortázar describes elsewhere as "a resounding, absolute silence."[2]

Los reyes is a short, poetic play whose style and form are somewhat anachronistic even in the multifaceted context of Cortázar's works. As we shall see, however, this work presents some ideas and images that play important roles in later books. The story that forms the basis of *Los reyes* is the classical myth of the Minotaur, half man and half beast, the product of the union of King Minos's wife, Pasifae, with a bull. According to the myth, Theseus is dispatched by King Minos to slay the Minotaur, whom Minos has imprisoned in a labyrinth, calming his evil appetite with a diet of young Athenians. As Theseus enters the labyrinth, Ariadne, the daughter of Minos, gives him a skein of thread so that he can trace his escape route.

Perhaps the most immediate inspiration for *Los reyes* came from Gide's *Thésée,* published first in *Les Cahiers de la Pléiade* and subsequently by Gallimard, both in 1946. We know that Gide was one of Cortázar's preferred authors. But we should not discount the possible influence of Borges, who in "La casa de Asterión" has his own version of the Minotaur myth. Gide offers a fairly conventional account. Borges, more adventurously, makes the Minotaur the narrator and hides that fact till the end of his story. But the labyrinth, so dear to Borges as a metaphor for an endless universe, is not employed to similar effect by Cortázar.

Written in poetic prose, Cortázar's version of this story is structured in five scenes, four of which are dialogues and one, occupying the pivotal third position, a monologue. The play, more an exchange of ideas than a drama of action, begins in a stiff, declamatory style. Minos sets the scene, speaking of his obsession with the Minotaur, whom he refers to as the insatiable tormentor of his nights (17). The ensuing dialogue in this first section is between Minos and Ariadne, who waxes now descriptive, now wistfully lyrical in response to her father. It becomes clear that for both of them the Minotaur stands for deep-seated and disturbing passions. The prison-labyrinth to which the Minotaur has been confined is imagined by his half sister Ariadne not as a hostile place but as one that is "clear and desolate, with a chilly sun and central gardens in which call-less birds fly above the image of [her] sleeping brother" (26). The Minotaur lives on the other side of a wall that separates their worlds, marking the line between "the black heart and the white sun," and she feels "the delight of horror," an attraction to and a fear of that other world (27).

In the second scene the dialogue is between Minos and Theseus, the one contemplative, the other ready for action and inspired by "Gods nourished by fearsome dialectics" (34). These contrasting personalities can also be viewed as complementary human types, a view encouraged by a Borges-like declaration made by Theseus that he is Theseus and at the same time Minos, and that this is "something that is ours, on our side of our kingdoms and our names" (38). There is some ambiguity here: the phrase Cortázar uses for "something that is ours" is *cosa nuestra,* which may be paraphrased more fully as "something that the two of us have in common, share privately" but is also a phrase that may turn one's thoughts to the Mafia. Both of the two men are said to be acting out their "meticulously woven destinies," and the Minotaur is bringing them to light "como envuelve el rocío en su delación plateada el tapiz de Aracné" (38; just as the dew envelops Arachne's tapestry in silvery betrayal). Despite the fact that Minos has imprisoned the Minotaur, he himself feels a prisoner: "I was obliged to incarcerate him . . . and he is taking advantage of my having to incarcerate him. I am his prisoner" (42). According to Minos, the Minotaur is something we carry in our hearts, "in the dark recesses of the will" (41).

The third, very brief, scene, which comprises Ariadne's monologue, is a crucial one in three respects. It marks the point beyond which the action passes into the labyrinth; it provides the structural nexus, the only monologue separating two pairs of dialogues; and it is thematically crucial because here Ariadne's desire for the Minotaur is made quite explicit. For it transpires that Ariadne has given the thread to Theseus in the hope that not he but the monster will escape and come to her. As the skein unravels, she anticipates the satisfaction of her secret lust for the Minotaur: "It arises from the depths I never dared plumb" (57). Despite the fact that Theseus patronizingly refers to the skein (in Spanish, *ovillo*) as a "woman's thing" (56), the clear implication is that this woman has an influence on destiny and is a none too distant relative of Arachne, the very weaver to whom Theseus referred earlier in his dialogue with Minos.

The idea that a powerful weaver of destinies is at work is so central and recurrent in Cortázar that it justifies a brief digression from our discussion of *Los reyes;* it is a notion to which we shall find ourselves returning on a number of occasions in ensuing chapters. The weaver is usually unidentified, sometimes sinister, and is not to be confused with the Christian God. She (for often the weaver is a female figure) is frequently invoked as a metaphysical force. Quite often the metaphor is applied to the storyteller, to the act of spinning the narrative yarn. For the moment, a few sample contexts will suffice to illustrate how important the concept of the weaver is. Both in the story "Casa tomada" (of which more in the next chapter) and in *Divertimento,* a work composed at about the same time as *Los reyes* but published only posthumously (see chapter 9), Cortázar again dwells on the image of the *ovillo,* the skein. Moreover, images of spiders (arachnids) are generally common in his works. In *Último round* (1969) there is a poem titled "Las tejedoras" (Weaving women) that paints a disturbing picture of ubiquitous, relentless, discreetly repulsive weavers of the fabric of death (98; "upper floor"). Recognizing the centrality in his works of the notion of the weaver, in that same book Cortázar includes a text of his that was written in response to the observations of a critic who had reviewed a collection of Cortázar's stories and had identified certain patterns in them; Cortázar accepts the validity of the reviewer's comments but adds that underlying those patterns are "the frightening designs woven in the shadows by the great Mothers" (31; "ground floor"). And again, to take a last example, in a short piece called "De otros usos del cáñamo" (Concerning other ways of using hemp), included in *Territorios* (1978; Territories), Cortázar notes the frequency with which he is inclined to evoke images of cords or threads when he writes, and he acknowledges that the myth of Arachne is probably an underlying factor; a little further on, recalling his portrayal of Ariadne, he adds: "The day came when I discovered that a cord could be an emissary of destiny. . . . But I couldn't yet know what I realized much later, the coded message, the long, long and sinuous *quipu* that

Ariadne was sending to her Minotaur brother . . . those were years in which I was tying up my personal secrets, the discovery of sensuality, the awareness of death, and I was unravelling books of short stories and novels, excitedly opening packages of imagination and poetry" (52).[3]

Now to return to our discussion of *Los reyes*. Scene four is the encounter between Theseus and the Minotaur. The latter, exploiting the double sense of the word *hilo* ("thread" and "trickle"), observes that "El hilo está a tus pies como un primer arroyo, una viborilla de agua que señala hacia el mar" (65; The thread is at your feet like the beginnings of a stream, a viper of water pointing to the sea), to which Theseus responds by declaring that Ariadne is that sea. The thread is the trickle of desire that will flow free in the encounter with Ariadne, while the serpent image of course evokes Eden and the idea of the forbidden. Yet the Minotaur, instead of following the thread that will lead him from confinement to the other space occupied by Ariadne, chooses to submit to Theseus's sword, for death means true liberation, "the final and ubiquitous freedom, the tiny and terrible labyrinth in every human heart" (72). As for Ariadne, the Minotaur will continue to excite her dreams "like a shining blue dolphin . . . like a free gust of wind," and she will turn to him again for he is impatient and exciting, "ensconced . . . in the perturbed maidenliness of her reveries" (73). The strength of the Minotaur, then, is metaphorical; the power of Minos physically to imprison him, and to have him killed, is an irrelevance.[4]

In the final scene, an exchange between the dying Minotaur and a musician, the former explains how his bodily death does not put an end to his symbolic vitality in people's minds: "Thus I seek access to men's dreams, to their secret heaven and its remote stars, those that are invoked when the light of dawn and destiny are in play" (81).

In *Los reyes* we find many thematic elements that will become Cortázar's stock-in-trade: the freeing of suppressed desires, an awareness of "otherness," a suspicion vis-à-vis what is rational and orderly, a sense of fate, the use of erotic imagery, and an exploitation of myth. The Minotaur is a mythical figure who in the hands of Cortázar becomes a representation of repressed passions; the Minotaur himself, surely speaking for the author, suggests the remedy: "sólo hay un medio para matar a los monstruos: aceptarlos" (71; there is only one way to be rid of monsters: accept them). The Minotaur may also be said to represent difference, individuality of a kind that is subject to the conformist pressures of authority.

Even in its many classical literary versions the story of the Minotaur in his labyrinth varies in matters of detail, and later versions only add to the variety. Yet, broadly, the interpretations throughout history of the symbolic import of the death of the monster at the hands of Theseus have been these: that it signals the victory of reason over blind ignorance, that of noble, spiritual qualities over base instincts, or the triumph of political principle over the exercise of arbitrary power.

Cortázar's *Los reyes,* as Roberto González-Echevarría aptly puts it, is more of a subversion than a version of the myth.[5] This critic argues that at bottom the work is about creativity, about "the violent birth writing." The Minotaur, it is argued, represents "immediate but naïve knowledge of man before the Fall," and his language is incoherent and symbolic. Theseus, on the other hand, represents logical, linear discourse. At the conclusion, neither is in control of the labyrinth and "writing is the empty labyrinth" that they have both left.[6] Another view, one which draws more heavily on sociopolitical realities of the time of composition, is espoused by Luis Bocaz, who reads the play as a veiled attack on Perón. Néstor García Canclini expresses a more commonly held view of Cortázar's subversive twist: that the Minotaur acquires a heroic aura while Theseus is reduced to mediocrity, a man who is "fearful of the new and a promoter of conformism."[7] Reference can also be made to an inversion of the classic Argentine theme of conflict between "civilización y barbarie," order versus unruliness, the Western, white, and urban culture versus the unreined, raw, and rural. From this standpoint the Minotaur ceases to appear grotesque and becomes a harmonious being who reveals ideal ancient Greek qualities.[8]

Critics have generally regarded *Los reyes* as an immature and not wholly successful work, albeit one that rehearses images and themes that are explored more successfully in the future. Juan Carlos Curutchet is one of the most openly critical when he says that *Los reyes* is too obviously imitative of the grand cadences of Greek tragedy; he regards the characters as too generic, believes the symbolism is too abstract, and says that there is an excessive reliance on being suggestive; the overall effect, he writes, is of a crude exchange of ideas being dressed up in images that are sometimes far too *précieuses.*[9]

Cortázar himself was evidently uneasy about *Los reyes;* for two decades after its initial appearance he resisted having it republished, and in an interview with Luis Harss he said that he still had a sentimental attachment to the work but acknowledged that it was written in "the style of an aesthete."[10] He further declared that *Los reyes* "has little or nothing to do with what I have published since." From a stylistic point of view, this may be a fair comment; from a thematic one, it is something of an overstatement.

CHAPTER 3

Winning by a Knockout

The Stories

My aim in this chapter, perhaps the most crucial chapter in this book, is to trace through samples the major themes and techniques in Cortázar's creative writing.[1] In doing so, I shall draw almost exclusively on his stories. They are the component of his work that has drawn the most unflinching admiration from readers, and they have inspired endless critical studies. Every one of Cortázar's interests, obsessions, and concerns is exemplified in the body of the more than eighty stories he published. This is not to imply in any way that they are monolithic or even narrowly focused. On the contrary, they are protean creations that resist attempts to reduce and simplify them. It is characteristic of them to be open to multiple interpretations, and many thrive on ambiguity, as if to prove the author's profound dislike of tidily convenient solutions. Since they tend to overlap with and intersect one another, stories discussed below under a given heading may reappear under another.

Fears, Fantasies, Phobias

A great number of stories, especially those of the first three or four collections, involve the insertion of fantastic, and often disturbing, elements into a context where everything else seems quite normal. Important among the many formative influences on Cortázar that are especially relevant to his early stories are the works of Edgar Allan Poe, widely read in Argentina and highly valued by Cortázar, who translated Poe's complete stories into Spanish. A second influence to note comes from the field of psychology: his voracious reading had included the works of Freud and Jung. Thirdly, the pressures of Cortázar's life in Buenos Aires as he worked for a publishers' association and at the same time prepared to qualify as an official translator drove him to such a state of nervous tension that he had a number of nightmares; these he then used as the basis for stories. Together, these factors help account for the way in which fears and phobias, and perhaps the working of Cortázar's own subconscious, are evinced in so many of the early stories.

"Casa tomada" (House taken over) played an important role in bringing Cortázar recognition. This can be attributed both to its intrinsic merits as a story and to the fact that it was brought to public attention in 1946 by Borges, the leading figure of twentieth-century Latin American letters, who published Cortázar's story in *Anales de Buenos Aires,* a journal of which Borges was then the editor and in which he published some of his own work. With other stories published at about the same time—"Carta a una señorita en París" (Letter to a young lady in Paris), "Lejana" (The distances) and "Bestiario" (Bestiary)—"Casa tomada" would later reappear as part of Cortázar's first collection, which came out in 1951 under the title *Bestiario.* Monsters, obscure threats, and fears are common features in the early stories, and they give more of a sense of oneness to *Bestiario* than can be identified in any other collection of Cortázar's stories.

In the tradition of the best short story writers, in "Casa tomada" Cortázar wastes no time with preliminaries. At once, the reader senses involvement with the predicament of the story's narrator, a middle-aged man who in confessional tones describes the domestic regime that he and his sister share and how that regime comes to be circumscribed, even threatened, by unidentified forces. "I had to lock the passage door," he tells her. "They've taken over the back part" (109). To this she responds in a low key: they will simply have to make do with the other. Irene (whose name associates her with peace, possibly also with the eighth-century oriental empress who was noted for her devotion to orthodoxy) is said by her brother to be born not to bother anyone. But later on in the story, when he finds that he has no choice but to close off yet another section of the house as the hostile forces advance, he too reacts in a similarly stoical manner, simply brewing some mate, as if to prove that fundamentally he is as accepting and impassive as his sister.

The reader is naturally led to wonder quite what these alien forces might be and why those affected by them accept their lot so blandly. But no clear answer can be found. In this, the very first story that Cortázar published, we are given a sense that ill-defined powers govern existence and that people are inclined to submit to such powers without questioning. Both are features that will recur on numerous occasions in his fiction.

The house is huge, comfortable, well furnished, and well located in Buenos Aires. The two who inhabit it have no financial worries since they live on income from family property in the country; as a result, he can amuse himself, like any normal Argentine of his sort, reading his French literature, while she can quietly knit. It appears, then, that in a number of ways these are typical bourgeois. However, it is conspicuous that the brother refers to their life together as a "matrimonio de hermanos" (107; a marriage of brother and sister). Indeed, they live, as might a long-married couple, in a quiet tedium of daily routines and conformity, save that he appears to have assumed parts of the traditional female role.

It is noticeable, too, that once the pair find themselves confined and forced to modify their routines, the brother occupies himself by going over a stamp collection, as if regressing to childhood.

What is one to make of the fact that, as they eventually leave the house, Irene abandons the garment she has been making and whose thread leads under the door to the skein, still inside the house? Does this symbolize a break with the past, or perhaps the end of the narrative text (the yarn that has been spun)? Could this again be Ariadne's thread? When Irene's brother puts his arm round her waist, is he simply comforting her or symbolizing the "outing" of their (monstrous) feelings for each other? Then again, his last act is to throw the key to what was their house into the gutter; is this a symbol of loss, recognition, or surrender, or is it a gesture designed to protect others from similar invasions, or even a means of preventing others from having access to the comforts that the brother and sister once enjoyed?

Paradoxical though this statement may appear, what is most clear and significant about "Casa tomada" is that it is full of ambiguity. Some critics have highlighted the theme of incest, which is not only present, as we have seen, in *Los reyes,* but also elsewhere; yet Cortázar, while accepting their right to make such observations and even acknowledging their accuracy, denied that he had ever introduced that theme intentionally. Other interpretations of "Casa tomada" have often tended toward the allegorical, relying on extratextual factors, so that, for example, the house is seen as representing an old aristocratic order that is under threat due to political and social changes in Argentina or, to be more precise, due to the rise of Peronism. It is even possible to argue that the house stands for the nation as it is being driven into a new relationship with the modern world.

In "Bestiario" a young girl, Isabel, who is frail and sickly, is dispatched to her aunt's house in the country, where she plays with her cousin Nino. Isabel, however, is preoccupied with a tiger that roams the house in freedom. One would suspect that this tiger is a figment of the child's imagination and that it would be tolerated by the adults as such, but in fact they all sense the tiger as something real enough to be avoided, taking care not to enter the room it is currently occupying. In the end Isabel uses the tiger as a means of revenge against Nene, another character who may have been making unwanted sexual advances to Rema, who is perhaps her aunt, in any event much loved by her. She tricks Nene into entering a room occupied by the tiger, and he does not reemerge. Is Isabel cruel and unjustly vengeful? Is she a disturbed child? Has she some strange power over or understanding of the tiger? How real is the tiger, and what is its symbolic value? One thing that is clear is that, like the invasion of "Casa tomada," the presence of the tiger is something out of the ordinary that is nonetheless accepted as if it were normal. Another thing that is clear is that Rema is grateful to Isabel for what she has done. This modern bestiary could be understood as having some moral implications. It is possible that incest is again implied in the relationship between Nene and Rema. And there are hints of Isabel's sexual awakening; exactly what are her feelings for Rema? Commenting on the frequency with which animals make an appearance in his fantastic works, Cortázar suggested that they were related to the world of dreams and to Jungian archetypes; he observed that the bull and the lion commonly returned in dreams and were always related to sexual taboos and power.[2] This story, like the one we shall look at next, is the product of one of his dreams. It is unlikely, however, that Cortázar had any moral intention in this or any other of the stories of his *Bestiario.*

In "Carta a una señorita en París" Cortázar uses a first-person narrator for the first time, and the story is in the form of a confessional letter.[3] In brief, the narrator looks after an apartment for a lady friend who is away in Paris, and one day, while traveling in the building's elevator, he vomits up a rabbit. This turns into a habit, even a predictable and agreeable one, but the narrator becomes worried about the condition of the apartment as the number of rabbits increases, and he tries to confine them to a wardrobe. In the end he tosses them all out of the window, and there is a strong hint that he throws himself out too, leaving a mess on the pavement for the city cleaners, rather than on the carpet for his housekeeper. The fact that the narrator manages to hide the rabbits from Sara, apparently the housekeeper, who otherwise is so meticulous about keeping things in order, suggests that they are really his problem, perhaps only his fantasy. Certainly he and Sara do not communicate much, nor do they share the same interests (indicated by his preference for jazz and hers for *pasodobles*). There are many references in this story to orderliness and to the narrator's lack of it, or at least to his having an abnormal sense of order. Part of the disorder that challenges the housekeeper involves the narrator's many papers, which might suggest that the narrator is a writer of some sort. It is also conspicuous that Cortázar, not a man given to cluttering his stories with redundant images and descriptions, chooses to draw attention to a portrait of Miguel de Unamuno that he has put on the wall. These allusions to writing open up the possibility that the story is a metaphor for creative activity: the rabbits are the creations that spring from the narrator in a miraculous and inexplicable way, leaving him slightly embarrassed and occasionally dissatisfied with them. In that light, the ending of the story can be read as the destruction of the created work; doing away with the rabbits is a way of putting an end to the story. But this literary speculation is no doubt encouraged by the extratextual information that is available to us: elsewhere Cortázar has described the process whereby his stories come into being, and it matches the interpretation I have given here.[4] We also learn from his interviews that "Carta a una señorita en París" began as one of the author's nightmares and that it was written at a time when he was minding an apartment for an absent acquaintance. Without such "illegitimate" information, that is to say, relying on textual evidence alone, "Carta a una señorita en París" comes across as the fantasy of a neurotic person, a story with a gruesome ending but with amusing and tender moments along the way.

Fear in one or another of its many manifestations is a latent force in a great many Cortázar stories. Characters are often apprehensive about being manipulated by forces they cannot identify or for reasons they cannot understand. Political power, authorial power, the power of destiny, or a godlike force are all implied at one time or another. But fear and excitement come simply with the unknown, whether hostile or not; Cortázar himself spoke of how the fantastic can bring a sense that there is "a frightening heartbeat which is not our own, an order that may use us at any moment for one of its mosaics" (*Vuelta,* 45). For the moment, we shall consider one further example of fear, in the Poe tradition.

In "Omnibus" Clara takes a bus ride to visit a friend for tea. The bus route leads to a cemetery, and Clara becomes aware that she is the only passenger on the bus who is not armed with a bunch of flowers. She feels increasingly uncomfortable as the others stare at her, until a young man, also without flowers, boards the vehicle and becomes the object of their stares. Some solidarity develops between the two, their hands touch and eventually hold each other. Once the other passengers have alighted, Clara and her new friend feel threatened by the driver and the ticket collector, like prisoners unable to get off or even change seats. The tension mounts, and they make plans for a quick escape once the bus reaches the end of the line. As the culminating moment approaches, the bus is portrayed like a raging bull, ready to charge; the driver tries to stop the pair but their escape is successful, and the bus doors give a parting snort as it moves off. Clara and her anonymous friend now enter a park, happy among the children and the ice creams. He leads her across the grass, toward a river. They pass a florist, and he buys her pansies (*pensamientos* in Spanish, also meaning "thoughts"). After he has paid the florist they walk on, each with some flowers but no longer hand in hand as they had been on the bus.

This is a straightforwardly linear story in which tension builds strongly and is finally released, but the underlying reasons for the tension have not been explained. On a simple level, it expresses the discomfort we all feel when we sense that we are different from the rest and the way we seek reassurance in the company of others who are in the same boat. Conspicuous and self-conscious, the two passengers allow things to get out of proportion, and they perceive hos-

tility where none exists. But the flowers, the motif of the journey (past a cemetery, no less), the arrival at an idyllic garden, the presence of the river, the ani-
mal-like portrayal of the bus, and the hands that meet each other are examples
of the many features that feed symbolic readings of this story. The flowers carried by the two at the end may signify their capitulation to the social norm; the
fact that these are pansies may suggest that thought is taking the place of
unthinking. The convergence of the hands suggests mutual support but also sexual contact; their separation at the end may signify that a certain type of relationship is possible only in adversity. The walk through the garden may signal a
return to innocence, but what, then, of the river that lies beyond it?[5] There are
possible links here with Cortázar's posthumous novel *El examen,* and certainly
there are some similarities with his story "La autopista del sur" (The southern
thruway) in *Todos los fuegos el fuego,* in which a couple caught in the alien world
of a fantastic traffic jam have a relationship that dissolves at the end.

Hands

A striking characteristic of "Omnibus" is the attention paid to the role of hands and
the suggestion that they behave independently of their owner's conscious will.
"Hands have always been very magical things to me," Cortázar said to González
Bermejo,[6] adding that an early girlfriend had told him that his hands were the most
interesting thing about him. To illustrate his point, Cortázar called upon the examples provided not by "Omnibus" but by an early story, "Estación de la mano" (Season of the hand), and one published in *Octaedro,* "Cuello de gatito negro" ("Throat
of a black kitten").[7] In the former, a hand enters through a window and befriends
someone who then becomes frightened because he dreams that the hand has
designs on one of his own, and he sees the hand playing with a knife; the visiting
hand realizes that this is happening, and leaves. The second story, a far more substantial and powerful one, is another Poe-like tale of horror, though it was published at a time when in general Cortázar was no longer writing in quite that
tradition. "Cuello de gatito negro" begins in the *métro,* a place of almost mystical
significance for Cortázar. The protagonist's hand, holding a rail, is approached by
another that belongs to a woman, as if fulfilling the steps of a ritual. The girl apolo-
getically recognizes that hands cannot be controlled: "There's nothing you can do
about them" (107). The two people are involved in a game, not an amusing one but
rather a pact that seems to be sealed at the moment when she looks him in the eye
as if she were waking up, and the train reaches a station with the signpost "Convention." The woman is frightened and asks the man to stay with her, and so he
accompanies her to her apartment, his hand holding hers as one would the neck of

a kitten. Inside the apartment it appears that the woman is now relaxed and relieved of the fear that was associated with being in the subway, the subworld, so to speak. The pair begin to converse about banalities, and for a while she seems to be in control of herself. But language breaks down when they veer away from everyday matters; when they attempt to talk about the ritual in which they know they are involved, about her obsessive fears, their sentences are left incomplete, or they find themselves using words that are vague and unrevealing. The woman closes her eyes, in tears. As the story progresses, the staleness of the atmosphere reminds the reader of the air in the subway. When they go to bed together, the couple's hands obediently carry out the desired movements in the dark, but after they have made love, she awakens in fear of the darkness. The man comforts her, but then her disquiet returns and she wants light. Cortázar makes subtle use of references to light and darkness. The absence of light is also oppressive and frightening, first for the woman, then for the man, who after several attempts to bring light to the bedroom fail somehow finds his hands round the woman's neck, squeezing it like a cat's.

Like many Cortázar stories, this one grew from a real-life incident: traveling on the *métro* one day his hand had inadvertently touched another passenger's, and on the basis of that he had imagined "a sort of nymphomania concentrated on the hands." He conceived the story as wholly fantastic but thought it had fatalistic overtones, for the woman is condemned to die a victim of an uncontrollable power. The idea of the autonomous hand is by no means exclusive to Cortázar, being found especially in nineteenth-century literature. The hand is extremely important for Cortázar; consider the part it plays, for example, in the story "No se culpe a nadie" (No one is to be blamed) or the novel *62: Modelo para armar.*

In Pursuit of Oneself

For quite different reasons, "El perseguidor" (The pursuer) and "Las babas del diablo" (Devil's spittle), two of the stories included in *Las armas secretas* (1959), were to prove to be milestones in Cortázar's development as a writer; thematically, both can be said to mark the path toward his *magnum opus,* the novel *Rayuela* (*Hopscotch*).

On one level "El perseguidor" is a sentimental homage to jazz, specifically to one of its great exponents, Charlie Parker: hence the story's dedication "*In memoriam* CH. P" ("CH" rather than "C" because the former used to have the status of a separate letter in the Spanish alphabet). Cortázar reincarnates Parker in the personage of a self-destructive drug addict called Johnny, a man whose behavior imperils his career and places a great burden on those around him, for he is volatile and frequently abusive. Yet he can also be tender, and when playing his saxophone he comes into his own, so much so that he seems godlike. It is through the free forms of jazz that Johnny, who otherwise appears to be incoherent, disorderly, and unappealing, finds a true way of expressing himself. In daily life, he is attended and protected by his wife and by his biographer, a music critic called Bruno. Bruno narrates the story, and in the course of it reveals how equivocal his attitude to Johnny is, because he serves and protects him, but he is motivated by a mixture of human concern and self-interest; after all, Johnny's life is Bruno's living.

Among the Cortázar stories published prior to this time few had been cast in so realistic a mold. "Los venenos" (The poisons), included in the first edition of *Final del juego* (1956), is something of an exception. That story, a good part of which is autobiographical, delves quite deeply into human sentiments. "El perseguidor" is also remarkable for its concentration on personal, human concerns. In his interview with González Bermejo,[8] Cortázar would later acknowledge that a transformation had come over him when he moved to Paris, a transformation that is reflected in "El perseguidor," for the story revolves around character, rather than vice versa. Although the earlier Cortázar (the Cortázar of *Bestiario* and *Final del juego*) had created believable characters and had felt personally involved with some of them, he had been at least as concerned with aesthetic matters and had sometimes sacrificed character development in favor of narrative effects. "El perseguidor" reflects the fact that Cortázar had, by the time he wrote it, been living in Paris for some years, and his life there had been much more intense, more filled with human experiences than the somewhat bookish and withdrawn one he had led in Buenos Aires. The emotional and intellectual readjustment represented by the move to Paris, his "road to Damascus," had generated a feeling that what was bothering him had to be expressed in writing.[9]

Though faithful in many ways to the biography of Parker, Cortázar projects onto Johnny some of his own preoccupations, such as his suspicion vis-à-vis our concept of time, the feeling that the *métro* is an environment that invites different modes of perception, and the belief that music may allow one to express what language will not. The main interest in the story centers on the dynamics between Johnny and Bruno although the contrast between them is not as clear as one might at first be tempted to assume. Moreover, we should note that the title in Spanish is ambiguous—"The pursuer" or "The persecutor." It is not at all clear that it refers only to the musician. In his music, Johnny is the pursuer of something that cannot be defined, something that Bruno's more intellectual mind can only glimpse, something that has to do with personal authenticity and self-expression. Although Bruno seems genuinely concerned about the way in which Johnny is destroying himself and wasting such talent, he pursues him out of professional interest, rather as *paparazzi* pursue the objects of their attention. Delving into his own motives, Bruno asks himself how far he is really concerned about Johnny's life. Isn't he really worried that Johnny might go his own way and end up undermining Bruno's conclusions in his book? Johnny is difficult, even incoherent, in his dealings with others, and yet, paradoxically, he provokes in Bruno a reaction that is at once patronizing and awestruck.

Bruno is always aware of the task that faces him as biographer and makes a number of references to his difficulties in writing. Except in the closing paragraphs of this long story, he insistently (and unusually, although perhaps one might ascribe it to the influence of French) uses the perfect tense, as if to remind the reader that this is a biography in the making, its subject as protean as are the means to capture it. Ironically, perhaps it is Johnny who expresses that particular dimension most clearly: "No one can say anything without you immediately translating it into your own filthy language" (261). It is as if Johnny were warning that once language takes over and the biography is published the "truth" is fixed, and falsified in the process.

According to comments he made three decades later to Prego,[10] for years prior to writing "El perseguidor" Cortázar had felt "pursued" by the idea of writing a story in which he would confront himself; already familiar with Charlie Parker's music, he settled on him as the focus for the story when, following Parker's death, Cortázar read a brief biography of him in a newspaper. This leads one to wonder what motivated Cortázar to call his protagonist Johnny Carter. A musicological explanation might be that it combines parts of the names of two other well-known saxophone players, Johnny Hodges and Benny Carter. Another explanation follows from the idea that in this story Cortázar is in some sense confronting himself: in other words, CH. P. becomes J. C. in order to allude to Julio Cortázar. This equivalence, however, must not be taken too literally, for it is clear that Cortázar is in Bruno as much as in Johnny. Thirdly, the initials perhaps allude to that most famous of persecuted people, Jesus Christ. Critics have been quick to notice a plethora of religious references in "El perseguidor," ranging from the description of Johnny as a god or an angel or a devil, to Bruno calling himself an evangelist or one of the damned, to the fact that Johnny calls attention to a wound in his side, or the fact that Bruno goes down on his knees before him, or the fact that the epigraph taken from the Apocalypse is associated with John, or the fact that there are some phrases and images in the story that have a biblical ring to them. This is not to imply for a moment that Cortázar sees himself in Christian terms; rather, Christianity provides a cultural framework that is exploited in the construction of the narrative, suggesting that the story's implications extend beyond the author's self-exploration to encompass all of humanity. It is important, however, to realize that one cannot read this story in terms of the simple dialectic opposition of the divine versus the evil.

Johnny and Bruno are complex, overlapping characters, both of whom may be assumed to reflect certain personal characteristics or concerns of the author. One becomes aware of these complexities, of the ethical grayness, so to speak, and, perhaps for that reason, when Johnny dies and Bruno declares the biography complete and final, one has an uncomfortable feeling of escapism, of matters being too tidily resolved. As Bruno puts it at the funeral: "The biography was, so to speak, finished. Perhaps I shouldn't be saying that, but naturally I'm just seeing it from an aesthetic angle" (266).

Many of Cortázar's stories were written in a single sitting, but "El perseguidor" was begun in Paris, halted by writer's block for some three months, and finished during a visit to Switzerland. By Cortázar's standards it is long, even rambling, and lacks the economy and drive that characterizes most of his stories. That said, its importance is not to be underestimated. Above all, this story is important for its themes: in "El perseguidor" we have the deepest exploration yet of what it is to be authentic, of the tension between opposites, of intellect versus instinct, of order versus spontaneity, all of these being matters that will be fully explored later on, especially in *Rayuela*. The author told Evelyn Picón-Garfield[11] that some time after the appearance of *Rayuela* he came to realize that its protagonist and Johnny had much in common and that, had he not written the story, he would never have been able to write the novel. "El perseguidor" was, he said, the beginning of a new phase of awareness of his fellow man. Ultimately, it would lead him into political involvement.

A Telling (and Seeing) Problem

If Bruno's difficulties in giving an account of his subject ("I'm just seeing it from an aesthetic angle") receive a certain amount of attention in "El perseguidor," the problematics of telling are put directly under the microscope in the second of these milestone stories. Whereas so many of Cortázar's stories, especially those of the early period, start by placing the reader beside the characters in a plausibly mundane situation that gradually acquires strange and unpredictable dimensions, at the very beginning of "Las babas del diablo" Cortázar forces upon the reader the realization that he is engaged in an artificial enterprise that is fraught with difficulties. How, the anonymous narrator asks, can one tell this story if the usual armory of language is inadequate and if invented forms will do no better? How is one to put images that are visual into words? Whatever the code used, can one ever be sure that one is doing anything more than telling one's own version of the truth?

After some two pages of such self-reflexive writing the "author" is suddenly set aside in favor of what masquerades as bare facts regarding a protagonist, a photographer called Roberto Michel, and a scene he has witnessed when taking photos beside the Seine. But that illusion of factual objectivity is short-lived, for the storyteller at the typewriter constantly reminds us of his own presence, with comments on the clouds and the pigeons that he can see through his window as he writes. In addition, the author behind Michel overlaps with Michel the "author," since the latter's experiences are recounted sometimes by the anonymous third-person narrator and sometimes in the first person; in other words, Cortázar wants us to identify the two creative artists, writer and photographer, with one another.

There are then posited certain other "facts" making up the scene observed by the photographer, who awaits perfect conditions and seeks the right angle to capture them through his art (through his perspective). However, it soon becomes clear that the photographer is faced with problems that are analogous to the writer's, that the camera's lens (*objetivo* in Spanish) is anything but objective. Just as the use of language constrains the writer, the camera constrains the photographer, framing the subject, selecting; as if to confirm the analogy, the writer sitting before the typewriter sees the clouds and pigeons framed by his window. Biographical data reinforce the association of Cortázar with Michel: both are, so to speak, half French and half South American, both are photographers, but most importantly, both are translators (by profession but also, by virtue of the nature of art, translators of reality). Moreover, Michel, as we shall see, is also a storyteller.

Michel sees a couple beside the river, a mature woman with a young boy; as he takes up his position and adjusts his focus, he invents a story to explain their presence, imagining that though they almost look like mother and son, this is a scene of early sexual experience for the boy, who appears to be nervous and tentative, while the woman is leading him on, perhaps only playing with him in order to leave him frustrated. Finding (from his point of view) the right moment, Michel takes the photo and is then confronted by the woman, who angrily (and unsuccessfully) demands that he give her the film, while the boy flees.

The third-person narrator has already assured us that Michel knows that photographers function by using permutations of their own way of looking at things, while Michel, for his part, tells us that "todo mirar rezuma falsedad" (all looking reeks of falsehood) and that all one can do is be aware at the outset that this is the case and do one's best to strip away the falsifying paraphernalia. Now that it is clear that the photographer and the writer are in the same boat, Michel the photographer/narrator offers an illustration of the difficulty: he tells us that the woman is "slim" and "svelte" (but at once an aside warns us that these words are "not right"), that her face is "white" and "somber" (but we are told that these words, too, are "not right"), and then Michel describes her eyes having recourse first to simile (they fix on their object like an eagle's) and finally to outlandish images (they are "two squalls of green slime"), images to whose outlandishness the narrator once again immediately calls attention.

Here Cortázar is gesturing ironically in the direction of his readers and himself: Michel is constructing a story with a satisfying ending that seems to tie up any loose ends, even a story with mythological hints like many of Cortázar's (for example, the eagle-woman who hovers over her prey, fluttering her wings as if about to steal another Ganymede). However, it appears that, in constructing his account, Michel's selective eye has eliminated a third player in this drama, a man wearing a gray hat and sitting in a car. It therefore seems that the act of framing the scene is like (in the other sense of that word) framing the reader: Michel's ordered explanation turns out to be false, and so he is justifiably said to be "guilty of literature" (220). Now the relevance of the story's title becomes clear. The cobweb patterns traced by early-morning dew (which, it should be noted, will be wiped out when the sun, in photographic terms the light level, increases) may be described, may be "looked at" in two ways: "las babas del diablo" (the devil's spittle) has its equivalent in the French "les fils de la Vierge," a phrase that, *translated,* becomes "los hilos de la Virgen" (the Virgin's threads). This alternative representation of the phenomenon signals a darker, alternative reading of the scene, one that includes the man in gray (maybe a homosexual or a pimp, about to corrupt a minor) who, like so many other gray figures in Cortázar's fictions, implies danger.[12]

However, the complexities of this fiction do not end there. Ill at ease, Michel leaves the river, returns to his apartment, and, still fascinated, enlarges the photo he has taken to life-size. He hangs it on his wall, where it dominates the room and seems to come to life (a possible reference to the Pygmalion myth). As it does so, caught in the middle of translating a sentence (whose meaning is in itself not irrelevant), Michel slips out of the picture: "de mí no quedó nada" (there was nothing left of me/mine) (222). The typewriter falls to the floor; the author "dies." Now the story, in Pirandellian fashion, seems to take on an impulse of its own, as if it were telling itself, with Michel swept frighteningly along like any other actor in the drama. But in a final paragraph the writer in the apartment, looking through his window at the changing images of clouds and pigeons, reasserts himself, and in doing so reminds us of Cortázar's theme. This is not simply another horror story, it is a story about the nature of artistic creativity.[13]

Given the many references to the processes and devices of both storyteller and photographer and to the evocative power of the static image, together with the repeated use of words related to seeing and the allusions to perspective, composition, and verbal narration, this is the most self-referential of Cortázar's early works. Here Cortázar faces his need to tell stories and the problem of how to tell them. "Las babas del diablo" is a meditation on creative impulses and processes, on art as translation, on the elusive nature of truth, and on the human impulse to order and explain. It feeds, like some of Borges's fictions, on the philosophy of idealism, on skepticism regarding language and the status of truth, in ways that seem to anticipate later writers (and critics). Previous works by Cortázar had never been as explicit in their thematization of the creative process, and this, together with its technical inventiveness, is what makes "Las babas del diablo" so important, heralding the writerly concerns of *Rayuela.* "Las babas del diablo" inspired the Italian director Michelangelo Antonioni's feature film *Blow Up,* (hence the title of the story in its English translation), though, perhaps fittingly, the differences between the two works are quite marked.

Interestingly, in the very last story of the very last collection that Cortázar published (*Deshoras,* 1982) once again he deals directly with the problems involved in telling stories. "Diario para un cuento" (Diary of a story) is structured as a series of diary entries spanning the month of February 1982, and it seems to be firmly rooted in Cortázar's own experience. "Diario para un cuento" is told in the first person, and the first entry in it evokes the writer sitting before his typewriter, surrounded by cigarette ends, and recalling his few encounters with Adolfo Bioy Casares, a contemporary of Cortázar's, a fellow Argentine writer, and someone Cortázar tells us he liked. The second entry begins by saying that so far the writer/Cortázar has been beating about the bush, but then he imagines Bioy quoting a short piece of verse in English that tells of Annabel Lee, a maiden who many years ago lived in a kingdom by the sea.[14] This elicits from Cortázar the comment, deflatingly, that it was not a kingdom at all but a republic, nor was her name Lee, but Flores; furthermore, his Annabel was no maiden, having been "deflowered" (a play on "flores") by a traveling salesman. In this way the seeds of what will eventually be a seedy story are sown. However, before any further progress is made, in the third entry the author talks once more of his difficulties in getting going with the story, and he takes a diversion via an obscure passage written by Jacques Derrida, in which he finds confirmation that his goal is unattainable: "I know," he says, "that I never had access to Anabel, nor will I ever, and that writing a story about her now, a story that in a sense *is* her, is impossible." But the story does indeed get going: Cortázar evokes the years when Perón was on the rise and Cortázar was working as a translator. Into his office one day comes a prostitute from El Bajo, an area close to the port of Buenos Aires, asking him to write letters for her to a sailor, and to translate his letter to her, written in English. As he does so, the translator becomes personally involved. He *composes* as much as translates the letters (rather as Cortázar is now composing as much as relaying Anabel's story). He also has a physical relationship with Anabel, which contrasts with his relationship with the middle-class Susana and recalls the opposition between respectable and bohemian lifestyles that Cortázar had explored in a story included in *Todos los fuegos el fuego,* "El otro cielo" (The other heaven).

Eventually, despite some continuing reminders of authorial awareness, such as a reference at one point to his purchase of "something by Borges and/or Bioy" (two authors who did in fact coauthor a number of works), Anabel's story seems to have taken over. It would be an exaggeration to say that that story has a dénouement: it lurches along into a confusion involving poison and betrayal. The translator realizes that he has lost control of Anabel's story and that he is no longer a player in it. The means by which he learns that he has been marginalized is the reports he receives from his friend Hardoy, a man in whom he insists he has absolute confidence. However, it is significant that Hardoy is merely another fictional character, imported from an early Cortázar story, "Las puertas del cielo" (The gates of heaven), a story that has some similarities with the present one. In his final diary entry Cortázar portrays a translator who is no longer visited by the other characters (one must surely think of Pirandello's *Six Characters in Search of an Author*). He is resignedly going back to translating patents and immigration papers, though he would have liked to round off Anabel's story. Cortázar's readers cannot tell what has been fiction; in "Diario para un cuento" the translator and author have fused into one, implying that writing is translation. Cortázar ends by summoning Derrida once more: nothing is left, neither the thing nor the experience of it; "Looking for Anabel in the recesses of time always brings me back to myself, and it's so dreary to write about myself even though I like to carry on imagining myself writing about Anabel" (509). After so many turbulent years as a public figure, it is interesting to see that Cortázar's last story seems to reaffirm his interest in writing, as such.

Children and Adolescents

Quite a number of Cortázar's stories inhabit the world of children. Cortázar saw children as spontaneous and intuitive beings uninhibited by the trappings of adulthood, the conventions and patterns of thought and action that limit adults. He often casts doubt on the idea that our world can be accounted for in terms of reason, of cause and effect. When children are used as a vehicle for expressing that doubt, they are portrayed as being able to accept phenomena without the demand for rational order or logical explanation; the fantastic and the fantasmagorical can take their place beside the real, for perceptions stretch beyond the confines of reason and language. In *Territorios* (1978, 108) Cortázar refers to children as "Eleatic" and "pre-Socratic." The adult worldview will eventually impose itself, however: in "Manuscrito hallado en un bolsillo" (Manuscript found in a pocket) Cortázar writes that "children look unflinchingly straight at things until the time comes when they are taught to locate themselves in the gaps between as well" (*Cuentos completos,* 2:66).

For Cortázar the transition into adulthood, a painful experience that has been dealt with by so many writers, marks not only a loss of innocence but also a loss of richness. Notable among the losses is the child's sense of playfulness. It is therefore understandable that many of Cortázar's adult characters, perhaps especially those who serve as his alter ego (one thinks especially of Oliveira, the central figure in *Rayuela*) are noteworthy precisely because they still cultivate that sense of playfulness and seem to be overgrown children. In one of his interviews, Cortázar said that everyone he had lived with had complained at one time or another about the degree to which he was still a child at heart. He acknowledges that they had reason to do so: "Faced with certain situations in which adults naturally tend to behave like adults . . . my reaction tends to be childlike, playful."[15] In another interview he confessed: "I am still very much a child and very adolescent in many things. . . . There's always been an adolescent side to all my emotional relationships."[16]

One can observe the writer's complicity with children in such stories as "Silvia" and "Las fases de Severo" (Severo's phases). In the latter, the ailing Severo is attended by friends and relatives gathered around his bed. Together they enact a series of bizarre rituals, while the reader angles for a rational explanation of these activities. Toward the end of this story a child turns to the narrator, who happens to be called Julio, wondering if what he takes to be a game is over and asking for reassurance that it has indeed been a game; Julio assures the child that it has. Perhaps the story has all been a game, and so the joke is on the reader, who has been struggling to make sense of it. Perhaps, though, declaring it all a game is simply a way of dealing with something that is rationally incomprehensible, because conspicuously, at the close of the story, the adults are said to be busying themselves with routine things, donning their slippers and starting to sip mate, which, the narrator wryly concludes, are "things that always help."

Fernando, the narrator of "Silvia," is surely a thinly disguised Cortázar, since he lives as an exile in Provence, has friends who are Argentine or at least versed in Spanish American literature, and demonstrates such empathy with children. When Fernando first arrives at the house of some of these friends their young daughter Graciela rushes into his arms and settles herself on his knee, as if expecting to be told a story. It seems, however, as if their roles are reversed. Graciela keeps referring to Silvia, the young woman who looks after the group of children of whom Graciela is one, tending to their cuts and bruises and other bodily needs and comforting them; apparently she is old enough to act like an adult, but still close enough to their world of cowboys and Indians for them to feel she is like an older sister. Fernando thinks he glimpses her in the firelight; he appreciates her figure and becomes attracted and absorbed by her as, all the while, he is engaged in conversation with the other adults about intellectual and artistic matters. When he asks the children about Silvia, they say simply that she comes along sometimes and that if he doesn't understand, he is silly; when he questions the adults, they dismiss Silvia as the children's imaginary companion, telling him not to let them string him along. But Fernando is smitten by curiosity and by Silvia, wishing both to understand rationally and to believe, because Silvia represents the lost power of childhood fantasy (and also arouses his adult lust). The rational explanation is that Fernando is getting drunk and that part of him is still credulously innocent and childlike. Yet the imagined Silvia grows in importance until she occupies his mind more fully than do the real adults. At a later social gathering, Fernando is obsessed with whether she present or not, and when, at last, she is no longer, his sense of loss is palpable. Graciela has the final word when he asks her if Silvia is there: "Mira que sos tonto. . . . Es la luna. . . . Qué adivinanza tan sonsa, che" (How silly you are! It must be the moon. . . . What a loony thing to think!) (21)

"Who is Silvia? What is she?" are questions that are familiar to us thanks to Schubert's setting to song a poem in German based on one in Shakespeare's *The Two Gentlemen of Verona* (4.2). Elsewhere in that play (3.1) Shakespeare writes in a way that appears to encapsulate Fernando's predicament:

What light is light, if Silvia be not seen?
What joy is joy, if Silvia be not by?
Unless it be to think that she is by
And feed upon the shadow of perfection.

The choice of Silvia as the name for the girl in Cortázar's story is probably not fortuitous but rather intended to call to mind the Schubert melody as a sort of leitmotif. Just as we know that Cortázar was often influenced by music, we also know that echoes of Shakespeare in his work are quite frequent.

Apart from any quest for the ideal love—"the shadow of perfection"—here in "Silvia" we have the child and adult worlds in contrast with one another, the one open to imagination and possibility, the other circumscribed by reason and social custom. The story also has a metatextual dimension, since it presents a fiction within a fiction. Graciela is told by her mother to go back to playing with the other children and stop telling Fernando stories, but Graciela grasps Fernando's face between her hands "to tear him away from the grown-ups," and she insists to him that she and the other children have not invented Silvia. Later, the mother chides Fernando for being gullible and falling for the children's version, and close to the end of the Cortázar's story, when Silvia seems to have vanished, the mother says that that is just as well, since they (the adults) had all had enough of "that story." In saying this she is no doubt alluding to the child's habit of inventing as much as to the specifics relating to Silvia. One might compare "Silvia" with other Cortázar stories that present a fiction within a fiction and use the embedded fiction to remind us that the outer one is no less fictional, no more deserving of trust: I refer to stories such as "La salud de los enfermos" (The health of the sick) and "La isla a mediodía" (The island at noon).

In many stories, then, including "Bestiario" and "En nombre de Boby" (In the name of Boby), the child's worldview is contrasted with the adult's. In a good number of them, however, the focus is on growing up. An early example is "Los venenos," a highly autobiographical story, which portrays an idyllic world of children playing in a garden; they are fascinated by a piece of fumigating apparatus brought by an uncle to put an end to an infestation of ants. The story also deals with first feelings of love: there is poison to harm the ants and poison to hurt the feelings of the child narrator. Beyond the ramifications of its title, "Los venenos" is a remarkably realistic and straightforward story; it is also an engaging and accomplished evocation of the edenic world of the children and the sensibilities of the child narrator. The interest in insects is typical of Cortázar; he sees spiders as weavers of destinies, associates rigidity and conformity with beetles, and hostility with ants. In some autobiographical passages in *Territorios* there are powerful evocations of lost innocence, of a lost sense of wonder (see, especially, "Las grandes transparencias" [Large-scale transparencies]), and in that same book (44) mankind is pictured fighting for liberty against the "horminids" (*hormiga* is "ant" in Spanish).

"Final del juego" (End of the game), the title story of that collection, is perhaps the most indicative of how Cortázar regards the passage from childhood to adulthood. It is about three sisters who play "statues" on an embankment for the benefit of a boy they see speeding by periodically in a train. They dub him "Ariel" (Cortázar's allusion to Shakespeare's sprite). Ariel drops a note telling the girls how much he enjoys the show and saying that he is most intrigued by one whose name is Leticia. But she is handicapped, and there comes a time when the truth about her condition must be revealed in a note that is passed to Ariel. In these new circumstances Leticia, who is likened by the author to a trapped insect, poses for him one last time. Thus the game is put away, the facts of life are faced, and the handicapped Leticia (whose name means "Joy") is left in tears. And so it turns out that her name has been ironically chosen: the description of her early in the story as "the happiest of the three of us, and the most privileged" (394) proves to be the opposite of the truth.

A psychological handicap is perhaps what dogs the life of the narrator of "Después del almuerzo" (After lunch), another story to be found in *Final del juego*. After lunch, the narrator, an adolescent, obeys his parents' instructions and takes "it" (or "him") on a bus ride into the town. Whatever one may like to assume "it" actually is (for its identity is never revealed), more important is what it represents in terms of an adolescent's fears, inhibitions, and sense of responsibility. At one point the adolescent tries to abandon "it," to break away, but in the end he returns home as anticipated and is even proud to have done so. The recurrent images of dead leaves in this story suggest that some of the problems are not exclusive to the adolescent or escapable in adult life.

Shortly before his death, in semblance an old man, Cortázar wrote a prologue to a collection of stories by a friend, in which he singled out the ability of children to strip bare the world of those who pretend to control them, thus rendering it derisory: "But adolescence emerges, slowly and bitterly; in that murky in-between state games enter an area in which prohibitions will be violated. . . . These are fake adults who cannot accept the rules of the game . . . the adolescent turns one last time toward his past in a final, desperate attempt at resistance."[17]

Among the stories that concentrate on young people, two stand out because they focus directly and solely on the sufferings of adolescence, the road to independence from a mother figure, and the achievement of sexual maturity. "La señorita Cora" (Nurse Cora) was first published in 1966, in the collection *Todos los fuegos el fuego;* almost twenty years later Cortázar published the story "Ud. se tendió a tu lado" (whose title, as will become evident, is not translatable) in *Alguien que anda por ahí*. Each is an interesting narrative experiment in which the style in some way represents the theme.

In "La señorita Cora," Pablo Morán, an adolescent, is admitted to a hospital for an appendectomy, but complications arise and lead to his death; the story is concerned with the relationship between the boy, his mother, and Nurse Cora, a triangular relationship in which the boy is the apex. The opening words, a monologue by the mother, at once establish her domineering protectiveness as she complains about the clinic's failure to provide a guest bed for her and about her "little boy's" disorientation on realizing he would be without her: "He is only fifteen and no one would believe it always sticking to me though now that he's in long trousers he's trying to fool everyone and pretend to be a grown man" (548). Her complaints center on "that hussy of a nurse," whose authority in the clinic is confused by the mother with rivalry for the care and attention of Pablo. His mother is an amusingly convincing stereotype: she is over possessive, a social snob, and unwilling to release her son into manhood; she has a henpecked husband whose behavior, in her view at least, is typically male; and she is jealous of Cora as a potential rival and garrulous to boot. Just as it seems that the story might slip into triteness, there comes the first narrative surprise: "Habrá que ver si la frazada lo abriga bien al nene, voy a pedir que por las dudas le dejen otra a mano. Pero, sí, claro que me abriga, menos mal que se fueron de una vez, mamá cree que soy un chico y me hace hacer cada papelón" (548; I'll have to make sure the blanket is keeping my baby warm, I'm going to ask them to have a second one handy just in case. Yes, of course I'm warm enough, thank goodness they've finally gone, Mom thinks I'm just a boy and creates so much fuss). In the middle of a paragraph Cortázar has moved from one monologue to another, from the mother to the boy. The blanket issue is seen from two points of view. So too are the mother's enforced absence and her protests against it. It becomes clear that Pablo's inclination to "pretend to be a grown man" is not all a matter of show, though she cannot accept that fact. Nevertheless, his wish to grow into independence is contained by boyish enthusiasm. Thus the noise of the lift evokes in him memories of an exciting horror film, and when his sweets are taken away by the nurse, one is not quite sure whether his indignation is caused by the fact of having them removed, as if from an irresponsible child, or because he simply wants to suck mints. Many actions and reactions point to Pablo's ambivalence: this young man still reads comics, blushes repeatedly at the slightest cause, has a voracious appetite that he feels he must deny, finds it impossible to talk about normal bodily functions, and is acutely embarrassed at his own sexuality. As the story progresses, the shifts of perspective become more sudden, taking place in mid sentence, and are sometimes not even signaled by punctuation marks. Moreover, more perspectives are involved than those of the boy and his mother: most importantly, Cora comes into play. When she does so, the sentence thread that links Pablo with his mother like an umbilical cord is replaced by a new bond, with the nurse, a bond that has both maternal and sexual overtones.

We have already seen that a union can be forged between Pablo and the women, first his mother, then Cora, by means of narrative style. Another respect in which language can be called mimetic in this story is in the changes of style— now puerile, now blasé, now composed—reflecting the protagonist's attitudes. Sometimes we see a loose interdependence of too many statements, in the manner of an enthusiastic, but not particularly articulate, child. In all senses, Pablo's style matures in the course of this story; the hospital stands for the school of life, in which he acquires self-assurance and independence, growing free of his mother and then even of Cora, to die with a sad and lonely dignity.

Cortázar admitted that he was very fond of this story and that he had identified closely with Pablo, having himself experienced similar feelings when being treated by a young woman dentist.[18] Furthermore, Freud, he says, confirms the adolescent tendency to project erotic fantasies onto caregivers. As he wrote the story, Cortázar *was* Pablo; he both loved and hated Cora. In *Último round* (149; "upper floor") Cortázar said that (at least until 1969) he had never written anything as erotic as "La señorita Cora."

All through his evolution, Pablo is viewed with sympathy; he is indeed adolescent in the original sense of the word, for his physical and mental anguish run in tandem. Other characters may view him with patronizing disdain (Marcial and, to some degree, Cora also) or insensitivity (his mother), but the reader is made to feel sympathetic throughout and senses that an awesome outcome is inevitable. One might perhaps compare this story with that of the boy on the boat in *Los premios* (*The Winners*), Felipe (see chapter 5). Lacking in experience but determined to assert his adult self, to "behave like a grown-up," he makes a rash sortie into the forbidden zone; his motives are recognized for what they are, but he fails to achieve his aims and provokes adult reactions that range from mockery and amusement to sympathetic understanding. To paraphrase the comments of one sympathetic (adult) fellow passenger, what makes him so engaging is that he is on the verge of change; he is aggressive, fearful, dimly aware of love; he senses that the time is near but doesn't know of what.

In another story in *Todos los fuegos el fuego,* "El otro cielo," the protagonist, who this time is an adult, is still seen as partially dependent on his mother. We see him in two contexts, the Buenos Aires of Perón and the Second World War, and the Paris of Lautréamont and the Prussian War, his passage from one to another being realized fantastically. His Buenos Aires self represents the epitome of middle-class behavior running along the expected channels, whereas in Paris his existence is bohemian and precarious. The two are linked by the common image of the arcade, in such a way that having entered the Pasaje Güemes in Buenos Aires the protagonist can exit from the Galérie Vivienne into Paris, break with conventionality and, most significantly for our present discussion, the expectations of his mother. Thus the arcade is, in a sense, a duct through which life passes, and what matters for us is that it passes from mother and wife relationships to one that is more free; "El otro cielo" is evidently concerned with broader issues than that of a son freeing himself from his mother's apron strings. Although the arcade is not quite a symbol of the umbilical cord, it is certainly an evocative image, one which suggests that the passage to the other side, to the alter ego, is related to the transition to adulthood. Interestingly, the transition to adulthood is here associated with a move toward greater authenticity of being; there seems to be some contradiction between it and the association that Cortázar more commonly makes between adulthood and loss of spontaneity and suppression of the instinctual.

It is within the Buenos Aires setting that Cortázar dwells somewhat on the adolescent crisis; the spectral figure of the South American who moves about Paris makes one think of the author's own passage to France and the transformation that experience brought about in him, a man nearing forty. Cortázar writes, as if in echo of the image of Pablo in "La señorita Cora":

Round about 1928 the Pasaje Güemes was the treasure cave that offered a delicious mixture of glimpses of sin and mint candy (590).

My mother always knows if I've slept at home . . . [her] present consists of a clear tacit signal that the offense is over, the son has returned to normal life at home with his mother (592).

It was to be another decade before Cortázar returned to the theme of adolescence as his central concern in what proved to be another experimental story, this time a more daring one: "Ud. se tendió a tu lado." The title of this story is ungrammatical, offering immediate proof of the way in which here theme and form are inextricably entwined. The ungrammaticality arises form Cortázar's inventive use of second-person pronouns. In standard Spanish there are both familiar and honorific (polite) forms of pronouns; in Argentine Spanish there are additional dialectal variants, which extend the palette. This is not the place to enter into technical details regarding how Cortázar deploys these devices in "Ud. se tendió a tu lado." The effect is to create ambiguity surrounding the identity of the referent and the narrative point of view adopted; in other words, the reader is not always sure who is being talked about and by whom. One wonders, for example, whether Cortázar is using both familiar and honorific forms to refer to a single person. If so, does the use of one or the other imply a change of attitude toward that person, and is that change of attitude on his own part or on the part of another character in the story? Is it perhaps the narrator's attitude that changes with the pronouns, or is it a case of authorial omniscience giving way, at times, to perspectives that are narrative-internal, that is, those of the characters in it? We have already noted that the title is strange. Also puzzling is the opening line, which may mean "When was the last time I/he/she/you had seen him/it/you naked?" Nor is this the end of the perplexities. The first paragraph is a long, single-sentence onslaught on the reader, comparable with the opening of "La autopista del sur" and some other stories; during this sentence, a succession of images of adolescent self-awareness—the locked bathroom, the croaking voice, the self-absorption—gives way to a flurry of childlike dependence: "a una costumbre de salto al pescuezo, de violento cariño y besos húmedos, mamá, mamá querida, Denise querida, mamá o Denise según el humor y la hora, vos el cachorro, el cachorro de Denise" (140; to the habit of throwing his arms around his mother's neck, of rough affection and slobbery kisses, Mommy, dear Mommy, dear Denise, Mommy or Denise according to the mood and the hour, you little puppy, Denise's little puppy).

This establishes the theme clearly enough as the ambivalence of adolescence. The vacillation between "Mommy" and "Denise" is, it seems, paralleled by the confusion of pronouns, and thus one is left wondering how far the child is still strongly attached to his mother and how far he is truly independent and self-reliant. By referring to both mother and son with second-person pronouns Cortázar achieves two effects: he places Denise and Roberto close together, and himself close to them. It is as though the two "you" forms bind mother and son into one being at times addressed as a child, at times as an adult; Cortázar, then, uses a dual form of address that is analogous to Roberto's use of "Mommy" and "Denise." Other characters in the story are kept at a distance by being referred to in the third person. Moreover, the confusion of second-person referents reflects, in a formal, linguistic way, the emotional, even physical link between those referents, the mother and the son; the "you" forms are functioning as a linguistic equivalent of the umbilical cord.

Inventive and highly successful though this story may be, we should note that the writer's self-awareness is also reflected when he explicitly states that ordinary language is not up to the task in hand: thus the characters are said to be engaged in "an almost incomprehensible exchange of monosyllables, laughs, and shoves from the new wave that no grammar could make clear and that was life itself laughing at grammar" (144).

The linguistic antics in "Ud. se tendió a tu lado" are more daring than the mid-sentence shifts of perspective in "La señorita Cora," and so are their implications. On the symbolic and thematic level the story has a good deal in common with the earlier story, although the mother, Denise, far from being protective, is liberated, forward-looking, and provides Roberto with the means to break away from her. Once again a boy is confronted with two women, a mother and a potential lover. Lilian, the lover, is much talked about but makes her dramatic entry only at the end. The mother here may be very predominant, but she is not the possessive mother figure of "La señorita Cora." Instead, she is inclined to suppress any such feelings (including a certain physical attraction), and she finally becomes impatient with her son's lack of independence. The difficulty of the transition to manhood arises very much from Roberto himself. Denise makes disparaging comments at the expense of other parents, attributing to them the protective characteristics of Pablo's mother in "La señorita Cora"; although Denise sees her son as a "puppy" and a "baby" she is at pains to push him onward toward adulthood. That so much of the action takes place in the water evokes a womblike environment in which, for example, Roberto dog paddles round his mother; yet this is also Denise, the woman who engages him in an adult conversation about sex and contraception and one for whom his own feelings are partly sexual. The adolescent must learn to swim by himself; nonetheless, seeing his uncertainties, at one stage a wave of protectiveness overcomes Denise, she mothers him and embarrasses him in the process; she will help him along the road to independence, despite herself.

During the course of the narrative there arises a need to buy contraceptives, but it transpires that Roberto does not have the courage to make a visit to the pharmacy, so that Denise, "the little baby's Mommy," must make it for him. Here a tender, but wry, recollection of how she once treated Roberto for a rash in the genital area has the effect of juxtaposing a clinical (Cora-like) involvement with her son and the implicit sexual involvement hinted at by the contraceptive and swimming episodes—she is both mother the nurse and Denise the accomplice in sexual adventure. The embarrassment with regard to purchasing the condoms is set beside the embarrassment of the treatment for the rash. Images from the time of Roberto's childhood are put beside the sprouting moustache and the visible Adam's apple, and in this manner the two occasions fuse: Denise is left thinking that "it was laughable and [she] smiled beneath the water, a wave covering her like a sheet" (143). The feelings of the two protagonists, both of them ambivalent, are finely captured and played off against one another. As a result, when the visit to the pharmacy does take place, it is as if both share the experience, so closely are their emotions bound together; apparently it is Denise who makes the visit, but once there she senses the embarrassment that Roberto would feel at finding himself having to deal with a young female employee. Moreover, Denise, her adult side laughing at her own quasi-adolescent evasiveness, buys alcohol in order to stall for time before blurting out her request to the shop assistant and surprising all present.

Once she is back home, and with the contraceptives now lying on his bed, Roberto makes half manly, half childlike overtures to his mother ("let me in"). She, meanwhile, is portrayed as virginal and seductive ("looking young in her low-cut white dress"). The sexual subtheme previously suggested in the water scenes is thus reinforced. The dreamlike paragraph provides the climax (145-46). Ostensibly it relates Roberto's first sexual experience with Lilian, but the images of incubus and succubus, the by now customary confusion of references by means of pronouns, and the reiterated allusions to childhood disorders all serve to implicate Denise as well in the experience. The final water scene links with the dream images also. Denise is face up; someone, perhaps Denise again, is face down. Roberto buzzes around her solicitously, while Lilian is still relegated to the fringe. He wills his mother to decide that the beach days are over and that it is time to return home, but she is not prepared to play Arachne for him: "If mother's baby has a bad throat, then it's time for him to find his own pills" (146).

Roberto's realization that his time has come brings back phrases that opened the story, producing the circularity that Cortázar is often seeking in his stories. However, if Roberto realizes what is inevitable, he yet does not have strength to act accordingly. Denise turns away from him in desperation at the impossibility of going back to a time when the bathroom door was left unlocked, when Roberto watched her dress with no more than childlike curiosity. The boy remains submissive, while the women stay on top to the end. But it is at this final juncture that Lilian steps forward to sit between them, as if by her action she were at last severing the umbilical cord.

Adolescence reappears in "Siestas," a story first included in *Último round*. It is also a major focus of the title story of Cortázar's last collection, *Deshoras,* published in 1982. There, he traces the beginnings of love in pages that echo the emotional atmosphere of "Los venenos," and he continues with passages (especially in the third section) that might almost be paraphrases of parts of "La señorita Cora" and "Ud. se tendió a tu lado." In "Deshoras" ("Unreasonable Hours") the boy Aníbal senses in Sara, the big sister of his best friend, Doro, that same amalgam of nurse, mother, and potential lover; but he does not feel he can express his interest and so he yearns for her in silence, believing that she is unaware of his feelings. The story begins with a first-person narrator, Aníbal himself, but soon switches to the third, a switch that will later prove to be crucial. Sara is a surrogate mother to Doro because of the physical incapacity of their mother. Sara's mothering extends to Aníbal, who is devastated one day when she comes into the bathroom and sees him naked. To compound his suffering, Sara then marries a man who takes her away. Years later when, for all their good intentions, Doro and Aníbal have lost touch and the latter has moved to Buenos Aires, become an adult, and entered into a business partnership, chance leads his path to cross with Sara's. After a brief moment of embarrassment they start to communicate as adults, and she reveals to him that years before, when she had come into the bathroom, she had already been aware of his interest in her and so had entered deliberately in the hope of curing him of his longing. It seems that now, as adults, they have reached the point where they will consummate the relationship. However, at this juncture the narrator reminds us of his identity by slipping back into the first person; by doing so he emphasizes that he has been telling a story, using words that for a while had "gone along astride reality" but that are now yielding to it in the form of his wife reminding him of things that need to be attended to about the house. The main point of "Deshoras," then, rather as in Carlos Fuentes's story "La muñeca reina" (The doll queen), has to do with levels of fictionality. In the dénouement of "Deshoras" the hopeless and idealized longing of Aníbal for Sara seems to be satisfied by means of the author's trick of suggesting that the two of them meet by chance years later as adults and become lovers; yet this adult encounter remains a literary one, "written" by the narrator, still ideal. One is reminded of the elusive perfection of Silvia, of the joy that may be had in imagining that she is "by."

Women Feared, Loved, Abused

The ambivalence of adolescents with regard to their mothers is only part of a larger picture in which Cortázar's women figures are by turns fearsome, protective, stifling, desirable, and even abusable. So far as love is concerned, broadly positive portrayals, such as those involving passion, sad evocations of failed affairs, and hopes of total communication, are counterbalanced by images of rape and violence. The explanation for such a polyvalent view of women is probably to be found in the extent to which the author exploits his subconscious, in particular as revealed by dreams. There are literary and psychological texts that undoubtedly fed this complex scenario, such as the works of Georges Bataille and Freud, to name only two.

The image of women in the poem "Las tejedoras" (Weaving women) is a daunting one indeed, one of inexorable, silent manipulators, of an oppressive Arachne. In the story "La salud de los enfermos" (The health of the sick) the mother figure, though entirely sympathetic, emerges as the power in control of a fiction-within-the-fiction, psychologically the strongest of all the characters in the story, even though physically the most frail. Her deceased favorite son, like that other mother's favorite son in "Cartas de Mamá" (Letters from Mother), is the motivating element in the drama. In the latter story, the closing pages show us her other son dutifully writing a letter to her, discarding a first attempt in favor of a second that asserts greater independence from her, only to be faced with the phantasmal presence of the favored son; it is as if "Mamá," rather than being senile as had been supposed, is mysteriously asserting her power. (Both stories are discussed more fully on pages 66–67.)

A little imagination applied to the surname of the protagonist of "Circe," Delia Mañara, will yield the word *araña,* which means "spider." Delia is certainly a schemer; she is already on her third suitor, the two previous ones having died mysteriously, and she is feeding him homemade, chocolate-covered cockroaches. She also has an uncanny affinity with animals and is able to predict their demise. One day Mario, her current fiancé, goes into the kitchen and finds the cat dead, with splinters in its eyes. Delia had predicted the cat's death, and Mario is disturbed by this; he breaks open a chocolate and sees what she has done. There are narrative signs along the way: the reluctance of members of Delia's family to try the chocolates, the fact that they cut them first, and the cockroaches that are seen in the kitchen. Delia has been attracting men in order to destroy them, an evil sorceress like her mythological namesake. "Circe" is one of the stories that Cortázar wrote to exorcise a neurosis, in this case, about food.

Many stories are about love affairs tinged with sadness, if not outright pessimism. "Las caras de la medalla" (The faces of the medal), discussed elsewhere in this chapter, deals with a couple who become close but whose relationship never quite comes off. "Todos los fuegos el fuego" (All fires the fire) is about two love triangles that culminate in death. "Vientos Alisios" (Trade Winds) is about a couple trying to recapture the enthusiasm of their early life together; they devise an elaborate game that will take them abroad on separate flights to a place where, provided that they respect their rules and things fall into place, they might rediscover each other. Lodged separately in the Trade Winds resort hotel, they trade lovers, and when the time comes for them to return home it is as if they have become their respective lovers. "Verano" (Summer) deals with somewhat similar territory: a couple with a stale marriage are spending a routine summer holiday and looking after the young daughter of some friends. One night, they are disturbed by the noise of a horse threatening to enter (a night mare?). The wife, who is terrified, believes that her fear and the threat of violence have come about because of the presence of the young girl. Her husband then forces her to make love. But later, routine resumes its sway. Cortázar explained to González Bermejo that the story was autobiographical, set in his house in Saignon, and that the horse represented his personal feelings at the time of a declining relationship. "Lugar llamado Kindberg" (A place named Kindberg) is not at all fantastic and is also based to a degree on personal experience; in it, a middle-aged man picks up a young female hitchhiker who rekindles his youthful passion but in doing so shows him what might have been. He then kills himself in a car crash. Both stories are in *Octaedro,* which, as some critics have noted, can be a depressing book because of its themes.

The violence associated with sex can reach disturbing proportions. In "Las armas secretas," a fine and relatively long story, Pierre and Michèle are lovers, but Pierre is a troubled man. Each time it seems that they are coming truly close to each other he is overcome by the sense that another being, a double, is invading his life and carrying him toward an ineluctable, unseen destiny. This feeling is accompanied by recurrent images, such as a shotgun, a glass ball, and strains of a song in German, by Schumann. Pierre tries to find rational explanations for what is happening. The reader also learns that Michèle is haunted by a past experience: she was once raped when France was under German occupation, and the rapist was killed. Though unaware of these facts, in the dénouement of the story Pierre is taken over by the personality of the German rapist and he reenacts the rape with Michèle, who seems to understand what is happening. At the end of the narrative all the strands and images come together, distasteful though the outcome is.

"Anillo de Moebius" (Moebius strip) in the collection *Queremos tanto a Glenda* (*We Love Glenda So Much*) is probably the most disturbing story of all. Janet, a prudish and virginal British girl, is cycling in France, where she is raped and murdered by Robert, an orphan and a social misfit. She struggles as he rapes her, but not to get away. He is sentenced to death but hangs himself, while she enters a kind of limbo, discovering a desire for him that, it is hinted, might be consummated beyond the grave. A real ambivalence is generated in the reader by the extraordinary beauty of the writing contrasted with the awfulness of its message. That, no doubt, was what Cortázar's intended, though there remains the disturbing implication that the girl enjoys being raped.

"Tango de vuelta" (A return tango) is in the same collection. It is a narrative full of authorial self-consciousness. Unhappy in her marriage, Matilde has abandoned her first husband, Emilio, falsifying his death papers in order to start a new life with Germán. She and Germán live comfortably and conventionally for some years until Emilio reappears, seduces their maid, befriends their son, and comes to get Matilde. In a violent ending she kills him and takes an overdose.

Boxing

Once Cortázar stunned a respectable lady who had asked him which he considered to be the most important moments in recent history by saying that he recalled two in particular: the birth of radio and the death of boxing. This anecdote he tells in "El noble arte" (The noble art) in *La vuelta al día en ochenta mundos*. In 1923 Jack Dempsey had defended his title against an Argentine challenger, Luis Angel Firpo, whom U.S. commentators referred to as "the wild bull from the pampas." Firpo lost, but not before crowds of people had gathered in Cortázar's house to listen to the radio commentary from New York; in those early days there were not many radios in Banfield, the suburb where the Cortázars lived. Julio recalls his wonder on that occasion, at the age of nine, and then goes on to analyze the fight and its implications: in its early stages Dempsey was thrown out of the ring and his supporters broke the rules by helping him back in, but the officials turned a blind eye to that and Dempsey retained his title. Up to that time, says Cortázar, boxing had been in its heyday; there have been great boxers since, but the atmosphere has never been the same. Cortázar appended a note to "El noble arte," recounting that in 1952 it all came back to him on a rainy day in Paris and inspired the story "Torito" (*toro* is "bull" in English). In general Cortázar was no great sports fan; the sports that most interested him were the individual ones, such as singles in tennis, where one could see individual destinies being played out.[19] He attended boxing matches in Argentina up to the early thirties. Trying to explain the appeal of boxing for him, he told Prego that he had evolved a view of boxing that set aside the violence and the blood, which repel so many people, and converted the sport into a game of skill. He personally was interested in the strategists and skillful movers, not in the big punchers.[20] He told Picón-Garfield that a good boxing match was "as beautiful as a swan," and spoke of sublimated violence.[21]

"Torito" is realistic. It is based on a real-life fight and life story, but it concerns another Argentine boxer, Justo Suárez, whose career also peaked in New York. In the story he is beaten by Peralta, abandoned by his girl, and left a ruin. The story is told by the boxer from his hospital bed to a visitor (by implication, the reader). Constant recollections of past glories are counterpointed by the persistent cough of the boxer in the present as he tells his story, dying of tuberculosis. Possibly there is some wider lesson here about how, when people are down, they get kicked, but fundamentally this story speaks of a closed world. Cortázar's empathy with his protagonist is obvious. The language of the story, full of slang and private vocabulary, no doubt makes it appealing to Argentine boxing enthusiasts. Linguistically, it has a certain amount in common with "El móvil" (The motive). "Torito" occupies several minutes in Tristan Bauer's dramatized documentary about Cortázar (1994; *Cortázar*); that fairly represents the author's interest in boxing, but it also makes for the most tedious part of an otherwise interesting film. Probably the best of the boxing stories is "La noche de Mantequilla" (Butterball's night), which is discussed in chapter 7.

Cronopio, Cronopio

Once, when he found himself alone in a theater, seated in its uppermost circle, Cortázar suddenly imagined he could see bloated green things floating around him, things that he immediately thought of as "cronopios." The idea continued to hover around him after that, and so he began to write short pieces about the cronopios —one hesitates to call them stories, despite the fact that they were gathered after his death in the *Cuentos completos*. Later the cronopios were joined by the "famas" and the "esperanzas," which came to Cortázar in a similar, though less precise, manner. Each type then gradually developed characteristics that distinguished it from the others. In the Paris of the early fifties, when Cortázar was neither well known nor particularly busy, he wrote some twenty such pieces, gathered in the *Historias de cronopios y famas* (*Cronopios and*

Famas). Several years later, the editorial director for a major Buenos Aires publisher read these pieces in manuscript and expressed an interest in publishing them, but also said that he wanted more material to fill out a book. During the intervening years between the conception of the cronopios and the approach by the publisher Cortázar had written two unrelated collections of short prose pieces while in Italy, "Material plástico" (Visual matter) and "Manual de instrucciones" (Instruction manual), and another while in Buenos Aires, "Ocupaciones raras" (Strange occupations). In response to the publisher's request, these four sets of pieces then came together to form the book titled *Historias de cronopios y famas* (1962). It is important to note that it was a *mariage de convenance* more than a unified artistic conception, because critics have sometimes been reluctant to face the fact that this book has no real message or cohesiveness. Coinciding in time with the appearance of *Rayuela,* the lighter and slighter book "was met by the heavy artillery," as Cortázar himself describes it.[22]

Historias de cronopios y famas progresses from a vague, "mythological" phase to a point where one can say that cronopios are spontaneous, free-spirited beings with a capacity to enjoy life, whereas famas are more conventional, less imaginative, in Freudian terms more anal. Esperanzas are somewhere in between the other two, and they are inclined to go with the flow. To take a single example that I hope will give a sense of the inventive playfulness of these pieces, under the grand title of "Lo particular y lo universal" ("The Universal and the Particular"), Cortázar tells of a *cronopio* who is carried away with enthusiasm while standing on his balcony and brushing his teeth; it leads him to squeeze an unusually large quantity of toothpaste from the tube. After having cleaned his teeth with an inordinate amount of it, he attempts to dispose of the surplus by throwing it over the balcony, sending blobs of pink toothpaste onto the hats of some famas who happen to be standing below, trying to have a serious discussion. They then appear indignantly on his doorstep, to berate him for spoiling their hats and being profligate with toothpaste.

Other sections of the book are no less entertaining. In "Simulacros" ("Shams"), members of a family are full of projects but confess to being short on Angst. Possibly a Sartrean joke is involved here, but that is as far as it goes. Their latest project is to construct a gallows in their front garden; this attracts onlookers from the neighborhood, but they eventually wander off disappointed because nothing is happening, and so life goes on. In "Perdida y recuperación del pelo" ("Hair Loss and Retrieval"), a cousin is in the habit of pulling out a hair, tying a knot in the middle of it, washing it down the sink, and immediately launching a recovery operation. This may involve enlisting the help of the rest of the family to sort through the many hairs to be found in the waste pipes; should the hair in question have made its way beyond their own lengths of pipe, they may have to go to work in order to earn enough money to buy the flats below and open up their pipes, and so forth. In "Progreso y retroceso" (One step forward, one step backward) a fly is jubilant on discovering that miraculously it can pass through glass, but things go wrong when a Hungarian scientist explains that this is a one-way process, and the fly trap is invented, ruining all hopes of a fraternal relationship with the insect. "Manual de instruccciones" tells one how to do such things as climb stairs (one practical problem in explaining the process is that there are two elements involved that are both called "foot"), how to cry (whatever motivates the crying is neither here nor there; one should concentrate on the appropriate facial contortions and on keeping within normal time limits), and how to sing (break all mirrors in the house, stand facing a wall, forget yourself, emit a note, wait till you see a cluster of surreal images, then go out and buy a dress coat, take lessons, and above all avoid Schumann).

If there is a unifying thread in these absurd pieces it may lie in their attempt to break with routine and the predictable; we tend to be creatures of habit, given to goal-oriented, rational behavior, and we take ourselves too seriously. As always, it is possible to extract social and political implications from these texts, but almost never very coherent or significant ones. Some critics have vainly tried to see *cronos* (time) at the root of the word *cronopio,* but the truth is that it and the other names are pure inventions. Cortázar, in confirming this, referred to Lewis Carroll's poem "Jabberwocky."[23] That was in the early seventies; many years later he told Prego that "in all this there's a friendly irony, there's no allegory . . . there was no didactic or moral purpose."[24] In *Historias de cronopios y famas* Cortázar is simply amusing himself and his readers, exercising his extraordinary imagination in a liberating, absurd, "pythonesque" manner. This collection, perhaps together with *Les Discours du Pince-Gueule* (The discourse of the Pince-Gueule) and *Silvalandia* (Silvaland)—all three owe a debt to Carroll—is the most carefree display of his humor. Other works by Cortázar provide evidence of plenty of humor, but he tends to use it as a counterbalance to pomposity or in poignant contrast with the tragic or horrific. Being funny is, as he liked to insist, often quite a "serious" business. Certainly this can be said of *Un tal Lucas,* a book that is sometimes compared with *Historias;* in *Un tal Lucas* Cortázar's use of humor is generally far more "edgy," more focused on an end beyond itself.

The Other

Rites of passage are everywhere in Cortázar's writing. Numerous images of such things as bridges, boats, and trains (not least among them, the *métro*) are associated with spiritual odysseys to "the other side," and with or without the aid of such signs several works openly foreground the theme of the personal journey. If there is one cohesive feature in all of Cortázar's writing, it is probably the idea of the unrelenting quest for something other and more authentic. Sometimes that other side is attained, but the price of doing so may be death. Sometimes another self, a double, is implicated in the quest. In due course we shall see a number of sophisticated and complex explorations of these things. All of them are crucial elements in *Rayuela,* for example, and a good example of their exploration in a short story can be found in "La isla a mediodía" (discussed on pages 62–65).

One of the earliest illustrations to be found in the stories is "Lejana" (The distances) in the collection *Bestiario.* This story is in diary form, so that the narrator, Alina Reyes, voices "her" views on what is happening; the games with words with which the story starts seem to be her own, and so are the views on what transpires. At the beginning there is an anagrammatic speculation based on her name, suggesting the permutation to which she is about to be subjected; her speculation is said to be "lovely because it opens up a way, but doesn't end" (119). Alina lives a comfortable middle-class life in Buenos Aires, manages and marries her dull but worthy fiancé, but even before doing so is haunted by an awareness of "otherness": while dancing with him in a comfortable salon, with a mixture of sympathy and revulsion she senses the presence of another being, an old beggar woman in Budapest (on another continent, in another season), and has the uncomfortable sensation of snow seeping into her shoes. She tries to forget the image of the woman, let her suffer alone, but here in Buenos Aires Alina thinks that what is happening to the woman in Hungary is happening to Alina, far away, to her other self (120). Dancing with her fiancé she feels warm and sensual, but the woman in Budapest is being beaten, and so Alina has an impulse to tell her fiancé that she isn't feeling very well. Despite much insistence on the imaginary status of the experiences in Budapest (in the diary entry for 25 January, for example, the frequency of words related to thinking, believing, or inventing is particularly conspicuous), those experiences seem to become ever more immediate. By the night of the twenty-eighth it is clear that her life as a socialite in Argentina is losing ground to the realities of Budapest; she is losing her sense of time in a way that parallels the breakdown of the sense of distance. She finds it surprisingly easy to draw her husband, an unwitting pawn, into "the game," and she declares that together they will travel to Hungary. In her final diary entry, dated 7 February, Alina records that she has again sensed the other woman's suffering: "I know they must be beating me again," but she also says that she has been indulging in fantasies that her marriage will cure, that her diary writing, her imagining, must come to an end: "That's enough thinking; it's time to start being" (124). This may appear to signify that now reality will resume its sway and Budapest will fade from the picture, that Alina and her new husband will live out their predictable life together. But in Alina's mind "starting to be" means confronting the reality of the other woman; she anticipates that the two women will meet on a bridge and look each other in the eye.[25] At this point Alina's first-person narrative ends and an omniscient third person steps in to narrate the final page of the story. We are told that Alina and husband go to Budapest, where she wanders the city without a clear direction until she finds herself facing a bridge; hesitatingly, with difficulty but ineluctably, she begins to cross the bridge, and at its center, with tears of mingled joy and suffering, she embraces the old woman and fuses with her.

A similarly fantastic transmigration, this time without social overtones, can be seen in one of Cortázar's most famous stories, "La noche boca arriba" (The night face up), in *Final del juego*. A motorcyclist has an accident in Buenos Aires, is hospitalized as a result, and, whether under the influence of drugs or engaged in some sort of dream or hallucination, he finds himself involved in human sacrifice among the Aztecs of Mexico. Once again the normal barriers of time and space have been transcended; the terminal fiction, that of the scene in Mexico, becomes dominant and more "real" than the Argentine one, the "endless lie" with which the story began: "El sueño maravilloso había sido el otro, absurdo como todos los sueños; un sueño en el que había andado por extrañas avenidas de una ciudad asombrosa, con luces verdes y rojas que ardían sin llama ni humo, con un enorme insecto que zumbaba entre sus piernas" (392; The marvelous dream had been the other one, which was absurd like all dreams; a dream in which he had been going along strange streets in an overwhelming city, with green and red lights that burned with no flames or smoke, with a huge insect buzzing between his legs).

A different approach to the idea of transition to the other is illustrated in "Axolotl" (*Final del juego*); this is one of Cortázar's briefest stories, and it is highly regarded by some people. The narrator is in the habit of going to the Jardin des Plantes in Paris, where there is an aquarium and a tank with an axolotl in it. Fascinated (like Marini, the airline steward who in "La isla a mediodía" stares through the window at his "golden turtle" of an island below), the narrator of "Axolotl" stares intently at the amphibian, is drawn toward an understanding of it, and eventually becomes one with it, looking out at an image of himself on the other side of the glass. Such is the confusion of man and axolotl created by Cortázar's skillful narrative that it becomes difficult for one to describe how the story ends. There is a self-referential twist, as there is in a number of later stories. Thinking about believing about imagining, the axolotl-man says: "I find consolation in thinking that perhaps he is going to write about us, believing he is imagining a story he is going to write about axolotls" (385). The problem with "Axolotl" is one that the author himself sensed.[26] In the third sentence of the extremely short first paragraph the narrator bluntly informs the reader that he is now an axolotl; the ensuing account of the transformation, or transmigration to the other—the axolotl—becomes an explanation after the event, not a preparation for it. This is another story based on personal experience. Cortázar told Prego about his fondness for animals and the fascination with which he had studied the axolotl in the Jardin des Plantes until he was overcome by a fear that made him want to run from the place. Some time later, when a pair of documentary makers had asked him to go back to the aquarium to film a scene, he had refused because the memory of that fear still haunted him. Cortázar told González Bermejo also about his obsession with "the impossibility of projecting ourselves for even a second into the structure of animals in order to get an idea, from their side, of the reality they perceive."[27]

Ways of Seeing

The impression made upon Cortázar by the visual arts, especially painting, is not to be underestimated. If, for example, it is clear that surrealism had a major influence on him, it is no less clear that among the surrealists the painters were at least as influential as were the writers. Cortázar went on record several times saying that he would have liked to be a painter, and in a passage in one of his books based on art, *Territorios* (1978, 86), he amusingly conveys the frustration he feels when his own impulse to wield a brush only leads to disappointing results. A similar frustration applies regarding music, to which we shall turn in a moment.

The role of art in Cortázar's writing clearly evolves over the years, and, as in so many aspects of his life, the sixties are transitional in this regard. Up to and including *Rayuela* (1963) art enters his works via passing allusions or references; to take just one typical example, a character in *Rayuela* is said to see the world as if it were as orderly as in a Van Eyck. Occasionally there are also important images drawn from art, such as Picasso's guitar, which is evoked by Persio in the novel *Los premios*. The references to art are many, and they are predominantly to painters of the twentieth century: for every Boticelli or Dürer there are several Magrittes, Bacons, and Ernsts. In his attention to art, as to literature, Cortázar was not systematic; instead he followed his tastes, often allowing one work to lead him to another. Frequently, this free-association process is reflected in the way he wrote. Although he did not systematically focus on any particular period in art, it is clear that twentieth-century art was the most important to him. It is also clear that his personal circumstances determined to some extent which artworks influenced him, particularly the fact that he was in Paris, saw certain exhibitions, and made friends with a number of practicing artists. In sum, the role he accords art in his works is a varying one and always very personal.

Change became noticeable when Cortázar launched upon a series of collaborations with a close friend, a fellow Argentine named Julio Silva. The collaborations began when Silva provided lithographs to complement text that Cortázar had written for his *Les Discours du Pince-Gueule* (1966), a rare example of a creative work that Cortázar wrote in French. Subsequently, the nature of the collaboration changed when Silva took the major role in designing the two collage books, *La vuelta al día en ochenta mundos* (1967) and *Último round* (1969), and then *Territorios* (1978). The sequence of composition shifts; art and photography become more central and eventually provide the inspiration for the writing. (These and several other art-related works are discussed in some detail in chapter 7).

Instead of describing or analyzing them, Cortázar's usual strategy was to contemplate artworks and allow his imagination to take him wherever it would. At bottom, it is the very strategy that he had learned as a child when looking at cloud patterns with his mother and building "texts" around them. As an adult, quite often the strategy led him to write texts that were analogous to the artworks he was contemplating. A good example is a story that appeared in a catalogue for an exhibition by the Venezuelan artist Jacobo Borges; borrowing its title from one of the artist's paintings, Cortázar calls it "Reunión con un círculo rojo" (Encounter with a red circle). He opens his story by taking advantage of the name Borges: dedicating the story at its start merely "To Borges," he entices readers to think of Jorge Luis Borges. Then, at the end of it (in a fashion that is, of course, suitably Borgesian) Cortázar reveals the true identity of the story's narrator. In doing so he also reveals the extent to which "Reunión con un círculo rojo" apes the deliberate narrative deceptions that are characteristic of the Jorge Luis Borges of stories such as "La forma de la espada" (The shape of the sword). But then, in a final, paradoxically ironic touch, Cortázar appends to his own story a (Jorge Luis) Borgesian footnote to the effect that the Borges he really meant was the painter.[28] "Reunión con un círculo rojo" is thus a consciously artificial text that gives a passing, playful bow in the direction of Jorge Luis Borges. It also contains other elements—such as hints of vampirism—that are typical of Cortázar. Its relevance to Jacobo the painter, as I have already suggested, is through analogy. In this story Cortázar has created a palpably threatening atmosphere that parallels the sinister quality of Jacobo Borges's painting with its circle of blurred, but evidently influential, figures, some of whom seem to be military. Quite literally, both story and painting are *vaguely* political works.[29]

"Siestas," is a story that is more inextricably rooted in art, and the proof of this is that it reads differently when bereft of the art reproductions that accompanied its first appearance, in *Último round*. There, it was punctuated by strange, unsettling landscapes done by Paul Delvaux, the Belgian surrealist painter. In one of them, a painting that in some ways makes one think of Bosch, a desolate landscape is peopled by nude women, two of whom have extraordinarily long hair and are embracing each other. In another, some young girls whose images suggest an amalgam of Boticelli and Cranach reveal their nude bodies in a slightly edenic environment. In a third, more starkly modern, a man dressed in a dark suit is looking out from a landing across a river to an urban scene; on the boards in front of him is a couch on which lies a woman with bare breasts, in a pose that might indicate seduction or abuse. Lastly, there is a painting of an alley beside a house, with a garden beyond; in the alley a dog seems to be confronting two lamps on the pavement. The story is perfectly self-sufficient without the presence of these images, but it is clear that they complement it, that their imagery has migrated to the story, and that the paintings probably led Cortázar to write it.

In "Siestas" two young girls begin to explore their sexuality with each other during the siesta hours when they are free of pressures from adults, and also by means of their individual fantasies. The title thus alludes literally to siesta time, but also indirectly to the dreamworld the girls may enter at that time. In the real environment the elder of the two initiates the younger, who proudly reveals that she has begun to grow pubic hair. Together, the girls fantasize over magazine images of a male model with a hairy chest. Their imaginations are also fed by pictures in a book they find hidden on a shelf (one is tempted to assume it is a book of pictures by Delvaux, though there is enough ambiguity in the way they are described to allow one to conclude that whatever images they are, they are provocative and perhaps pornographic). In her dreams, the younger girl is troubled by the image of a man with a sinister arm, lurking in an alley. By the end of the story that fantasy seems to have become reality, and she faces rape.

The "I" of the Beholder

Though Cortázar's dreams are made of the stuff of language, it is arguable that his approach to most phenomena is essentially a visual one. The act of looking (signaled linguistically by his use of the Spanish verb *mirar* as opposed to *ver*) is vested with an almost mystic import. *Mirar* connotes a cluster of virtues, including candor, innocence, understanding, true feeling, honesty, and love. *Mirar* is an act that comes more naturally to children than to adults. The questions that Cortázar poses are: what constitutes this act, how does one see, and what does seeing mean?

"Orientación de los gatos" (Orientation of cats) in *Queremos tanto a Glenda* is another story dedicated to a painter; it was written for the catalogue of an exhibition of the paintings of Juan Soriano in Mexico. The importance of the act of looking in this story is stressed by the recurrence of the verb *mirar* several times in its opening lines and of other words related to the visual throughout the story. An initial triangle is established in which the narrator is looked at frankly and openly by his wife Alana and their cat; these last two look equally openly at each other; but the narrator cannot do the same, cannot reach them: "mujer y gato [mirándose] desde planos que se me escapan" (329; wife and cat looking at each other on a level that is beyond me). He feels a need to give of himself, in a way that reciprocates her need when she looks at him. For a while music promises to provide a bridge to a deeper knowledge of this woman whom the narrator loves, then it appears that art might do so. When looking at pictures in a gallery she seems to be more unconsciously herself, more attainable, the pictures serving as a third point between the two people; in other words, a new triangle has been posited. In front of the canvases her look changes as if she were a chameleon; and so, without her being aware of it, the narrator senses that he is on the verge of seeing her in a new light, that his love for her is capable of "encompassing the visible and the invisible, accepting the directness of Alana's gaze with no uncertainty from locked doors and barred passages" (330). Then she stops at a last picture, which portrays a woman with a cat. The narrator sees her become statuesque, and he also observes that the cat is just like their own. It is as if she has been petrified by his gaze, lost to him like another Eurydice. It is another example of the sort of frustrated search that Cortázar is so fond of thematizing (the prime example being Oliveira's search in *Rayuela*); in the manner of some surrealists, a woman is cast as the intercessor. Alana (whose name implies *alas* [wings]) flies away from being apprehended by her husband. She has "entered" the picture and taken her place beside the cat Osiris (named after a complex Egyptian deity who protected the dead but also, paradoxically and appropriately, is associated with light). The narrator now understands that the facilitating triangle of communication (narrator-picture-wife) has also been lost. Wife and cat continue their tacit communion, able to see beyond the window, and looking back at the isolated narrator who cannot do so.[30]

Frozen and Framed

Photography and the idea of a fixed image undergoing change or taking on life are treated in a number of stories, including "Las babas del diablo" and "Apocalipsis de Solentiname." Cortázar also wrote texts to accompany the work of several photographers. More generally, the communicative powers of the static visual image are invoked throughout Cortázar's work and perhaps thematized to greatest effect in one of his best "political" stories, "Graffiti." ("Graffiti" and "Apocalipsis" are discussed in chapter 6.)

Straddling Cortázar's fascination with painting and photography is a story in his final collection, *Deshoras* (*Unreasonable Hours*). Called "Fin de etapa" ("A Place to Stop"), it is a tale of stasis and mobility. In one sense, the title refers to the end of a phase in the protagonist's life, her breakup with a man called Orlando. In another it can be understood as signaling a halt on a journey: quite literally, Diana stops off for lunch in the course of a drive home. These two ideas—the arrival at a watershed and the arresting of movement—are associated with a crucial transitional moment in time, high noon. In a "parenthesis," Diana stops in a small village, and, breaking with Orlando's ritual of having lunch at twelve, she visits the local museum, where, she has been warned, "there's not much to see" (426). Revealingly, she feels a vague need to "ver las cosas como quien es visto" (see things like someone who is being seen). She discovers that the museum is installed in a house in which each room leads into the next; Diana now embarks on this spatial sequence, this other journey. Her first impression is that the paintings are of abnormal size and are more like photographs, but then she understands that it is their hyperrealism that makes them look as if they were based on photographs. As she is drawn along through the sequence of rooms and paintings, it is as if they begin to lose their separateness from each other. She has a recurring feeling that rather than going through the village, the village is going past behind her back, while there she is, alone in the utter solitude of midday, with the light at its most unforgiving, allowing no shadows, with time "paralyzed" (429). Yet the light on the pictures somehow does not correspond to the reality of midday light. Moreover, she feels as though she were no longer looking from inside (ambiguously rendered as "included as a spectator on the inside") but approaching a painting "from the other side." A museum official tells her that they close at noon but invites her to resume her visit in the afternoon; she leaves the museum with only one mysterious room left to see. In the street a boy ask her the time, a narrative device that serves to emphasize both the reentry into reality and the symbolic importance of noon. It is a moment for thought and decision. She wonders whether the artist has not deliberately isolated the last picture in the remaining room because it stands for "another style, another phase in his work"; why should she "break the sequence that was lasting as a whole in her?" (428). During her first visit to the museum she had seen the figure of a man with his back turned, but now, back in the museum after noon, she notices for the first time that in one picture there is a figure of a woman dressed in black with her face half turned. "No había nada que la distinguiera demasiado de lo anterior, se integraba en la pintura como el hombre que se paseaba en otras telas, era parte de la secuencia, una figura más dentro de la misma voluntad estética" (There was nothing special to distinguish her from what had gone before, she was as much a part of the picture as was the man who was around in other paintings, she was a part of the sequence, one more figure within the same aesthetic design). Here there is a revealing ambiguity surrounding the pronoun "she," which could refer equally to the pictured woman and to Diana; just before this, Cortázar exploits a similarly ambiguous object pronoun, so as to suggest that light is invading both her (Diana) and the room. Diana then realizes that the woman is dead, "her immobility inexplicably more intense than the fixing of things and people in the other paintings" (431). A stunned Diana now finds herself in the street, and soon she is speeding away in her car toward the city, where she expects that a new and comforting order will take over, "a new phase" (432). But, becoming aware that this is a cowardly route to take, she doubles back to the village and reenters the museum, to find that there are still traces left of her earlier presence. A disturbing cry she has previously heard is still unexplained, but she settles down in expectation of whatever yet remains to be seen. The final sentence of the story emphasizes her refusal to move: she has, in effect, adopted the stasis of the pictures, is now the observer and the observed, just as the phrase "see things like someone being seen" seems to have promised.

Cortázar was asked by Prego whether Magritte and De Chirico had been a source of inspiration for this story;[31] he replied that Taulé was the starting point, but that he admired the other artists mentioned and that it was possible that they had had an unconscious influence on what he had written. The background was that Antoni Taulé had asked Cortázar if he would write something for a catalogue. Cortázar's response to Taulé is illustrative of his methods: he recalls that he had replied that he would like to, but would have to see whether any ideas came to him; he told Prego that he then kept huge reproductions of Taulé's paintings hanging in his house for a few weeks, glancing at them as he moved about or whenever he stopped reading, until suddenly he found himself seated at his typewriter and watching Diana arriving at the village.

Before we leave this initial discussion of the visual—so important an aspect of Cortázar's work—a word must be added about "Queremos tanto a Glenda" ("We Love Glenda So Much"), in which movement and stasis are related to the world of cinema. This fine story, also a late one, is about a film star called Glenda Garson, a name obviously adapted from that of the British actress Glenda Jackson. Glenda Garson's fans worship her to such a degree that they construct an ideal image of her, stealing her films and editing out unsatisfactory elements. One should not forget that "fan" is a derivative of "fanatic." When she announces her retirement, her fans believe that they have reached the point of "perfection," by which is meant not only the ideal but the final, complete, *per-*

fected ending. Unfortunately she later decides to return to the public eye and in doing so threatens the fixity of her image. Her fans cannot tolerate the unpredictability of a rolling camera, preferring the invariability of the still. The story strongly suggests that their remedy is to kill her. The narrator, an avid fan, explains that Glenda is being offered "one last, inviolable perfection," the status of a finished product.

These acolytes not only deify the film star, they elevate themselves to the level of creators of images, of a myth, and thus, when their "mission" is accomplished, the narrator can report that "we experienced the elation of the seventh day" (336). There is a blind, quasi-religious fervor here; there is talk of heresy, there is reference to inquisitional strategies, there is a chantlike repetition of the words "We love(d) Glenda." There are also a significant number of Christian references, for example in the story's final sentence with its hieratic talk of worshiping Glenda, of preserving her from the fall, of the devotion of the faithful, and the finality of the cross. Glenda has become a martyr to their cause. It is surely also meaningful that a leader of the group is called Irazustra (stirring thoughts of Zarathustra). Besides fanaticism, there is also megalomania. The fans' espousal of a monolithic view, their censorship of what does not please them (and especially their censorship of a form of art), their dismissal of public protests, all these things convey a sociopolitical message. And yet it is just as clear that Cortázar is speaking of how fictions are constructed and acquire currency, of how slippery truth is.

Figuras

At about the time of publication of "Queremos tanto a Glenda" (the book of that name dates from 1980) and *Deshoras* (1982) it happened that Glenda Jackson starred in a mediocre feature film called *Hopscotch*. That this film's title should be the same as that of the English translation of *Rayuela,* Cortázar's *magnum opus,* would strike most people as a curious coincidence; Cortázar, however, saw more extensive correspondences and for him it all amounted to a "beautiful" confirmation of the arcane workings of the *figura.* And so he opened *Deshoras* with a piece titled "Botella al mar" ("A Bottle Thrown into the Sea"), subtitled "Epilogue to a Story." From Berkeley, California, where he was teaching for a while, he addressed an open letter to Glenda Jackson, whom he did not know. He compared the letter to a message in a bottle thrown into the water in San Francisco and making its way to London. Just as, in the earlier story, he had made a gesture in her direction, so he believed that she, in the film, was making one in his. He describes the readers of his story and the spectators of her movie as the "ingenuous bridges of communication" between author and actress. As if that were not enough, in the film she played a person who was in love with an older man who was the author of a book called *Hopscotch,* whom she nevertheless killed; conversely, she had been the adored idol in "Queremos tanto a Glenda" whom Cortázar (now assumed to be the narrator of that story) had killed. Her participation in the film, he concludes, is not an act of revenge but of perfection, constituting the completion of "a beautiful symmetry" (425). Cortázar concludes "Botella al mar" by saying that he is still writing, and she still acting, always the same person beneath her various disguises. This conclusion may suggest a different faith, a faith in the preservation of personal integrity within a process of change. Having crucified Glenda in the earlier story, he now resurrects her.

There were many occasions when Cortázar spoke about his notion of the *figura,* one of the earliest being in conversation with Luis Harss (*Into the Mainstream*), another in his interview with Alain Sicard in 1979 (reproduced in the special issue of *Drailles*). Regardless of any logical or physical laws, Cortázar held that some people had an enhanced awareness of the possibility of what he tended to call "interactions" or "constellations" of behavior. The actions of one person could enter into a relationship with those of another, even if that other person were in a different time and place. As a result it seemed that certain patterns or designs were involved, though they always operated above or beyond the control and ken of people caught in them. Such patterns or designs he termed *figuras.* The following discussion of another story, "Todos los fuegos el fuego," will illustrate the concept.

"Todos los fuegos el fuego" begins with a Roman proconsul raising his arm in a hieratic gesture and thinking *ironically* about the projection of that image into the future: thus he will be represented in a statue. He lowers his arm and a gladiatorial contest begins in the arena before him, watched by his wife, Irene, who offers him a routine smile. The second sentence of the story informs us that Irene does not know what is going to happen; we educe from it that the narrator does, and possibly the proconsul too. However, she has a sense that the die is cast and that the course of events will be "cruel and monotonous." There is cruelty indeed, for the proconsul has arranged a contest in which her preferred gladiator will die. Sarcastically, the proconsul tells her that since she dislikes the games and yet has honored him with her presence, he has taken pains to offer her what she likes best. Sycophants proclaim his greatness: "You have brought the very shadow of Mars to our humble provincial arena," to which the proconsul replies, in contrastingly modern language: "You haven't seen half of it yet" (580). That linguistic contrast paves the way for what follows: narratively, there is a contrasting other half, now broached in the story's brief second paragraph. With no warning the action switches to Paris and to modern times; Roland Renoir answers the phone, and there is a lot of interference on the line. He has a minimal conversation with

Jeanne, enough to convey that he knows her well, to hint that he is tired of her, and to establish that another woman (we shall come to see her as *the* other woman, Sonia) has just left Jeanne's company. With that the action once again switches abruptly to Rome. In a minor flashback scene Marco, the gladiator, stands in the arena waiting to play his appointed role. He watches for the proconsul's gesture that will begin the contest, haunted by comments made to him in the hours preceding the fight and by images that have come to him in a dream, of a fish and of broken columns. He is a simple, instinctive man. Marco hopes that the proconsul's wife might give him a smile, as she has done on a previous occasion. His adversary, a huge Nubian, now appears, and Marco begins to glimpse the meaning of the images that are haunting him: the Nubian is armed with a net that appears to have scales. Irene tenses up inside. Her appearance is of a smiling and condescending person who might even be enjoying herself, but she has read the signs: the proconsul, having sensed that she has lusted in the past for Marco's body, is staging the man's public death, which she is obliged to witness. There is a price to be paid merely for imagining. In Paris a corresponding flashback scene is taking place: Jeanne is about to make the phone call to Roland. As she does so, her hand touches a bottle of tranquilizers. When he answers, she senses his irritation and feels foolish, as if she were talking to herself.

The following switch back to Rome takes place in mid paragraph, signaling the way in which the action and reactions of one setting will now increasingly spill over into the other. The two love triangles develop a number of parallels. Roland and the proconsul share a certain callousness, but at bottom they will both be affected by the outcome. The real communication in Rome is tacit, non-verbal; there is failed verbal communication in Paris (failed technology too, indicated by absurd noise on the telephone). Marco duly dies, Jeanne commits suicide, her death not quite engineered like that of Marco, but brought about by more subtle, modern means. Each group of three now becomes two. Just as there are premonitions of death in Rome, so there are in Paris: in addition to the tranquilizers already mentioned there are references to cigarettes and also a phrase that emerges from the interference on the telephone line, referring to the Gare du Nord (North Railway Station). In the closing scene fire breaks out in the arena, engulfing everyone; it is as if the same fire has spread to the Paris bedroom, where perhaps one of the cigarettes has been its vector. The firemen, who vainly try to save the protagonists of the Paris scene, comment on the adverse wind from the north.

The published English translation of this story misconstrues the meaning of the title in rendering it as "All the Fires the Fire." A better rendition would be "All Fires Fire." This version of the title elides the verb and the articles, but that only serves to emphasize the point that fire is universal. To paraphrase, all fires are instances of the phenomenon fire. This is one of Cortázar's most accomplished stories. At its deepest level, the action in two settings and two time periods is essentially the same. There are many parallels in structure and character development, with the result that one story seems to mimic the other, speak of the other.

Seconds Out (or "In a minute there are many days.")

My subtitle here refers not to boxing but to time. In "Todos los fuegos el fuego" we saw how Cortázar can violate divisions of time and space in pursuit of a *figura* and in the process say something about human life and behavior that transcends those divisions. We turn now to another story that was published in *Todos los fuegos el fuego,* "La isla a mediodía" (The island at noon), one of whose themes is time in relation to the familiar, to routine and meaningless habit. As if by chance, Marini, an airline steward, has glanced through a window in the tail of the plane in which he regularly travels, and he has noticed an island below him, in the Aegean. It is a beautiful and enticing image, like a turtle clearly outlined against the sea. By comparison, life as a flight attendant is colorless, obliging him to hand out standard food trays, with a standard smile, to standard passengers. Dealing with passengers from exotic places might be expected to be interesting, but when a Syrian does summon him, it is only to ask for the ubiquitous tomato juice. This rounding down of difference is coupled with a mindless adherence to a schedule. The airline, like any other, must depart and arrive according to schedule, its flights are programmed according to a rigid pattern, and there are many routines with which Marini and other airline personnel must comply in the approved manner and at the appointed time. Off the plane Marini has a meaningless life too. He has a girl in every airport, but cares about none of them. The stewardesses come and go, and he has well-oiled strategies for seducing them. But in that moment during each scheduled passage over the Aegean island, his existence takes on a different color. He comes to long for that moment, rejects the offer of changing to a more popular run to New York, and is seen by his fellow crew members as a man who is losing touch with reality. And so it is. Looking down at the island on one occasion he imagines some fishermen who must be looking up at "that other unreality"; flying over the island at noon feels to him as unreal as if he were imagining that he was doing so (565). When one of his girlfriends timidly announces that she is pregnant, Marini is unmoved: "La desconsolada decepción de Carla no lo inquietó; la costa sur de Xiros era inhabitable pero hacia el oeste quedaban restos de una colonia lidia . . ." (Carla was disappointed and disconsolate, but her news didn't bother him; the southern coast of Xiros was uninhabitable, but to the west there were relics of a Lydian colony . . .). What does a reader expect of a semicolon if not that what comes after it relates closely to, explains, or expands what comes before it? But here there is no rational, causal link, for mentally Marini has departed, leaving the concerns and processes of the modern world behind. Cortázar uses the same little punctuation device to signal Marini's distance from normal, rational, human behavior when Carla later announces that she has decided to marry a dentist in Treviso. Marini sends her some money to pay for an abortion, but his mind is on the island: everything else seems unimportant compared to his moments contemplating it through the plane window. He learns the Greek greeting "Kalimera" (Good day), tries it out on a girl in a nightclub, and seduces her. He reads about the island and longs for the opportunity to visit it.

As the story goes on, the paragraphs open with increasingly broad references to time: "Eight or nine weeks later" gives way to "As time went by," to emphasize the passage of hours, days, and months during which Marini's existence has no real meaning; then "Ese día" (That day) heralds a paragraph in which Marini will make the transition to the island. He has borrowed money, done his homework, is obsessed with going, and, very importantly, the reader wants him to do so. He senses that the moment of encounter is near and thinks "Kalimera." Now there occurs the transitional set of sentences upon which the whole narrative depends. In the plane, lips pressed against the window as if in a kiss, Marini thinks of how he will complete the various stages of the journey:

> Sonrió pensando que treparía hasta la mancha verde, que entraría desnudo en el mar de las caletas del norte, que pescaría pulpos con los hombres, entendiéndose por señas y risas. Nada era difícil una vez decidido, un tren nocturno, un primer barco, otro barco viejo y sucio, la escala en Rynos, la negociación interminable con el capitán de la falúa, la noche en el puente, el amanecer entre las islas. Desembarcó con las primeras luces . . . (He smiled, thinking how he would climb up to the green patch, plunge naked into the sea in the northern bays, fish for octopus with the men, making themselves understood with gestures and laughs. It was easy once you made up your mind, a night train, a boat, then another dirty old one, a stopover in Rynos, endless negotiations with the captain of the felucca, a night on deck, under the stars, the smell of aniseed and lamb, dawn among the islands. He disembarked as the light was coming up . . .) (567)

We have traveled from the putative ("he would . . .") to the realized ("he disembarked . . ."). Marini seems to have arrived, as we hoped he would. But in between there is the harmless-looking cliché "It was easy once you made up your mind," which does not state unequivocally that Marini took the steps listed (all of them described without a verb); what it does do is leave open that possibility, like a piece of bait that the unsuspecting reader, eager to see Marini's wish fulfilled, is ready to swallow. And then Cortázar reinforces that supposition by emphasizing the physicality of Marini's experiences. He has Marini smell the aromas of the island, feel the wind and sand against his skin, swim in an erotic encounter with the womb of the sea: "La isla lo invadió y lo gozó" (The island invaded and took him). All this, of course, is in stark contrast with the senseless, unfeeling sexual encounters of the pre-island Marini. He now loves the present island more than any of the many women in his past. That island represents all that his airline existence does not. He feels that he has found his spiritual and sensual home and that he will never leave it. Yet one notices that when he takes off his watch to swim he does not discard it but puts it in a pocket, understanding that his old self will be difficult to put aside completely. At this point, watched by Marini, a plane buzzes overhead and crashes into the sea; a dead man is brought ashore, and the local people rush to him. It is somehow as if Marini could visit the island only as a dead man.

Rationally one can point to the narrative trickery and assert that Marini never left the plane, other than in his imagination; his material self stays on the plane, while his ideal self travels. Marini's experience could be related to a common one that we all recognize: in our minds we undergo intense, compressed experiences, as if we had been unaccountably released to travel headlong through time and space, when the rational truth is that only a few moments have passed, and they have been spent walking down a road or sitting in a chair. Or again one may suppose that the plane does crash and that Marini has had a premonition of death. But this is not the point. The story is important as a metaphor and has a number of implications. When Cortázar drops Marini into the sea, he creates endless ripples of significance. Marini rejects the meaningless hours for the meaningful *moment*. His epiphany occurs at noon, with the sun at its zenith; there are shades of Icarus here.[32] He leaves the horizontal plane (and here I am punning deliberately) to take flight along a vertical one that is diametrically opposed; in doing so he rejects the binary, striking out toward a third point. The airline represents routine and empty relationships. It is also technology, whereas the island is nature (likened to an amphibian—able to negotiate both air and water). It is also significant that the American tourist on the plane is said to be one of many, and she is impervious to the delights of Greece. For there is a cultural argument here, too. The airline, in its own way defying space and time, is ostensibly bringing tourists to their cultural roots, but in doing so it is destroying those very roots, erasing cultural differences, planting a Hilton hotel in every city, bringing the invading hordes of "Gengis Cook" (the marauding Genghis Khan + Thomas Cook, the travel agent). Lastly, Marini's flight is irrational and leads from the rational into a world of the senses and intuitions, the watery world, which, as his name surely implies, is his destiny. Does it matter whether

Marini "really" visited the island? And what, symbolically, are we to make of his "death"? Is it a release from life, a complement to it, the onset of the other half of life's day, a transition to a better form of existence, the attainment of the much vaunted "lo otro" (the other/otherness), the price that must be paid for that? Such suggestions would be in line with Cortázar's thinking in the early sixties, a time when he was attracted by certain ideas in Buddhism.[33]

Somewhat similar, though less richly suggestive, is another excellent story from the same collection, "La autopista del sur" (The southern thruway). A few words from an Italian newspaper are ironically placed at the start of it: "Gli automobilisti accaldati sembrano non avere storia. . . . Come realtà, un ingorgo automobilistico impressiona ma non ci dice gran che" (505; Hot and bothered motorists seem to have no story. . . . When you come down to it, a traffic jam is impressive but doesn't amount to much). It is a Sunday afternoon and cars trying to return to Paris on a major thoroughfare are backed up. Time as recorded on their wristwatches or measured by their radio beeps is losing all relevance. No one has a name, but people can be identified by the cars they drive; the makes and models seem to reflect their personalities, professions, or social status. Hours pass and progress is limited to a few feet. A banana skin on the road becomes a means of gauging progress. The sun is oppressive, people get out of their cars and begin to establish contact, night draws near. So the narrative continues, stretching the duration of the jam to fantastic proportions, replacing the heat with snow. Fellow voyagers who are moving nowhere, the people in the cars begin to reveal their personalities: for example, Ford Taurus is an organizer; the old couple in the Simca are recluses. Food and water are passed around and bartered, a scouting party is organized to seek provisions, a black market develops, rumors run rife of events further up the line, "outsiders" appear, a scythe is thrown by a hostile community. Life begins and ends on the highway: a man dies and a council of responsible community members deliberates on what to do with his body, eventually "burying" it in a car trunk. Peugeot 404, an engineer, has started a relationship with Renault Dauphine; she becomes pregnant (we are now into months) and the two start to think of their future life together. Then, capriciously, this order that has become accepted and normal breaks down: the cars advance and gather speed, changing positions in relation to one another; Peugeot and Dauphine lose contact as they head back to Paris, a shower, clean clothes, and the old life.

Contrary to the statement in the Italian newspaper, this has been a momentous traffic jam. Again Cortázar is playing with time here, not by elevating the moment to a symbolic level, but by having his story opt out of the habitual order of time in favor of a fantastic one measured by banana skins, meteorological shifts, and human crises. In the unpleasant, depersonalized environment of the highway he begins to turn his car-characters into human types and have them play out the human condition; it is a social journey a little like the one he narrates, though in broadly realistic terms, in his first-published novel, *Los premios.* As for most characters in the novel, once the special experience is over, the participants in the traffic jam revert to normalcy. The adventure has been a static one, moving only on a fantastic level. In adverse circumstances, people make do, life "goes on." The society that develops on the *autoroute* becomes familiar and reassuring, and for Dauphine and Peugeot it comes to matter a great deal; when that society breaks up, one feels a certain disorientation, some sense of loss.

Suffering Fiction

People also accept a new order based on imagination, on fiction, in "La salud de los enfermos" (The health of the sick) in *Todos los fuegos el fuego.* The title is based on a Latin phrase sometimes seen in Catholic hospitals, *Salus infirmorum.* Cortázar clearly appreciates its ambiguity. Like many stories, this one begins obliquely. Cortázar feeds the reader a red herring when he refers to the sudden sickness of Aunt Clelia, for her sickness is tangential to the theme of the story. But he does drop a broad hint about its driving force when he goes on to talk about how Clelia's illness unleashes a moment's panic in the family because they have no plan to cope with it. The story gravitates around the supposed needs of *Mamá.* She is growing old and somewhat delicate, so that when Alejandro, her favorite son, is killed in a car accident, the rest of the family rallies round to protect her from this sad news. An elaborate fiction grows as they invent explanations for Alejandro's absence, build an imagined life for him, and write letters purporting to be from him to his mother, letters that are read to her by a daughter. The mother, however, suspects the truth, and the tables turn as she begins to play along with the fiction in order not to destroy the well-intentioned illusion that her loved ones have created for her. They themselves have become slaves to that illusion, it is their form of sickness, and the mother is now protecting them by playing along with it. When the time comes for the mother to take her secret understanding to the grave, the first worry of the rest of the family is how they might convey the news of her death to Alejandro. The site of suffering, then, has shifted from the physical infirmity of the mother to the psychological dependency of the others. We are left feeling that everyone is sick; we were invited to believe that it was an aunt at the beginning of the story, then that it was the mother, but the other members of the family, their friends, and the doctor, Bonifaz (whose name suggests that he puts a good face on things), have truly suffered in creating the fiction to protect the mother and in becoming slaves to it. Hence the ambiguity of the title.

Illness and death are common themes in Cortázar, apparent in stories such as "Torito" (about a boxer dying of tuberculosis), "La señorita Cora" (about a boy dying of postoperative complications), and "Liliana llorando" (Liliana weeping). In this last story, which opens *Octaedro,* the narrator has a terminal illness, which he is keeping from his wife so that she will not suffer too. He imagines how life will be for her and her family when he is dead, how his place will be taken by his closest friend. Then he is given an unexpected reprieve when the doctor discovers that a mistake has been made in the diagnosis, but by now the imagined posthumous order is in place. To save his wife from suffering, once more, the narrator hides his lease of life from her.

"Cartas de mamá" (*Las armas secretas*) also has some similarities with "La salud de los enfermos." Luis and Laura are married and living in Paris. One reason why they are there is to escape family opprobrium. Laura was once involved with Nico, Luis's brother, who died of tuberculosis, but even before his death had become involved with Nico, and when the two of them married, it caused a stir. *Mamá* suddenly writes from Argentina in terms that indicate that Nico is still alive and about to travel to Paris. At first Luis tries to keep this news from his wife, but other letters continue in the same vein, Laura becomes aware of the problem, and the two of them come to the conclusion that *Mamá* is becoming senile. But evidently Nico is real enough to occupy their guilt-ridden minds, and apparently Laura is still drawn to him. In some sense they believe in the return of Nico, for both Laura and Luis go independently to the station to meet him. There they see a man who resembles Nico. Returning home, they talk about Nico as if he were in their presence. This story is told by a self-conscious third-person narrator, who frequently refers to his search for the truth. Self-deception (by characters and writers) is involved. Truth is subjectively perceived. Reality, it seems, is not only made up of what is tangible or visible or linguistically expressible. The return of Nico is a fiction embedded in other fictions.

Acting Out

Deception, the stock-in-trade of theater, is also thematized in several stories. In "Los buenos servicios" (At your service) a humble Frenchwoman, Madame Francinet, is visited by a woman of higher social standing who engages her to help in the house of some rich people. Her first task is to look after some spoiled dogs. Among the people she meets is a Monsieur Bebé, who treats her with a little more consideration than do other members of the household; later she is inveigled to enact the role of a grieving mother at a wake. This she does quite well, in fact it is as if she oversteps the limits of her role because it becomes part of her, and she is reprimanded for that. Her emotional involvement arises from the discovery that it is Monsieur Bebé who has died. Using a simple, unpretentious style, Cortázar manages to get under the skin of Madame Francinet. He once recounted that when writing the story he *was* Madame Francinet for a few days. This is not the only time he successfully uses a woman narrator, and women are the protagonists of a great many stories that, though narrated in the third person, bring the author into close approximation with the female figure, as, for example, in "Recortes de prensa" (Press cuttings), discussed in chapter 7.

In some respects "Los buenos servicios" is a social story. The respectful working-class woman enters the world of the rich. At first she feels out of place, and she does not fully understand their ways. She is willing to do what is asked of her, perhaps naïve, certainly unaware throughout of the homosexuality of some of the people she is encountering in this other world. However, she gets carried away during her big scene, dissolving into tears over the body of her "son," Monsieur Bebé. In this she is overstepping her part, and the man in charge holds her back before she has a chance to bestow a kiss on the corpse. In the background there are men lurking who do not seem to her to fit the scene, and she is frightened. She should keep to her role, dramatic and social, and she should mind her own business. Something sinister seems to the reader to be afoot. Another aspect of this story gyrates around the idea of acting and appearances; in "Los buenos servicios" there is much emphasis on colors, show, dressing up, and disguise. About her experiences, Madame Francinet says that "it seemed better to me than going to any theater" (196). When she first crosses the threshold of this house she is made to put on an oversize apron (a costume), and, led by someone called Alice, it is as if she were entering a wonderland. Later, Madame Francinet is more lavishly decked out for her star performance. She describes the butler of the house as having gray sideburns "like they have in the theater" (196), says that the lady of the house is so dressed up that "she looked like a cake" (197), and that Monsieur Bebé and his friends "juegan a disfrazarse" (play disguises/pretend to be what they're not) (200). Madame Francinet has fully entered the drama by the end, but her understanding of what has been happening is illusory.

Behind the Scenes

The suggestion that sinister forces are at work is strong in many of Cortázar's works. An explicitly theatrical setting in which to explore that theme is found in "Instrucciones para John Howell" ("Instructions for John Howell") in *Todos los fuegos el fuego*. A man called Rice enters a theater on a dreary afternoon in London, witnesses the first act of an indifferent play, and during the first interval is approached by a man who invites him backstage, presumably for an audience-reaction interview about the play. There three mysterious, bored-looking men are somehow expecting him. Rice is told that no time is to be wasted before he takes over the leading male role in the second act that is about to begin. The man who tells him this speaks mechanically "como si prescindiera de la presencia real de Rice y se limitara a cumplir una monótona consigna" (570; as if he were setting aside the presence of the real Rice and were simply fulfilling carrying out a tiresome order). When Rice protests that he doesn't understand, the man replies that it is better not to. He also predicts that the play will improve. Rice feels under pressure to comply with the wishes of these faceless people ("the man in gray"; "the tall one"). The outline of the plot is explained to Rice and he is equipped with a wig and other props. Protesting that this is absurd, he threatens to create a fuss onstage, to which the tall man replies that that would not be in very good taste and that he is sure that Rice would not behave in such a manner. As he protests that he is no actor, they agree that indeed he is not, he is John Howell. Once on stage, Rice begins to find his rhythm and even enjoys himself. At first he behaves in ways that seem obviously appropriate, but gradually he tries to influence the action according to his own wishes. At one point his opposite number, Eve, comes over as if to kiss him during the play and whispers into his ear, "Don't let them kill me" (572). In another interval Rice faces the men again backstage. His freedom of action now seems further constrained: he can do what he likes in the sense that there is room for a certain amount of the unpredictable; he can vary details, but he must follow instructions. Thus Rice, crossing the barrier between reality and fiction in the tradition of Pirandello, is caught up in a controlled game that mimics the game of life, echoing the "All the world's a stage" theme. He cannot know the outcome, but he has a degree of free will. He is subject to the dictates of a powerful trinity of men. When Rice oversteps his part, he is ejected from the premises; he returns to the stalls to find that the original actor who was playing Howell is back in the part. At the end of the story the two of them are fleeing together in fear through the labyrinthine streets of London, forced constantly to choose a direction, crossing a river that may be the Styx or the Rubicon or represent some form of baptism. Levels of reality, the power of fiction, destiny, anonymous controlling powers, the pressures to conform, the limits of free will: many of the major themes in Cortázar are implied in this rich and complex story.

(A) Culture under Threat

Another spectator who flees at the end of a performance is Lucio in "La banda" (The band) in *Final del juego*. He goes into a cinema "como buen porteño" (like a good citizen of Buenos Aires) to see a European art film and finds himself in a theater full of fat women and children, facing an unannounced concert to be given by a women's band. Half of the band is there for purely decorative purposes, not playing a note. Caught between disbelief and indignation, Lucio betrays himself as something of a snob, not only a cultural one but also a social one: he observes, for example, that, judging by their complexion and garb, the fat ladies look like cooks in their Sunday best and that their gestures are the sort Italians use. There are many references in "La banda" to actual places and to the realities of life in Buenos Aires during the Perón era. The band is from the *alpargatas* factory (*alpargatas* are simple, rope-soled shoes; there was such a factory, and "Alpargatas, Sí" became a rallying cry). The concert program, including a fake march-past, is vulgarly popular and vaguely militaristic. Thus far, the story seems to be alluding to the assault on high culture by the hoi polloi of provincials and immigrants. But the story veers away, perhaps not entirely successfully, toward wider and deeper implications. Once the concert is over, Lucio duly sees and enjoys his film, then he leaves the theater and keeps thinking about everything but the film; he is angry because of the way his thoughts are so occupied, but, because he is from Buenos Aires, he takes the easy route and does not protest. In terms of narrative structure, the narrator begins by downplaying his own part, as if Lucio's story were true, recounted to him by Lucio himself; at the end of the narrative the narrator steps forward, a second time, to tell us that the conclusion of Lucio's story is harder to tell, "becomes difficult to transcribe."[34] The narrator now openly mediates, glossing Lucio's experience:

> De pronto le pareció entender aquello en términos que lo excedían infinitamente. Sintió como si le hubiera sido dado ver al fin la realidad. . . . Lo que acababa de presenciar era lo cierto, es decir lo falso. Dejó de sentir el escándalo de hallarse rodeado de elementos que no estaban en su sitio. Porque en la misma conciencia de un mundo otro, comprendió que esa visión podía prolongarse a la calle (Suddenly he thought that he understood the experience on a level that went far beyond it. He felt as though at last he had been allowed to see reality. What he had just witnessed was true, that is to say, false. He stopped feeling outraged at being surrounded by things that were not in their proper place. For in the process of becoming aware of this other world, he understood that that vision could spill over into the street). (351)

Lucio has been lucky to escape back into the familiar. The narrator's final words postulate a different ending: Lucio returns to the theater and discovers that the concert never took place. But then the narrator says that records prove that there was indeed such a concert in that theater on that day, so that the fact that Lucio fled abroad may have something to do with an illness or with women.

One is bound to think of Cortázar's own flight from Argentina and of his disaffection with the rise of Perón. But it is too simplistic to equate Cortázar with Lucio; Cortázar also fled some of the things that Lucio represents. Moreover, there is a literary side to this story in its treatment of the nature of truth and the status of stories.

"Las Ménades" (The Maenads), also from *Final del juego,* covers similar territory, and again in the context of a performance. It more clearly invites interpretation as an allegory of Peronism. In this story a condescending protagonist attends a symphony concert of popular classics and observes that the maestro has cleverly constructed a program that is calculated to please a lowbrow, middle-class audience. The story is narrated in the first person, but the narrator maintains his role as a distanced spectator of the action as long as he can. His detached, sophisticated, almost rational approach to music contrasts with the unbridled enthusiasm of the undiscerning majority. It is the maestro's anniversary concert, and much adulation is heaped upon him, but this develops gradually into hysteria until a group of women, led by one in red, invades the stage and attacks him in a bloody orgy, "unable to hold themselves back a moment longer, as if amid that panting of love that had been going on between the masculine body of the orchestra and the huge, submissive female auditorium the latter had chosen not to wait for virile pleasure" (323). It is not at all unusual for Cortázar, especially the early Cortázar, to draw on classical mythology, but only here and in "Circe" does he use a mythological reference in a title. The Maenads are the frenzied attendants of Bacchus, but Orpheus seems also to be implied in this story. So, too, is Hitler: the maestro raises his arm in a stiff, hieratic gesture and the masses go wild. The story contains a great deal of animal imagery, implications of bestial behavior, and cannibalism. It seesaws between the witty superciliousness of the narrator-protagonist and the horrific reality he is witnessing. A blind man, who manages to retain his dignity throughout, perhaps stands for those in society who turn a blind eye to what is happening or cannot see for themselves; he is trampled to death in the frenzy, while the narrator, who does see, tries not to get involved. At the end people begin to adjust their dress and regain their composure, but the final image is of the woman in red, who is licking her lips. "Las Ménades" seems to warn against the perils of manipulating the masses and the consequences of sitting on the fence. In a number of ways, "Las Ménades" can be compared to "Queremos tanto a Glenda."

As a coda to this section, let me add a brief comment on the fallout from another story with more clearly social implications. "Las puertas del cielo" (The gates of heaven) is a portrayal of a friendship but also a reflection of a social milieu, a seedy world. Cortázar reported in the seventies that the story had incurred the wrath of Peronists and said that he now agreed with them, that it was a story he hated, and that it had obvious political implications but faithfully reflected his feelings of alienation at the time when it was written.[35] He had been exasperated at the way in which the proletarian masses were taking over the capital; these are the monsters portrayed in the final scene of the story, and Cortázar was there in the person of Hardoy, the lawyer, as an observer and chronicler.

Flesh for the Elusive Idea (and an Antidote to the Spider's Bite)

Cortázar's greatest regret was that he was not a musician. He said, "if I could choose between literature and music, I'd choose music."[36] If he had to choose between taking books and records to the proverbial desert island, he went on to say, he would take records. This is an extraordinary affirmation for a writer to make.

Cortázar had reached a certain level of proficiency on the piano when young, taught by the aunt who lived with him, but in retrospect he viewed his playing level as artless and mechanical. He became fascinated with the music he heard in the early days of radio. As a student he had discovered jazz; a famous photo of him shows him trying to play the trumpet. Feeling that his musical talents were no more significant than his painterly ones, he settled for incorporating both art forms in one way or another into his literature. He speaks often of the musical qualities of language, of its "melody," its "rhythm," its "swing." He tells us that he assuaged his frustration at not being a musician by writing poetry. He entitles a section of his first collection of poems "Preludios y sonetos," emphasizing their musical affinities. In his second collection he compares poetry's communicative qualities to those of music that reaches the listener through headphones, in its purest form. In an interview published in February 1981 in *Le Monde de la Musique* (31) Cortázar compares the short story to a well-rounded movement of a sonata. His love of music is evident everywhere.

We have just seen examples of the use of concert settings in the stories "La banda" and "Las Ménades." One of the most memorable chapters of *Rayuela,* a chapter whose self-sufficiency makes it seem like a short story, is set at the piano recital given by one Berthe Trépat. There, as in "Las Ménades," one's enjoyment is enhanced by having some familiarity with the classical music repertoire. In *Rayuela* one benefits from a similar knowledge of jazz. There are three basic ways in which music functions: as a system of background references, as a leitmotif, and as a structuring device. In *Rayuela,* for example, jazz provides a backdrop for most of the conversations, sometimes serving as a counterpoint to what is being said or done. A great many names of musicians and numbers are quoted, together with some lyrics. When discussing "El perseguidor" we saw how jazz provided Johnny with a way to break out of the confines of his normal life and express himself in a code that does not depend on words. Generally, a large part of the appeal of jazz for Cortázar came from its improvisational qualities, its freedom to take off in whatever direction one fancies. This explains why he preferred the cool jazz of the fifties to the traditional variety. Music as leitmotif (in the very loose sense in which I am using the word here) is quite common in Cortázar's work. The most famous example is in "Reunión" ("Meeting"), in *Todos los fuegos el fuego,* in which Cortázar has Che Guevara listen intermittently to a Mozart quartet (discussed in chapter 7).

We find music in "Las caras de la medalla" (The faces of the medal) in *Alguien que anda por ahí* where it reflects the personalities of the two protagonists and tracks their relationship with one another. In an international agency where Javier has come to work, the first thing that is noticed about him is the way he listens to music on a transistor radio while he is working. Mireille, meanwhile, has been known to whistle Mahler in the elevator. Javier's old relationship is on the rocks, and soon he an Mireille begin to find common ground. Javier is fond of jazz and other music. They attend a piano recital together and agree on the Schubert but not on the Bartók. As the relationship grows, they take musical stock. Both like Mahler, Brahms, and medieval music, whereas only Javier likes jazz; they have yet to tackle the Renaissance and the baroque, plus Pierre Boulez and John Cage; it is predictable that Mireille will not like Cage, and probably not Boulez the composer, but probably Boulez the performer. They reach a point where they both begin to sense that their relationship has reached its limit: "It was as if Mireille were asking of Javier what he was asking of Mireille . . . we had made our way along a road with no one wishing to force the *tempo,* break the *harmonious balance*" (201; my italics). They fail to consummate the relationship (it seems that spiritually she cannot give him what he wants, and physically he cannot satisfy her). They drift apart, Javier to a girl who likes the Rolling Stones, and come back to each other again , but still unsuccessfully. Eventually they part company. As the story ends, a more explicitly autobiographical note is struck: Javier consoles himself by writing stories in which there are no medallions with faces looking in opposite directions, and the fictionality of this resolution of the problem is admitted: "but, of course, they are only texts" (205).

Cortázar does something rather similar, but more accomplished, with the narrative ending of "Deshoras," the imagined satisfaction of unrequited love through the exercise of writing. "Las caras de la medalla," narrated partly in the third person and partly in the first person plural, is also an interesting narrative experiment. I will very briefly mention two other stories that use music in a similar way. In "Vientos Alisios" (Trade winds) a couple decides on a strategy they hope will take them back to the days when their relationship was fresh, the days evoked by hearing "Blues in Thirds," and in "Las armas secretas" the Schumann song "Im wunderschönen Monat Mai" is constantly in the background of the story, set in a France invaded by Germany.

Much the most adventurous use of music occurs in the story titled "Clone" (*Queremos tanto a Glenda*). After the readers have had the pleasure of reading the story, they come across an appendix that explains its genesis and structure. The musically literate reader will already have been alerted by the opening words of the story, "It all had to do with Gesualdo" (383), a reference to the sixteenth-century Italian madrigal composer who murdered his wife (apparently not without provocation). Cortázar's story is about a small choir that is in trouble because of personal intrigues, and the story is intriguing enough in itself. In the long explanatory note that follows it, he says that he wrote the story after setting himself a new narrative challenge, that of basing its structure on Bach's *Musical Offering,* more precisely, on a recorded performance of that work under the direction of the harpsichordist Millicent Silver. Cortázar went to the beach with a photocopy of the record sleeve, on which the structure of Bach's piece was described, and waited for ideas to come to him: "Absentmindedness, dreams, and chance imperceptibly weave their future tapestry" (393). The self-imposed task required that eight characters be created to match the eight instruments of the recording ensemble, but the idea of the ensemble itself also had to be represented; it seemed evident to him that, given the brevity that is fundamental to the genre of story, his eight characters would need to be involved with one another by some device that suggested their association prior to the start of the narrative. A chance conversation brought Gesualdo to mind, and so he devised the idea of a vocal group that existed before the story started. He began by distributing voices according to the pitch of the instruments on the record: a soprano for the flute, for example, a bass for the bassoon. The singers were to be based in Buenos Aires and would be giving the final concert of an international tour. The harmony would be breaking up. Cortázar felt that he would have to match the entries of the voices to the pattern of participation of the instruments. Then the idea came to him that in the final scene there should be one voice missing and that the missing voice should be the root cause of the demise of the choir. Gesualdo, still in the back of Cortázar's mind, provided the final piece of the jigsaw puzzle: Franca and Gesualdo were to be the spider and the fly in this web. (We have already seen some evidence of how frequently Cortázar evokes images of weavers, and of Arachne the spider woman. In *La vuelta al día en ochenta mundos* (21) he writes of "the webs of life in which we are at once the fly and the spider," suggesting that people both construct their stories and are victims of them. He appears to be marrying a recognition of superior, determining powers with Sartre's "Man is what he proposes.")

Each part of "Clone" corresponds to a movement in the music, and the writing attempts to parallel the musical form of each. For example, the second movement is a *canon perpetuus* that in the recording (Bach did not specify instrumentation) is given to a flute, a viola, and a bassoon; in the second section of the narrative a soprano, an alto, and a bass take part, and their "voices" enter in canon. After providing full details of the sequence of movements and the corresponding instruments, Cortázar's concludes his explanatory note by saying that his musicological knowledge is based on an attentive reading of record sleeves and that he knows nothing about singing. "Clone," a late story, provides an excellent example of how Cortázar's approach to story writing had grown more self-conscious over the years.

CHAPTER 4

Break

Cortázar on Literature

With the exception of some of his early writings, Julio Cortázar harbored no pretensions about being a literary critic or theorist. Like several other prominent Latin American writers, however, he was not averse to expressing his ideas about literature and the creative process, and he was encouraged to do so with increasing frequency as his reputation grew. This chapter provides an account of Julio Cortázar's own ideas about such things as genre and the creative process. This is not the place to attempt to discuss those ideas in relation to other theories of literature (if, indeed, his can be said ever to achieve the grandness of a theory), nor do I intend to deal at any length with his formative influences; the aim is simply to summarize what Cortázar said and believed.

A good deal of what he did have to say is built into his creative works, where it can be observed in varying degrees of explicitness. We have already seen something of the thematization of the creative process in short stories such as "Las babas del diablo" and "Diario para un cuento"; in the chapter that follows we shall see similar kinds of evidence appearing in the novels, indeed sometimes functioning as an overarching framework for them. Here, we shall look at what Cortázar wrote and said outside his creative literature.

Much can be learned from the *Obra crítica* (Critical works), the posthumous three-volume publication that conveniently makes available many pieces of criticism and essays on literary and sociopolitical matters that Cortázar wrote over a period of some forty years and published in all manner of outlets. The first such volume consists of a lengthy essay on the novel dating from the author's years as administrator of the Cámara Argentina del Libro (Argentine Publishers' Association), the time when he was also in the process of writing the stories of *Bestiario.* The essay is titled *Teoría del túnel* (Tunnel theory); its subtitle is *Notas para la ubicación del surrealismo y el existencialismo* (Notes on the place of surrealism and existencialism). This essay, couched in a rather sanctimonious and insistent style, is thought to be the product of Cortázar's lectures at the Universidad de Cuyo. It is a somewhat unusual account of the evolution of the novel, one that at bottom serves as a kind of personal manifesto, prescribing the route that, after a few experiments, will lead its author to write *Rayuela.*

Acknowledging that he is a neoromantic, Cortázar argues that contemporary literature must change radically. He attacks aestheticism as an end in itself, saying that it must be put at the service of a greater goal: a new human dimension in which people live and exploit their possibilities to the full. In the confluence of existentialism and surrealism (which was enjoying a certain vogue in the Buenos Aires of the mid-forties) he sees the opportunity for such progress.[1] Literature, he says, is inextricably linked to human identity. Cortázar notes the high regard in which the surrealists held the count of Lautréamont, but says that they did not sufficiently recognize the crucial fact that for Lautréamont literature (poetry) has ceased to be a means of expressing one's existence and instead has *become* existence, the expression of the ultimate reality. Cortázar describes surrealism as above all a worldview[2] and states that the most enlightened of the surrealists understood that any sort of fetishism represented the opposite of what surrealism was really about; aware of this, they adopted a surrealist weltanschauung. Just as the surrealist rejects established and logical procedures, so the heroic existentialist accepts the fact that he is alone and assumes responsibility in the light of the absolute lack of beliefs on which to rely. Cortázar adds that those who maintain a surrealist worldview frequently seek relief from existential anguish in humor. There can be no modern novel that is worth its salt without the influence of surrealism, and that influence is revealed in such things as the use of poetic language for nonornamental purposes, the exploration of extremes, the use of dreams, and the presence of elements that are "non-Euclidian." Cortázar rejects any idea of surrealism as a school, as a phenomenon that is in any way fixed; instead, under his broad, resolutely nondoctrinaire definition of it he subsumes such things as cubism, futurism, ultraism, Freudianism, and existentialism.

It is typical of reactionary mentalities, he says, that they mask their fundamental cowardice behind dogma. "Everything that is orderly and sure . . . is past and lifeless, it is what holds sway by means of the deaf game of least effort, through fear, through codified conventions and laziness."[3] It is clear that here Cortázar is projecting his own concerns onto the novel; one can see evidence of many that would motivate his subsequent work.

Another writer recognized as important in *Teoría del túnel* is Rimbaud, to whom Cortázar had devoted a separate short essay ("Rimbaud") in 1941, under his pseudonym, Julio Denis.[4] In that essay Cortázar contrasts Mallarmé and Rimbaud, the former never satisfied with his quest for perfect poetic form, the latter taxed by a problem not simply of a poetic but of a human order. According to Cortázar, Rimbaud's "Je est un autre" (I is another) surprisingly demonstrates that there is a point of contact between Rimbaud and the surrealists, to be found in their common belief that the unconscious is a ruling force in poetry.

Cortázar returns to the subject of the novel in "Notas sobre la novela contemporánea" (Notes on the modern novel), first published in 1948, and in "Situación de la novela" (1950; The state of the novel) to express much the same views in a less didactic style than he employs in *Teoria del túnel*. Some passages from the first essay are taken verbatim from *Teoría del túnel*. Some of the language of "Situación de la novela" could almost have served as material for *Rayuela;* for example, he writes that "novels presuppose and search out man's imperfect system, using the imperfect system of language."[5] Cortázar's view is that in the nineteenth century characters and readers shared a common culture but did not share each other's personal destiny. Novels were read at that time as a form of escapism; they evoked nostalgia for a lost Arcadia, critically portrayed the social order, and pointed toward some form of utopia. The modern novel, however, is read in order to discover oneself in the present.[6]

An important essay dating from 1954 is "Para una poética" (Toward a poetics).[7] Drawing on the work of the late nineteenth-century anthropologist Lucien Lévy-Bruhl, Cortázar asserts that there is a primordial human inclination to approach the world poetically, through image, metaphor, and analogy. That inclination has been swamped by the rationalist approach, but underneath there remains the urge: "The very man who rationally concludes that life is full of suffering senses an vague pleasure in voicing this by means of an image: life is an onion that must be peeled as one cries."[8] The poet is a "primitive" in this good sense and perhaps has been left to go about things in his own way on the grounds that what he does is of no great consequence or threat to the prevailing ethos. One can understand why Cortázar fixes on this particular quotation from Lévy-Bruhl: "The essence of participation lies . . . in erasing all duality . . . the subject is at once himself and the being in which he is participating."[9] Cortázar sees the mystery of poetry as part of the mystery of mankind, not as a surface phenomenon related to language and style. Moving on from the general argument to the particularities of poetry, Cortázar points out the value of metaphor as opposed to simile, the former being a simple expression of a sudden leap into another way of being ("una irrupción en otro ser, en otra forma de ser").[10] Here he quotes (one of many instances of this quotation) a statement that Keats made, in one of his letters, to the effect that should a sparrow come close to his window, he would share in its pecking.[11]

The kind of poetry that interests Cortázar sets its sights beyond the achievement of formal structure. The kind of poet who interests him is a sufferer from existential anguish, one whose work is an expression of disenchantment, unsettling, ambitious, characterized by "an existential stammering that is restless and pressing."[12] Only the poetic strategies previously identified (analogy, metaphor, imagery) can serve these ends. The poet is a metaphysical magician, an "evoker of essences," a person driven by a thirst for otherness.[13] Words (and here again there is a foretaste of *Rayuela*) are the "the poet's troubling need." The implications of this phrase seem to be two: that a writer cannot but struggle with the mediating effects of a linguistic code, but that paradoxically (and to adopt phraseology that became modish two decades after Cortázar's essay) the medium becomes the message.[14] Cortázar goes on to talk of the poet as a magician who rejects the discursive method and makes "an ineffable transition," an ontological shift to being the object, to "lo otro" (otherness).[15] He mentions Poe, Rimbaud, and Baudelaire as antecedents of this process. This epiphanic form of knowledge has nothing to do with explanation or scientific progress; Cortázar illustrates his point by saying that plastic light switches allow the passage of the same current as did the porcelain ones of days gone by. Finally, the poet is above all open, receptive like a lightning conductor. Cortázar concludes his essay by quoting from García Lorca: "Yo no soy un poeta, ni una hoja, / pero sí un pulso herido que ronda las cosas del otro lado" (I am not a poet, nor a leaf, but I am a wounded pulse that skirts the things on the other side).[16]

The reference to Poe indicates that even in those days Cortázar's notion of "poet" was not necessarily confined to the practitioner of the kind of writing that, due to its formal characteristics, one would unquestioningly label "poetry." Later, it becomes quite clear that Cortázar sees the poetic as a quality of all kinds of writing and particularly as one found in good short stories. Though increasingly skeptical and disrespectful of conventional demarcation lines between literary genres—his collage books of the late sixties loudly proclaim as much—Cortázar did talk and write quite a lot about generic differences.

The short story is the subject of a key address that Cortázar gave in Cuba in the early sixties and that was subsequently published under the unassuming title of "Algunos aspectos del cuento" (Some aspects of the short story).[17] As one reads this essay, it is important to bear in mind that its author was the "new" Cortázar, the man who had become widely known as a short-story writer, the man for whom the Cuban Revolution had been a cathartic, transforming experience. Speaking of his own stories, he explains that almost every one of them written up to that time is in some way fantastic and sets out to counter the idea that things are real because they can be accounted for in the sort of scientific and philosophical terms that were taken for granted in the eighteenth century. According to those, the world is governed by a more or less harmonious set of laws and principles, relationships of cause and effect, and clearly defined psychology. Everything has its place. Cortázar, by contrast, is suspicious of such a naïve concept of reality. He intuits a more elusive and secret order of things, and he credits Alfred Jarry, the man who said that the exceptions were more interesting than the rules, with steering him toward that viewpoint. Cortázar insists that he is only talking about his own writing. He also states his belief that there are characteristics that are shared by short stories in general, but in the same breath calls it a very indefinable genre.

The novel is an open structure (not in Eco's sense but in the sense that it is not subject to limits), whereas the short story is founded on the idea of limitation. (On another occasion, in a more playful mood, Cortázar said that there were no rules governing the novel, except that it should not be too heavy for the reader to hold up.) The two genres, novel and short story, can be compared, respectively, with movies and still photographs. The short-story writer aesthetically exploits the physical limits of the genre. Photographers and short-story writers alike fix on significant images that speak of wider things or launch the spectator or reader toward those things. And here Cortázar also uses an analogy with boxing that would become famous: the short story must win by a knockout, whereas the novel may win on points. The story has to do its business quickly, but the novel may take its time, achieve its effect cumulatively. The story writer, knowing that time is not on his side, works vertically, seeking depth, condensing and compressing. A bad story is one that lacks these qualities; stories fail because of poor technique, not because of their subject matter. A significant (effective) story is one that "bursts out of its own limits with the sort of explosion of spiritual energy that all of a sudden sheds light on something that goes far beyond the trivial and occasionally dreary anecdote it is telling."[18] Meaning is directly related to the degree of intensity (*intensidad,* the pent-up energy awaiting release) and tension (*tensión,* the tauhtness of the telling, the story's technique).

Speaking of his own writing, Cortázar says that he does not often choose his subjects, but that they tend to present themselves to him; most of his stories (at least up to that time) were written "regardless of my will, above or below my reasoning consciousness, as if I were only a medium through which some alien force were passing and making its presence felt."[19] The subject of the story, whatever its origin, always has an exceptional quality in that, like a magnet, it attracts a constellation of feelings and ideas to it. That exceptionality depends on the subject's interaction with the writer, his personal values and culture, for no subject is necessarily good or bad. The successful text has "dynamics that cause us to break out of ourselves and enter a system of relations that is more complex and beautiful."[20] It is this capacity that explains Cortázar's personal list of favorite stories, which he then exemplifies; the list includes Poe's "William Wilson," Maupassant's "Boule de suif," Borges's "Tlön, Uqbar, Orbis Tertius," Tolstoy's "Death of Ivan Ilich," and Hemingway's "Fifty Grand." Lasting short stories, says Cortázar, are like seeds of huge trees that grow in our memory.

Once the writer has his subject and senses the various dimensions of its significance, the challenge is to convey to the reader that sense of significance and recreate in the reader, who may be indifferent and is most often passive, the feeling that led the writer to begin the story. The reader must be engaged, obliged to keep reading, and isolated from the surrounding world by involvement. He must emerge from the experience enriched. The only way to achieve this is by means of the intensity and taughtness (*intensidad, tensión*) referred to above. Unnecessary description must be eschewed, transitional phrases be eliminated. Cortázar quotes Poe's "Cask of Amontillado" as an example of such a story, saying that it projects the reader into the thick of the drama after only three or four sentences. Kafka or D. H. Lawrence, on the other hand project the reader into an atmosphere that Cortázar, rather confusingly, now dubs "*tensión.*"

In an important coda to his speech, Cortázar relates what has previously been said to the situation in contemporary Cuba. He says that professional skill as a writer in itself will not guarantee results if that writer is not committed to something beyond the aesthetic. But conversely, and more importantly (given the context in which Cortázar was speaking), good intentions, passion, and revolutionary fervor will lead to nothing if the writer lacks the requisite writing skills. Furthermore, "to write within the revolution . . . to write in a revolutionary manner, is not, as many suppose, necessarily to write about the revolution itself."[21] He then advocates openness and artistic freedom, berates those who see art as didactic, as a means of promoting an ideology, and warns against the "facile demagoguery" that prescribes themes and demands that literature be written in forms that are accessible to everyone: "One is not doing the common man a favor if one offers him literature that he can assimilate with no effort, passively, like someone going to the cinema to see cowboy films."[22]

"Del cuento breve y sus alrededores" (Concerning the short story and its contexts) appears in the miscellany *Último round.* Here some of the same territory is revisited, though the focus is more on how Cortázar himself comes to write a story. He refers to Horacio Quiroga's precepts for the short-story writer; Cortázar respects those that advocate economy (the idea that the story is like a novel "without the padding"; the notion of—as Pound put it, speaking of poetry—maximum of meaning in a minimum of words). He is also persuaded by Quiroga's exhortation to tell the story as if to a small circle of intimates and as if one might have been involved in it. This is a particularly significant point, bearing in mind Cortázar's skill at involving his own readers; they identify with the narrator, and even when that narrator narrates in the third person, have a feeling that the narrator is very close to the protagonists. Cortázar reports that, when confronted by Ana María Barrenechea's view that he too infrequently used a third-person narrator, he had to prove to her that in fact he often did; together they deduced that when he did so it came across as a disguised first person. He goes on to assert that the hallmark of a great story is its "autarky," its self-sufficiency, likening such stories to bubbles freeing themselves from a clay pipe. The narrator, whether first person or third, is in the bubble, not in the pipe. When writing in the third person Cortázar is at pains not to distance himself from the action.

He then talks of being invaded by his subjects and of writing as a means of exorcism. Many of his stories, perhaps most stories, in particular fantastic ones, are the product of neuroses and nightmares. (We know this to be literally true in Cortázar's case, at least during the first half of his career: he became neurotic due to pressure of work in the years before he left Argentina and has identified a number of his stories as the product of nightmares.) As Cortázar writes a story, he enters into a trance-like state from which he emerges exhausted and disoriented, as if he had been making love, and there is sometimes a sense of disenchantment on his return to the status quo. Poe, he reminds us, wrote many of his best tales in such an *état second*. Cortázar attempts to convey an understanding of the process by quoting the famous words of a child who once explained how he went about drawing by saying: "First I think, and then I draw a line around my think."[23] Recalling the time when he wrote the story called "Una flor amarilla" (A yellow flower), Cortázar says that he began with an amorphous idea about a man finding a child who resembles him and has an intuition regarding immortality. He wrote the first scenes without a hitch, unaware of where he was heading; had someone told him at that point that there would be a poisoning at the end, he would have been astounded. The story did indeed end with a poisoning, but reaching that conclusion had been like unraveling a skein. Cortázar goes on to claim that his stories often have no "literary" merit, in the sense that they come to him without his making a conscious effort. No doubt the practice of several years allows him to narrate with ease what comes to him as if of its own accord. This sort of writing is then compared to Baudelaire's concept of the magical properties of poetry. The story depends on qualities that characterize poetry and jazz: tension, rhythm, internal pulse, the irruption of the unforeseen within a framework of the familiar. For fantastic literature to be effective, he adds, the exceptional must be accepted as if it were a process of osmosis, realized without the exceptional displacing the familiar framework into which it has broken. He returns to the subject in "Del sentimiento de lo fantástico" (Concerning the sense of the fantastic).

That piece and "Del sentimiento de no estar del todo" (Concerning the sense of not quite being there) are both in the earlier miscellany *La vuelta al día en ochenta mundos* (Around the day in eighty worlds). The title of the second refers to Cortázar's sense of being both adult and child and of inhabiting a zone between the two, only partially participating in his circumstances: "I write by default, because of dislocation . . . from an interstice" (32). This man-child is a *cronopio,* an eccentric rather than a gentleman, a person struggling to make sense of his life and under attack for being too intellectual.[24] The time may have passed when people believed in an oversimplified idea of reality, but now the *realista ingenuo* (the naïve realist) has been replaced by *ingenuo realista* (the realistic naïf) (34).

According to Cortázar, a gentleman's agreement has come into operation between man and reality: man is left in the comfort of his routines and in exchange agrees not to keep prodding and questioning. Cortázar clearly feels he must do his share of the prodding. "Del sentimiento de no estar del todo" is a text that resists adequate summary. It includes an account of Cortázar's indignation when, as a child, a friend returned a loaned book to him unread, saying that it was too fantastic. He also speaks of his own poems, describing them as "petrificaciones de . . . extrañamiento" (petrifications of . . . estrangement), as ways of capturing what he sees "instead of." He doubts that great poetry can come about without such a sense of estrangement from familiar, accepted perspectives. That estrangement amounts to a sort of eccentricity that is shared by humorists, anarchists, and social misfits, not to mention many writers.

A second section of the essay explains how his stories and novels can also be seen as expressions of estrangement. Fundamentally they share a common purpose and *Rayuela* is "in some ways the philosophy of my short stories" (35). However, there is a difference in writing strategy: whereas the stories, like the poems, are written with the writer in a state of altered consciousness, almost automatically, as if the texts were writing themselves, the novels are more consciously constructed, with moments of altered consciousness along the way. It is important to recognize, however, that the construction of the novels is carried out through an associative rather than a logical process.

All these ideas are repeated and expanded in interviews. Cortázar also talks of writing less and less "well." This can be understood in general as a process of rejection of traditions, clichés, or formulas. He abandons grandiloquence, introduces ordinary language, does not cultivate style for its own sake, and works to efface any possible distinction between style and content. He does not generally change the text of stories once they are complete, but when he does revise, it is usually a question of applying Occam's razor. Cortázar tells González Bermejo that in the mid-seventies he is still basing his story writing on exactly the same inspirational process as forty years previously (the initial, poorly defined idea, and then the writing that carries itself along).[25] The subjects come to him in such a way that there are times when he almost feels ashamed to claim authorship. He likens the story to a sphere, something that is perfect and self-contained, with no loose ends. Writing stories is also a musical operation involving rhythm and euphony,[26] not in the sense of using fine words, but related to the melodic flow of the syntax: the purer the melody, the more complete the communication with the reader. Once launched into the writing of a story, it is like riding a bicycle: problems arise when one slows or interrupts the onward drive. In a letter to a critic he explains that he has always written as if in response to an impulse and that the rational elements in his work reveal themselves after he has said what he has felt driven to say.[27] If his stories have changed over the years, he says, it is because the collections from *Alguien que anda por ahí* on involve more every-day situations with which readers can easily identify, as if they were possible protagonists in them. Much is also said by Cortázar in interviews about his novels, but that will be explored in the next chapter.

CHAPTER 5

Winning on Points

The First Three Novels

Los premios

In 1960, by then well known for his work as a short story writer (*Bestiario, Final del juego,* and *Las armas secretas* had all been published), Cortázar surprised his readers with a long novel, *Los premios* (*The Winners*). The main characters in this book have all won the lottery, the prize being a cruise to an undisclosed destination. As the novel opens, they gather in the appointed meeting place, a café called The London. It is as if the reader were witnessing a conversation between two men, both teachers at the same school, and both of them winners of the lottery. As they sit chatting in the café, they observe other customers, wondering who among them will prove to be fellow prize winners; a young couple enters, and Cortázar moves the eavesdropping microphone, as it were, over to them, thus beginning a new chapter. By way of this relay technique, the process of introducing characters continues until all the passengers have been presented and the reader has been made aware of their varied social backgrounds and expectations. (All Cortázar's novels are characterized by the early introduction of a number of characters en bloc, and some critics have taken him to task for it, saying that he fails to distinguish adequately between them. The author himself acknowledged this tendency, for example in his video interview with Saúl Sosnowski, *Espejo de escritores.*) One or two of the winners seem to sense already that there may be some indefinable, but significant, purpose behind the cruise upon which they are about to embark; the impression, as a dentist called Medrano puts it, is that "esto va a terminar de una manera . . ." (it's all going to end up in . . .), or, as López, one of the teachers, says, that there is something in the air, "una especie de tomada de pelo pero en un plano por así decirlo sublime" (28; as if we were having our legs pulled, but in a sublime sort of way).

Once on board the *Malcolm,* the passengers are faced with crew members with whom they can hardly communicate. Those crew members who do speak a language that is shared by some of the passengers are hermetic, at best polite but unforthcoming; others, who do not speak a comprehensible language, are suspected of being of obscure Nordic origins, perhaps Finnish. Early in the voyage the youngest passenger, a boy called Jorge, dubs the rank-and-file crew members "lipids" and their officers "glucids"; these playful names are promptly adopted for general use by the more adventurous among the passengers and by the author (ever willing to assume a child's perspective). The passengers are able to learn a little about the previous captain of the ship, but nothing about the current one; their requests for information about other matters, such as their destination, are fruitless. Japan is rumored to be on the itinerary, provoking excitement among some passengers and skepticism among others. Most significantly, the passengers are prevented from having access to the stern of the boat, and when they press for an explanation they are told that it is because there is an outbreak of a mysterious strain of typhus. It is this prohibition that serves as catalyst for most of the action in *Los premios.*

Among the winners we find the following people: the two teachers (Dr. Rastelli, pompously grandiloquent and subject to somewhat ridiculous donjuanesque fantasies, and his younger colleague, López); Medrano, a dentist, who has just abandoned his lover; Paula and Raúl, old friends from well-to-do backgrounds, who share a cabin and mutual trust, but are not sexually involved with each other; Nora and Lucio, two young lovers; the Trejo family, led by a domineering wife and including the adolescent Felipe; Jorge, a younger boy, in the company of his divorced mother, Claudia, and their strange friend, Persio; Don Galo Porriño, an arrogant self-made man of Galician origins; and finally the Presuttis, a family group from an area of Buenos Aires famous for Italian influence and soccer supporters.

Thrown together on the boat, these people reveal the determining power over their characters and behavior of the different classes and areas from which they come. Many critics have seen represented here a cross-section of Buenos Aires society, even to the extent of attributing social types to particular zones of the city.[1] Cortázar deftly and ironically caricatures these people in the early pages of *Los premios,* and for the most part they play predictable roles in the action. But there is, throughout, an ironic awareness of what is happening, revealed by the author in several ways and occasionally expressed even by some of the characters themselves. For example, Paula and López play with one another in what she recognizes is a standard courtship routine: "a crazy situation, but somehow an inevitable one, as if they were marionettes who were bound to strike the usual blows. . . . Both could play the game and hopefully Punch would be as good at it as Judy" (237).

The hand that works the puppets is, quite obviously, Cortázar's, but this is not to say that he wrote *Los premios* with a clear sense of direction from the start. At the end of Spanish-language editions of this novel there is a note (for some reason omitted from the English translation) in which Cortázar explains that he began to write the book while on a long sea voyage himself, as a means of guarding his own privacy. After the initial idea the novel acquired its own shape and pace, and he came to feel that he was being led along by it, discovering what happened next as if he were the book's first reader. That final note to *Los premios* has a playful tone, and may arouse suspicions that in it Cortázar was talking tongue-in-cheek; but there were also other occasions when he spoke in similar terms about the development of *Los premios.*

It will be clear from the foregoing that in this novel there are signs, relatively muted ones, of the author's self-awareness; that is something Cortázar would bring to the fore in texts like "Las babas del diablo" and *Rayuela.* In *Los premios,* the most overt device that Cortázar uses to draw attention to the story-in-the-process-of-composition is Persio. Cortázar "fleshes out" the main characters by two basic means: he uses omniscient authorial descriptions of their physical characteristics and behavior and, above all, he adroitly constructs conversations in which the style of the language, as much as its content, betrays the characters' identities. Some of the most amusing examples, the most caricaturesque, are moments involving Atilio Presutti: for example, his effusiveness on seeing how well the cabin bathrooms are equipped. It is worth noting here that Atilio's nickname, "El Pelusa," links him with the pieces of fluff that become attached to people and clothing in the course of a novel Cortázar had written a decade before, *El examen;* there they can be associated with the proletarian supporters of Perón who, in the eyes of people like Cortázar, were invading Buenos Aires in the late forties and early fifties. (*El examen* is discussed in the chapter titled "Down, but Not Out.")

Of all the characters in *Los premios,* Persio is the most enigmatic. The other characters, even those who appear to be one-dimensional, are all credibly and sufficiently drawn; Persio, by comparison, is not at all rounded, and his presence among the other passengers always seems provisional. Unlike all the others, Persio exists on two levels, as a passenger and as a detached observer of the whole situation. As a passenger he does not play a prominent role, interacting primarily with Claudia and Jorge, the two with whom he has come on the voyage; even with those two, his exchanges seem eccentric, while other passengers perceive him as a strange and uncertain presence. Thus, on one occasion when the passengers are all gathering, "only Lucio and Nora were missing, not counting Persio, because Persio never seemed to be missing anywhere" (126). Persio's second level, as a privileged observer, is recorded in a series of italicized sections that are interpolated between the chapters of what is otherwise a novel with a traditional, linear narrative structure.

In these italicized sections devoted to the thoughts of Persio, sections whose cryptic and imagistic style contrasts markedly with the easy readability of the rest of the book, Persio adopts a seagull's-eye view of the boat and all that is happening on it, seeking a design, a *figura*. In the process he toys with any number of perspectives, be they divine, logical, or visceral; a "crystallization," he claims, must be possible, coinciding perhaps with the Portuguese railway system or with the image of a guitar painted by Picasso; the lottery winners, like stars, must surely form "constellations." As we near the last of Persio's passages, it becomes easier to follow their drift, and they appear to be more clearly relevant to the role and viewpoint of the writer. The fact that Persio usually works for a publisher is not irrelevant.

The difficulty in understanding the passages devoted to Persio (which both the critics and the author have tended, somewhat inaccurately, to refer to as monologues), coupled with the fact that they interrupt what is otherwise an easily flowing novel, tempts the reader to skip them. Mario Benedetti says quite bluntly that these passages are "very boring";[2] he was not alone in criticizing their inclusion in what has in other respects been regarded as a highly successful novel. In the closing note that I referred to above, included in Spanish language editions of *Los premios,* Cortázar acknowledges that some of his acquaintances (disparagingly referred to as "people who like to get their amusement in a straight line") had been troubled by the intrusion of the Persio passages. The reference to reading "in a straight line" clearly portends the hopscotch technique that was to characterize Cortázar's next and major novel, *Rayuela.* In response to his straight-reading critics he says that the Persio passages came to him ineluctably at the points at which they appear in the narrative, to serve as a sort of overview of all that was happening on board; he adds that the language in which they are couched seeks to express a different dimension, aims at something different. But the truth is that the problem with the Persio passages goes beyond their inherent difficulty, which in itself is the product of a quest to create—through the inhibiting medium of language—an order that is elusive and mystical in nature. Steven Boldy rightly points out that Cortázar does not adequately integrate the two narrative components, as he does so cleverly in some stories and in *Rayuela.*[3]

After a while on board, the inevitable love interests develop. We see that Claudia and Medrano sense a spiritual affinity that seems to promise something deep and lasting. We find that Paula is a little manipulative, a clever and well-read woman who has rebelled against her aristocratic background; Felipe, the adolescent, lusts after her, as does López, who becomes irrationally, but understandably, jealous of her cabin mate Raúl. The latter is intelligent, an intellectual who is somewhat detached from the preoccupations of the other passengers, a homosexual who makes gentle overtures to Felipe, who in turn is flustered, unsure of his own sexuality. In fact, Felipe is to lose his innocence to one of the sailors, whose name, Orf (Orpheus?), and whose quarters below deck invite thoughts of the underworld. Plied with fierce rum and tobacco, Felipe falls into the clutches of Orf, a man with an immense tattoo of an eagle (Zeus, disguised as an eagle to carry away Ganymede?; Felipe actually tells Orf that in Buenos Aires he buys a tobacco he understands is "pleasing to the nostrils of Zeus") (262). Tobacco, or more precisely the pipe, seems in this novel to promise homosexual love: both Raúl and Orf offer Felipe a pipe, evidently a phallic symbol.

Other mythological allusions are numerous. Paula says that Felipe is another Dionysos (363); Raúl likens the frustrating search through the passages of the boat to the trials of Tantalus (361) and to a trip to Hades (308), and elsewhere he anticipates a likely appearance of a Charon look-alike with serpents all over his arms (188). As a group of the men explore below deck, it seems to them that the whole boat consists of passages, in short that it is a labyrinth; and at that juncture Raúl quips that "all we need now is the Minotaur" (190). This last reference may be read as Cortázar poking fun at himself: mythological allusions pepper his early works, and his first major publication, *Los reyes,* had been a version of the story of the Minotaur. It is important to realize that here, as in most of his work, when Cortázar invokes mythology it is by loose associations and not by straightforward reincarnation of myths.[4]

One of the most important features of *Los premios* is the revealing effect that prohibition and lack of information have on the passengers. Some are spurred into action by the unknown: they try to find a way to the stern, they confront the authorities with their dissatisfaction at the restrictions placed upon them and the poor flow of information, they challenge the status quo. Anger, rebelliousness, curiosity, and playfulness all have a part in motivating the characters who make up this group of recalcitrants. By the end of the novel, the passengers have resolved themselves into majority and minority groups. The majority (Don Galo, Rastelli, most of the Trejos and Presuttis) blandly acquiesce and set their sights no higher than on having a quiet and undemanding time; they accuse the minority of dissidents of rocking the boat unnecessarily.

After some fruitless attempts to find a way through to the stern and in view of the fact that young Jorge is ill and a doctor is not forthcoming, things get out of proportion, the rebels arm themselves and storm their way through, and Medrano reaches the stern, where he is shot. "Todo eso tenía un aire de cosa ya sucedida, de novela de kiosko" (It all had the air of something that had happened already, an air of pulp fiction) (418). Atilio and Raúl retrieve the body, and it is carried back to a cabin. The next day the passengers gather in the lounge, the conformists in one group and the troublemakers—the *malditos* (cursed)—in another. The authorities announce that the cruise has been suspended and the passengers are to be flown back to Buenos Aires. It becomes clear that the death of Medrano will be passed off as an accident and that the voices of those who refuse to sign a declaration to that effect will be lost under a wave of conformism and official denials. With that, the passengers disperse to their usual locations and social positions. The cruise has never got beyond the bay of Buenos Aires, and the voyage of personal discovery has had an impact only on a minority of the passengers.

Apart from Felipe, the most interesting cases of personal development are those of Atilio and Medrano. In the course of the novel, Atilio has grown from a figure of fun into one of heroic stature (Cortázar, in his final note, declares himself amazed at the transformation). Among those who make their way to the stern, Atilio is the only one whose motivation is entirely selfless: his only concern is to do what is best for the sick Jorge. In one of his interviews, years later, Cortázar summed him up this way: "For all his ignorance, his ingenuousness, his bad taste, [he was] one of the few truly honest people, willing to do whatever was necessary for things to turn out right."[5]

But Atilio will return to his nest: the proof is to be seen in the tasteless brick-colored suit that marks him off socially as he stands with his newfound friends, the *malditos,* on the quay and they declare that they must all see each other again. As to Medrano, who is the best character according to Cortázar,[6] for him reaching the stern signifies breaking away from the superficiality and selfishness of his former life, reaching the other side, realizing that his abandoned lover represents his former self: "Ahora hacía las paces consigo mismo . . . un saldo de cuentas del que salía por primera vez tranquilo, sin razones muy claras, sin méritos ni deméritos, simplemente reconciliándose consigo mismo, echando a rodar como un muñeco de barro al hombre viejo" (Now he was making peace with himself . . . settling the account and coming away calm for the first time, with no clear reasons, no pros or cons, just reconciling things with himself, tossing away the old self like a clay doll) (420). This is a scene of self-discovery in death that has more than a passing resemblance to the epiphany of Marini in "La isla a mediodía."

The idea of the journey of discovery and return to origins has been with us for a long time, as has the ship-of-fools motif. It is taken up in the works of other writers from the River Plate area: Cristina Peri Rossi's *La nave de los locos,* 1984 and Daniel Moyano's *Libro de navíos y borrascas,* 1983. It is also to be found in other works by Cortázar: in the story "La autopista del sur" he again strands a number of strangers together in chance circumstances, a traffic jam of fantastic proportions that leads them to reveal their personal qualities until, just as arbitrarily, it dissolves and they speed back to their everyday lives. Shortly after the publication of *Los premios* in Argentina, Katherine Anne Porter published her *Ship of Fools,* which met with great success in the United States; the English translation of Cortázar's book appeared somewhat later, and some unthinking critics accused him of plagiarism.

We have seen that on a social level Cortázar paints a representative sample of Buenos Aires society, that on an individual one he uses the time on the *Malcolm* to take some of his characters on a voyage of self-discovery, and that, broadly, he groups his characters into the accepting and unimaginative on the one hand and the questioning and creative on the other. Narratively, through Medrano, and metanarratively, through the device of Persio, he raises metaphysical and literary issues that he will explore more deeply in the following novel.

Rayuela

> El hombre no es, sino que busca ser, proyecta ser, manoteando entre palabras y conducta y alegría salpicada de sangre y otras retóricas como ésta"(Rather than being, man seeks to be, plans to be, flailing around amidst words and actions and joy smattered with blood and rhetoric like this). *Rayuela,* chapter 62.

While García Márquez's *Cien años de soledad* (*One Hundred Years of Solitude*) has been a more popular book, there is little doubt that the work of greatest literary significance among those of the Boom period—and quite possibly the most significant novel ever to come out of Spanish America—is Cortázar's *Rayuela* (1963; *Hopscotch*), the novel—some would say antinovel—that brought Cortázar notoriety and drew international attention to his work. Surely no other novel in the history of Latin American letters has ever won so much critical attention. In 1984, when a new edition of it was published in the wake of Cortázar's death, its editor rightly described the bibliography on *Rayuela* at that time as "truly terrifying."[7] If that was so in 1984, it is all the more so today; no one can be sure of having read everything that has been written about *Rayuela.* In what follows I shall offer some of my own observations about *Rayuela,* aware that others have probably said it all before.

Until the early sixties, Cortázar's reputation was based on three collections of stories published during the previous decade and characterized by fantasy and horror, some of them open to allegorical readings and several of them dealing with the world of children. In one or two of them one can detect seeds that became flowers in *Rayuela;* one of the most important among these seminal stories is "Las babas del diablo" (*Final del juego*). Here the author foregrounds the act of writing as a theme and at the same time demands that the reader put considerable effort into the act of reading and making sense of the story; both of these characteristics become mainstays in *Rayuela.* We can also find embryonic signs of them in the novels that were written before *Rayuela.* In *Los premios,* for example, otherwise largely traditional and linear in form, Cortázar included a surprising and not wholly successful series of interludes devoted to Persio, a character who from his privileged vantage point seeks some wider, superior, transcendental perspective on the action; reading these interludes one has an enhanced awareness of an authorial presence, and one feels a need to work in order to find meaning. When, in a later chapter of the present book, we consider the author's posthumous publications, especially *El examen,* a novel that was completed in 1950, we shall see other early signs of what was to come.

Rayuela is in three consecutive parts titled, respectively, "Del lado de allá" (From over there), "Del lado de acá" (From over here), and "De otros lados" (From other places), this last part being subtitled "Capítulos prescindibles" (Dispensable chapters). The novel is some six hundred pages long. Chapters 1 to 36 make up part 1 of the book, the one titled "From over there"; from a geographical standpoint, "there" means Paris. Though there are few direct references to it, the time is the fifties. The protagonist is one Horacio Oliveira, an Argentine intellectual malcontent who spends his time wandering the streets or drinking, smoking, listening to jazz, and talking with his motley group of friends (almost all of them émigrés like Oliveira himself), who call themselves the "Club de la Serpiente" (Snake Club). Oliveira rails against what he himself best exemplifies: a worldview determined by Western dualism, reason, habit, received ideas (and, since he is Argentine, that includes many ideas received from Europe). His analytical detachment sits uncomfortably with his feeling of a need to be involved in a way he can feel is authentic: "'Lo malo,' pensó Oliveira, 'es que además pretendo ser espectador activo, y ahí empieza la cosa'" ('The trouble,' thought Oliveira, 'is that I want to be an active spectator too, and that's where things start to get difficult') (chapter 90). He is a man who is better at thinking than at being, a man who half acknowledges his own "moral diseases" (chapter 2). His literary ancestors include protagonists of existential works but also some clowns; in the context of Cortázar's own works his clearest precursors are Medrano in *Los premios* and Johnny Carter in "El perseguidor."

Oliveira is the link to the second part of the novel, chapters 37 to 56, the only person to appear in both parts 1 and 2 (with the possible exceptions of his paramour, Maga, and of Morelli, a character whose ideas seem to hover throughout the book, rather as did those of Persio in *Los premios*). In the second part of *Rayuela,* we find Oliveira back in Argentina, presumably having been deported from France. The third part, comprising the "dispensable chapters," consists of chapters 57 to 155, and these are not associated with any geographical space in particular.

Clearly, then, there is a sense in which we are invited to see it all from the angle of a narrator who is in (and probably from) Argentina. These and other narrative features, such as the fact that Oliveira's thoughts and activities, especially in part 1, are sometimes narrated from the standpoint of an omniscient third person and sometimes by "himself" in the first person, lead to a blurring together of Oliveira and the author in the reader's mind. Biographical factors, too, invite one to associate the exiled Argentine intellectual Julio Cortázar with his exiled Argentine intellectual protagonist. Finally, we have the author's own statement to that effect to González Bermejo: "En realidad Oliveira se me parece mucho en el plano personal" (The truth is that on a personal level Oliveira is very much like me).[8]

Somewhat as in "Las babas del diablo," in *Rayuela* Cortázar is quite open about the artificiality of the enterprise and the gauntlet he is throwing down to his readers. Cortázar opens the book with what amounts to a kind of manifesto: he tells us that in its way *Rayuela* is several different books in one. He suggests two ways of reading it, though he allows that yet others are possible; and he reminds us that as readers we are free to do as we wish. Of the two ways suggested, one entails starting on the first page and reading through to the end of chapter 56, at which point, says Cortázar rather disparagingly, there are three pretty little asterisks that mean "The End." If the novel is read in that straightforward manner, the third part of the book, proportionally more than a third of the whole, is simply omitted.

The second way of reading *Rayuela* comes as a surprise: it involves beginning at chapter 73 (that is, after "The End") and jumping around according to numbers that appear at the conclusion of each chapter. If the reader who is following this second approach gets lost, he can consult a "Tablero de dirección " (Guide table) that is printed at the start of the book and lists the bizarre order of chapters that characterizes this second approach. For example: 73, 1, 2, 116, 3, 84, 4, 71, 5, 81 . . . 138, 127, 56, 63, 88, 72, 77, 131, 58, 131.

The difference between the two suggested readings, however, is much more than a matter of ordering information. This can be illustrated by briefly describing the experience of reading the first five chapters in the *tablero* sequence. Chapter 73 begins with the word "Sí," as if in answer to a question or expression of opinion that has not, of course, been read. It goes on to talk in obscure, almost nightmarish terms about hostile forces and pressures, the "cloying substances that keep us on this side." Thus far the narrative voice has been in the first person plural. An unidentified first-person singular continues expressing Angst, talking of being cheated, caught between "infallible equations and the machinery of conformism," wonders if literature can do anything to facilitate an escape from all this, talks of the necessity of invention as a means of arriving at truth, and seems to favor contemplation as a means of self-knowledge. Someone called Morelli is mentioned, and there are a number of recognizable cultural references. In short, a good deal of what one later realizes that the novel is about is heralded right at the start of the book, but at that initial stage the reader is left in some confusion and can glean little more than the implications of the style of this initial chapter, that is, that the book is going to deal with serious matters in a challenging way. (Even with benefit of hindsight, the initial chapter makes fairly demanding reading). At the end of chapter 73, the reader is sent to chapter 1. Also somewhat cryptic, this chapter is narrated in the first person by a narrator who tells of his search for someone called Maga. Paris, mentioned only *en passant* in the previous chapter, now occupies the foreground as the place where the narrator and Maga meet by chance. The cultural references multiply. Other characters and a club are mentioned, but not contextualized for the reader's benefit. There is also a strikingly absurd moment when the narrator is searching for a lump of sugar that has fallen under a restaurant table. Chapter 2 carries on in a similar vein, allowing the reader to piece together a slightly clearer picture of the relationships between the characters and their various activities, but things remain disconcertingly vague. However, chapter 116, albeit very indirectly, provides information that can be read as orientational. It consists of edited notes by Morelli, who seems to be a writer and an intellectual; his notes refer in part to ways of narrating and contain one or two particularly revealing passages if taken to refer to the work that the reader has in his hands. There is a quotation from Georges Bataille ("Il souffrait d'avoir introduit des figures décharnées, qui se déplaçaient dans un monde dément, qui jamais ne pourraient convaincre" [It suffered from the introduction of fleshless figures moving about in a crazy world that would never be convincing]) that aptly sums up the state of things in *Rayuela* ; and there is further clarification in what seems to be a statement of intent: "Basta de novelas hedónicas, premasticadas, con *psicologías*" (Enough of hedonistic, predigested novels based on *psychology*). In other words, the reader seems to be being told that *Rayuela* will work in an unconventional way. Chapter 3 takes us back to Paris, to the world sketched previously, but this time the narration is by an omniscient third person, and we can deduce that a man called Horacio Oliveira is the one who was the first-person narrator in previous scenes.

This cursory account of the initial sequence of chapters gives an idea of how the reader must piece together information and conveys some sense of how the ordering of chapters colors one's understanding of the text. Either approach to reading *Rayuela* requires effort on the part of the reader, but the second radically changes the reader's experience. For example, the second approach omits chapter 55 as such, though the text of that chapter does appear, verbatim, embedded in chapter 133, one of the many chapters that are left out if one adopts the first approach to reading the book. More crucially, the second approach leaves the reader caught in an endless loop, because, as can be seen in the sample of the *Tablero* quoted above, at the end chapter 131 leads to chapter 58 and this to chapter 131, and so on.

The optionality of the extra chapters that make up the third part of the novel explains why they are called "dispensable chapters." But one must ask whether in practice the reader has significantly greater freedom of choice in approaching *Rayuela* than in dealing with novels that are presented in a less unconventional manner. True, Cortázar extends an invitation to his reader to steer his own course through the book, but at the same time he stirs the reader's curiosity as to what the second reading might be like; he challenges and guides (provides a guide table). So, at least by implication, there seems to be a preferred reading. Moreover, we have two sources that prove that Cortázar worked very carefully to arrive at the particular order established in the *Tablero:* his comments in various interviews with critics and his own working notes made during the process of composition and compilation. The latter were collected as the *Cuaderno de bitácora,* which was the author's "log book" of notes, published separately some time after the novel, under the editorship of Ana María Barrenechea, a friend of the Cortázar's and a professor in Buenos Aires.[9] Far from being capricious, then, the order specified in the *Tablero* was very carefully thought out.

The fact is that the "dispensable chapters" are anything but dispensable. If included, and particularly if included in the *Tablero* order, their effect is to amplify the world of the novel in dramatic and surprising ways, enriching the reading experience in terms of both ideas and moods, and often forcing the reader to reconsider what he has read in a previous chapter. Without the "dispensable chapters" the novel is less digressive, more closely focused, more linear, more traditional, though even then not without its share of puzzles and surprises. With them, the reading experience is peppered with seasonings that range from the unpalatable to the delicious; it is never bland. For example, at one point the tension is broken by a report from a London newspaper about the risks to the male anatomy that come with using zip fasteners; at another the emotional tension is amplified by a sequence of chapters dealing with abuse and violence. In the "dispensable chapters" can be found quotations from writers and philosophers about the meaning of existence; there is a highly eccentric and bizarrely expressed plan for world peace; there are erotic passages in *glíglico* (a kind of nonsense Spanish created by the author); there is an obituary that is totally serious in tone but ludicrously misspelled; and there is a letter to the press remarking on the shortage of butterflies.

Whether pathetic, anticlimactic, incongruous, contradictory, absurd, meditative, or erotic, these chapters are not, as some have argued, assembled in a loose collage, but instead form a very carefully woven web that crisscrosses with the chapters in parts 1 and 2, a web that formally and symbolically hints at the climactic scene in which Oliveira will try to set up a defense system based on a network made of twine or, indeed, at the fictional web in which the reader is caught.

While in theory it would have been quite possible simply to issue the novel with the chapters printed in the *Tablero* order, thus saving the reader a certain amount of irritation at constantly having to jump about, significant losses would have been entailed. One consequence would have been that the first approach to reading would then have become difficult, if not impossible, unless the now inserted dispensable chapters were accompanied by an invitation to skip them (which itself would constitute a modification of the experience of the first reading). Secondly, and much more importantly, the second approach to reading relies for part of its effect precisely on having the reader feel constantly displaced, physically obliged to carry out the interpolations; the constant shifting, the interruptions to the flow caused by having to seek out the "dispensable chapters," together with their unpredictability of content and style, serve to remind the reader that he is caught in an artificial construct, never to be allowed to get carried away by the illusion of a free-standing reality through fiction that is so dear to more traditional novelists and readers. In making this statement I do not mean to imply that in the early sixties self-conscious fictionality was anything new, even in Latin American literature, but Cortázar's novel played a major part in bringing such self-consciousness squarely to readers' attention and there was a subsequent rash of self-referential writing, coupled with a rehabilitation or rescue from oblivion of some earlier writers whose work was also in that metafictional vein. Macedonio Fernández and Leopoldo Marechal may be cited as examples.

The absurd and unconventional nature of many components of the second approach to reading *Rayuela* might justify our calling it the *cronopio* approach. Several things become ever more clear: that this approach is one that entails adventurous reading; that an adventurous approach to reading is the sort the author favors; and that any other approach to reading would, so to speak, be out of order. (In passing, we may also note that the more passive approach to reading is analogous to the attitude of the majority of the passengers on the boat in *Los premios,* faced as they are with a forbidden zone, one that a minority, rather like *cronopio* readers, actively explores.) This brings us to the important and somewhat paradoxical conclusion that the author trumpets his invitation to readers to make their own way freely through the text but in fact seems to defy them not to take the *cronopio* approach, the second approach to reading. And once taken, that approach proves in fact to be very controlled, very manipulative (in a pardonable sense), so much so that the readers' experience may be unusual, but their freedom is scarcely less constrained than by traditional authorial expectations of the act of reading.

The theme of authorial control, we should note, is alluded to in a number of Cortázar's works, in particular in a story that also dates from the early sixties, "Instrucciones para John Howell" in *Todos los fuegos el fuego* (1966). Its protagonist is a theatergoer who, having sat through the first act of an indifferent play, is invited backstage and then induced, if not coerced, into becoming a performer in it, told that he has freedom to act in matters of detail, but given to understand that he is subject to direction by superior powers. It is a story that doubtless has metaphysical and religious overtones, but literary ones also. (Note that in chapter 90 of *Rayuela* Oliveira observes that being an actor means abandoning the stalls and that he himself feels born to occupy a seat in the first row.)

Another noteworthy aspect of the opening of *Rayuela* is the appearance of two lengthy quotations that seem to be from other writers' works. Both, however, are surely not to be taken at face value. The first quotation, perhaps invented by Cortázar and falsely presented as authentic, in the manner of Borges, might have come from the pen of the latter's Pierre Menard, one of whose works is said to have been "a literal version of a literal version" of a work called *Introduction à la vie dévote*. Cortázar's own "source" supposedly derives from a form of biblical exegesis that has passed through two translations and then been edited and published in 1797 (surely a significant date, since at that time the Enlightenment was drawing to a close). The style of the passage concerned is convincingly out of date, the tone extremely serious. The modesty of its "author," Abbot Martini, rings false, for his aims are somewhat grandiose: inspired by a wish to serve young people and contribute to the general betterment of human ways, he claims to have compiled a cocktail of maxims and moral precepts that are not merely the basis of Christian behavior but also satisfying food for thought for the most intellectual of minds.

These things alone should alert most readers to the trickery that is afoot, and even the most unsuspecting among them will surely be made suspicious of the second quotation, which also looks as though it might have been invented by Cortázar. That second quotation is attributed to someone called César Bruto. The conflation of Caesar and Brutus in one name may be quite possible, but it is bound not to pass unnoticed; furthermore, if one takes into account the Spanish overtones of the adjective *bruto* (oafish, coarse), the passage's colloquialisms, its misspellings and appalling style, and not least its subject matter—ostensibly it comes from a book called *What I Would Like to Be If I Wasn't What I Am* and from a chapter of that book titled "A St. Burnard Dog"—Cortázar's playful and irreverent intentions become obvious. Another irony seems to be implicit in the choice of the St. Bernard, a dog that brings salvation.

César Bruto is, in fact, the pseudonym of Carlos Warnes, an Argentine humorist. Cortázar will call on him again, much later in *Rayuela.* When Oliveira disembarks in Buenos Aires (chapter 38) and his friends eagerly ask him what it was like in Paris, part of his zany reply involves quoting César Bruto once more: "Si a París vas en octubre / no dejes de ver el Louvre" (If you go to Paris in Octoober / you must not miss the Louvre). The awfulness of the rhyming of *octubre* with Louvre, when the latter is mispronounced with a heavy Spanish accent, brings to mind a similar joke based on appalling rhymes by, again, Borges, in the course of his story "El Aleph."

Two crucial characteristics of *Rayuela* have thus been heralded, its playfulness and its artificiality. The reader is going to find that nothing can be taken for granted, that the rug is constantly being pulled out from under his feet. Though the exclusive approach to reading (by which I mean the first of the two approaches suggested by the author, the one that excludes the "capítulos prescindibles") itself provides plenty of evidence of authorial trickery and playfulness, that impression is significantly enhanced if one takes the approach that does include them.

Among the most important of the "capítulos prescindibles" are those that deal with a character called Morelli. Morelli, an old man, is a writer who commands the interest of the group of intellectuals who people the Paris-based section of the book; he is the focus of many of the discussions that take place when they gather together to form what they refer to as the "Club de la Serpiente" (Snake Club). But Morelli more often comes to the reader's attention in a quite direct way, via the "dispensable chapters," many of which present his ideas, sometimes in a manner that suggests one is reading his original notes, sometimes through the mediating comments of an anonymous narrator. If a lot of Cortázar's worldview and experience can be said to lie behind the character of Oliveira, it is even clearer that Morelli is a barely disguised device for presenting the author's views, in particular those that have to do with writing and reading. Perhaps, too, Morelli is based on the figure of Macedonio Fernández, an eccentric and iconoclastic Argentine writer of the generation before Cortázar, one whom the latter is known to have admired and whose influence he acknowledged.

Assuming the *cronopio* reading, Morelli's ideas are presented consecutively in chapters 116, 71, 74, 115, 137, 97, 79, 62, 124, 141, 60, 109, 151, 145, 112, 154, 95, 107, 61, 105, 94, 99, and 66, that is, in more than twenty chapters. Of these, probably the most programmatic for *Rayuela* is number 79, a "very pedantic note by Morelli," in which he talks of attempting to compose a "*roman comique*" that will suggest new values and contribute toward the discovery of the true nature of mankind. Most novels (by which one understands novels in the nineteenth-century realist and naturalist traditions) fall short of such discovery because they leave the reader in a self-contained world (and the more self-contained it is, the better the novelist is judged to be). The reader cannot be allowed to sit comfortably in his armchair "sin comprometerse en el drama que también debería ser suyo" (without getting involved in the drama, which should be his, too) (chapter 99). Here one is reminded of an early Cortázar story, "Continuidad de los parques" (The continuity of parks), in which the reader reads about a reader reading about a character who then steals up from behind to attack him as he reads, making him a participant in the drama.[10]

What Morelli advocates is something analogous but more esoteric, a text that demands that the reader become an accomplice ("*lector-cómplice*"). Such a "hieratic" text is likely to irritate the majority of readers, who are accustomed to the more accommodating demotic presentation and therefore likely, says Morelli, to give up after a few pages and complain at having spent money on the book. Such readers are dubbed "*lectores-hembra*" (female readers). This, it must be made clear, does not mean "women readers"; indeed, one of the exemplary "*lectores-hembra*" portrayed in *Rayuela* is a man. All the same, in later years Cortázar felt the need to apologize for his choice of terms, saying that he should have talked of "*lectores pasivos*" (passive readers). In the interview with Picón-Garfield he says: "I ask the women of the world to forgive me for having used such a *machista* term, one that so reflects Latin American underdevelopment. . . . I did it quite ingenuously, and I have no excuse.[11]" The choice of "*lector-hembra*" speaks of another era and to some extent an earlier Cortázar; it reflects a perception of male and female behavior that is no longer thought tolerable in some cultures, though it is a perception that has deep and tenacious Hispanic roots.[12]

In *Los premios* Cortázar had already made fun of passive readers whose main concern is to see how it all turns out in the end and who expect to be led along by the nose and served easily digestible literary fodder. Morelli-Cortázar's blueprint is, by contrast, for a text that will be disorderly, provocative, and incongruous, one that instead of providing a gripping linear narrative will force the reader to participate actively in constructing the experience. Morelli's past works are said always to have a loose thread at the end, dangling outside and "apuntando a un tal vez, a un a lo mejor, a un quién sabe, que dejaba en suspenso toda visión petrificante de la obra" (pointing to a perhaps, a maybe, a who knows, that left any petrifying idea of the work up in the air) (chapter 141). Somewhat as what Umberto Eco talks of the "open novel," Morelli resolutely resists the idea of closure, cuts the systematization of characters and situations at its roots, is forever experimental, self-critical, and innovative, and above all advocates a text that functions as a vehicle for self-discovery for writer and reader alike. The writer must view the reader as "mon semblable, mon frère" (a person like me, my brother); it will be necessary to make the reader "un cómplice, una camarada de camino. Simultaneizarlo, puesto que la lectura abolirá el tiempo del lector y lo trasladará al del autor. Así el lector podría ser copartícipe y copadeciente de la experiencia por la que pasa el novelista, *en el mismo momento y en la misma forma*" (an accomplice, a fellow traveler. Make his experience simultaneous, since the act of reading will abolish the reader's time and place him in the author's. In this way the reader might become a fellow participant, a fellow sufferer in the experience the author is going through, *at the same time and in the same way*). Any literary device can be used to achieve this, providing that there is a sense of immediate, lived experience, a sense of "matter in the process of gestation." Morelli's "comic novel" will make use of such things as anticlimax and irony, avoid messages, and provide the essentials to enable the reader to explore, to search for something he may not find. The reader becomes the focus: "Me pregunto si alguna vez haré sentir que el verdadero y único personaje que me interesa es el lector, en la medida en que algo de lo que escribo debería contribuir a mutarlo, a desplazarlo, a extrañarlo, a enajenarlo" (97; I wonder if I shall ever manage to convey that really the only character who interests me is the reader, insofar as some part of what I write should help change him, displace him, surprise him, alienate him). Cortázar made the point in similar terms in one of his interviews, well in advance of the time when reader-response theories came into vogue; he adds that writers should "fight against the passiveness of the consumer of novels and short stories, against the inclination to prefer predigested products. The renovation of the novel . . . must aim to create a reader who is as active and committed as is the novelist."[13]

In other chapters Morelli dwells on the need to undermine conventional forms and usage. The normal logic of literary discourse, according to which one thing leads to another, explains another, must give way to a constellation of elements whose relationships with one another are changeable and multiple. One thinks of Mallarmé's uncompleted *Livre,* of the novel with pages that can be shuffled. And, like Mallarmé and so many others before him, Morelli is worried about language; he advocates language that is as unaesthetic as possible: clichés and formulas must be expunged, as must polished literary language used for decorative purposes, in favor of language as a means for communication and exploration. Etienne, a member of the Club de la Serpiente, exlains that "lenguaje quiere decir residencia en una realidad, vivencia en una realidad. Aunque sea cierto que el lenguaje nos traiciona (y Morelli no es el único en gritarlo a todos los vientos) no basta con querer liberarlo de sus tabúes. Hay que re-vivirlo, no re-animarlo" (99; language means living in a reality, inhabiting a reality. Although its true that language betrays us [and Morelli is not the only one who proclaims that to all and sundry], it's not enough to try to free it from its taboos. You've got to re-live it, not revive it). Here there arises a fundamental paradox, which is recognized quite frequently in Cortázar's work: language is the writer's means of communication; the only option to voice one's mistrust of language is by using the very language one mistrusts. This may seem to be make the whole undertaking futile; as Etienne puts it (attributing the idea to Morelli): "No se puede denunciar nada si se lo hace dentro del sistema al que pertenece lo denunciado" (99; You can't denounce anything if what you are denouncing is part of the system you are using to do it).

If language is the expression of a worldview (word view?), then it must be attacked first in order to shake readers out of their mental habits: "Una incitación a salirse de las huellas" (99; An invitation to get off the beaten track). The dominance of reason and science, the tendency to see the world in terms of binary oppositions, in fact, the whole Judaeo-Christian cultural heritage must be fought against in the drive to reach something that is more intuitive, more authentic, other, yonder (to borrow a term used by members of the club). Any form of categorization, such as those that are used in Western thought and language, is an obstacle to (as the text has it) turning oneself inside out like a glove so that one has raw contact with reality, without myth, religion, or systematization to get in the way. Morelli-Cortázar's aims are thus both literary and ethical. "Destroying" literature (*"desescribir,"* literally, "unwriting") and regenerating language are seen as necessary first steps in order for one to be able to approach this state of unmediated oneness with reality, even though (to insist on the caveat) "denunciaba, utilizándolo a su modo, el material formal; al dudar de sus herramientas, descalificaba en el mismo acto los trabajos realizados con ellas" (he was denouncing the materials in his way; because he mistrusted his tools, at the same time he was disqualifying the work done with them) (chapter 141).

What is presented in theoretical terms in the metatext (Morelli's ideas) is, to a large degree, put into practice in the text (the rest of the novel). This two-tier division might itself be thought a capitulation to the kind of dualism from which an escape is so insistently advocated, were it not for the fact that Morelli "spills over" as a character into the Paris section of the text; he has an accident, is helped, and later visited by members of the club. Oliveira even gets the key to his apartment (and perhaps by implication the key to his way of seeing things), and it is Oliveira, Cortázar's alter-alter ego, so to speak, who is most responsible for the fact that theoretical discussions relating to Morelli's ideas take place in the club.

Thus one may say that in the course of the novel its own rationale (though Cortázar himself would probably have flinched at the use of that word) and the very process of reading it are thematized, foregrounded, forced upon the reader's attention. One reads about what one is reading and why one is reading it in that way. It is not surprising that such an overtly metafictional style has led to Cortázar's work being seen as part of the tradition of Cervantes and Sterne or that it has been studied in comparison with the work of modern writers like John Barth.

But if *Rayuela* constantly thematizes its own composition, it also tells a story of sorts, the story of its protagonist, Oliveira. Despite its length, there is not a lot of action in *Rayuela,* and such action as there is is presented in a manner that avoids allowing a clear sense of chronology, partly due to the fact that the reader, if taking the *cronopio* approach, plays hopscotch with the text. As a result, any attempt at summarizing the action risks leaving the impression that it is more clearly sequential than it in fact is. However, the essentials are these. Oliveira has come to Paris dissatisfied with his own life and country and is being supported by money sent from Argentina by a brother, supplemented by his own casual earnings in Paris. Most of his energy, however, goes into wandering the streets of Paris, often in the company of Maga, his girlfriend from Uruguay, whose acquaintance he makes one day by chance, significantly at a bookshop. If not wandering the labyrinth of Parisian streets, Oliveira is involved in labyrinthine discussions with his fellow intellectuals in the Club de la Serpiente. These discussions are heavily charged with cultural references to art, literature, and above all jazz, which seems to be playing as a background to all their delib- erations. (Cortázar appears to be determined to drop the name of every great jazz musician known to mankind in the fifties; his clearest homage to that music is found in chapter 17.) The discussions among members of the club often are self- indulgent and pretentious. Most members are men, and of the two women, Maga is distinguished by not being an intellectual, and she is treated with a certain degree of patronizing derision by Oliveira and the others, yet acknowledged for her ability to take life as it comes, intuitively and unhampered by the analytical and cultural baggage that so determines the behavior of the others. The most intellectual of the group are Etienne and our hero Oliveira, a man who, in the words of the former, is "capable of finding metaphysics in a can of tomatoes." It is true that Oliveira is interested in the big issues. He is driven by a sense of dis- satisfaction to engage in a search that is unsystematic and for something he is not able to define. Were he able to define it, he says, he would not have to search for it. At one point, asked why he is in Paris, his answer (narrated in a mixture of reported speech and privileged access to his thoughts) is this: "Bueno, él era un argentino que llevaba un tiempo en París, tratando de . . . Vamos a ver, ¿qué era lo que trataba de? Resultaba espinoso explicarlo así de buenas a primeras. Lo que él buscaba era . . ." (Well, he was an Argentine who had been in Paris for some time trying to . . . Now let's see, what was it that he was trying to? It was tricky to explain it just like that. What he was looking for was . . .) (chapter 23).

Oliveira lives with Maga, who has a child whom she leaves in the hands of a foster parent for some time but later brings home, to Oliveira's irritation. Maga wants to acquire the culture that Oliveira has, and she has a passion for singing *Lieder* by Hugo Wolf. Oliveira has also another lover called Pola, but she becomes terminally ill, and he abandons her. Rocamadour, Maga's son, who has been ill for some time, is found dead by Oliveira. Members of the Club de la Serpiente arrive one by one, and Oliveira tells them that the baby is lying dead in the room. But no one tells Rocamadour's mother. The emotional tension builds as they engage in one of their discussions while Maga remains painfully unaware of the tragedy; when she does discover it and breaks down, Oliveira slips away rather than helping her. (Immediately after this distressing chapter the reader is sent to the one that reports on the dangers of zip fasteners; by comparison with what has just been read this seems facetious and insensitive, forcing the reader to make a huge emotional adjustment). Later, when Oliveira returns to the apartment, he finds her gone and another member of the club there. At a subsequent meeting of the club, Oliveira, sensing the opprobrium, stamps out his cigarette and with it his membership, telling them all to go to hell. He then descends to a place below a bridge where he meets up with some tramps in whom he and Maga had taken an interest; he gets drunk, is arrested while one of them is performing fellatio on him, and is carried off in a paddy wagon. Thus ends part 1 of the novel.

In part two Horacio Oliveira arrives in Buenos Aires, following a stopover in Montevideo to search fruitlessly for Maga (whose fate has become a matter of speculation—she may have drowned in the Seine). He is met by his old friends Traveler and his wife, Talita, who manage to find him work with them at a circus. Horacio now lives with his old girlfriend, Gekrepten, a homely and unimaginative woman, ("an unmemorable girl" is how Oliveira refers to her in chapter 1) just across the way from Traveler and Talita. Oliveira becomes increasingly obsessed by his relationship with Traveler and Talita, in some way seeing her as a bridge to his friend, whom he later will describe as his *Doppelgänger*. The circus owner then decides to acquire a lunatic asylum, and the three friends continue to work for him there. Some time later, descending once again, this time to the morgue in the basement of the asylum, Oliveira kisses Talita; then, believing that he will be attacked by Traveler, he retreats to his room, where he sets up a bizarre defense system based on twine strung across the room, ball bearings, and bowls of water. Traveler appears and falls victim to a certain amount of slapstick, but he is not as hostile as was feared and even tries to calm Oliveira down and protect him from the other people. This last crucial scene leaves us with Oliveira perched on the windowsill, looking down at a hopscotch pattern drawn on the ground below, on which Talita is standing—or is it Maga (for he has been confusing the two)? The ending is unclear; we may, for example, suppose that he physically jumps and dies or that he does so and survives; he may land in the heavenly zone (i.e. the longed-for "yonder" he has been seeking all along, symbolized by the top of the hopscotch pattern—in the Spanish version of the game one progresses from "earth" to "heaven"); he may figuratively leap into madness or into human (or even political) commitment; or, to take a more pedestrian view, he may simply stay put until they tell him that his behavior has cost him his job. These are possibilities that the text encourages the reader to consider.

Thus, at "The End" Cortázar portrays Oliveira thinking of Maga in association with the idea that he might at last achieve the object of his search, be able to make the transition to that longed-for other state identified by various terms and symbols in the course of the novel: the center, the axis, the kibbutz of desire, the land of Hurqalyã, Eden, paradise, and, of course, yonder. The impossibility of finding an adequate term is faced early in the novel; at the end of chapter 2 Horacio confesses that he almost always ends up referring to the "center" without being at all sure of what he is talking about; he complains that in using that term he is falling into the inevitable trap of using the terminology provided by the Western cultural tradition, that there are many alternative terms he could call upon in an attempt to identify his goal, but that the "*desconcierto*" (discomfiture) that drives the search for it is always the same.

Just as he closes the novel by associating Horacio's search with Maga, Cortázar opens chapter 1 with a question that does the same: "¿Encontraría a la Maga?" (Would I/he find/meet Maga?). It is a question whose grand implications cannot be apparent to the reader except in retrospect and whose grammatical subject is not immediately identifiable at the time when it is posed. That subject, it turns out, is Horacio, and the question refers both to his metaphysical search and to a more banal one: he and Maga prefer to meet by chance, even after they have made their first acquaintance.

An important part of Oliveira's complex and conflictive attitude toward Maga is his sense that she has much of what he lacks: intuitiveness, an absence of awareness of time and space, a closeness to things, emotional honesty, disorder, freedom from his own cultural baggage. The best Horacio can do is artificially promote such qualities, but Maga simply has them. According to Oliveira she swims through metaphysical currents with the ease of a swallow circling a belltower (chapter 21). Maga has been compared by many critics to Breton's Nadja, who similarly relies on chance encounters, is frank about sex, is associated with the underworld, plays with words, and relies on intuition rather than learning.[14]

It is striking that we learn little about the fictional Maga from her own actions and words: instead we learn from the comments of others, especially Horacio. While it is true that no character in *Rayuela* is accorded any real physical description, Maga, more than most, comes over as an elusive idea of a person; and this despite the fact that she carries out explicitly described physical acts (most significantly her lovemaking with Oliveira and her attention to the needs of her baby). Her name reflects this ethereal quality: "Maga" is "Enchantress"; hence her central function as a focus for Horacio's search. Her real name is Lucía, which connotes light: "uncultured" though she may be, she lightens his way, is his guiding light. At one point Oliveira tells her that he loves her because she is elusive, because she is on the other side, "allí donde me invitás a saltar y no puedo dar el salto" (over there where you are inviting me to jump to, and I can't make the jump) (chapter 93).

The idea of the search, so fundamental to *Rayuela,* is also symbolized in the game of hopscotch, as has already been suggested. The religious origins of this ritual game, now simply a children's playground activity, extend beyond the heaven/earth dichotomy and the journey from the latter to the former and encompass the idea of transgression, breaking the pattern, crossing the line, in short, sinning. The layout of the hopscotch is not unlike that of a church. Even the word *rayuela* can be said to contain hints in this direction: the phrase *pasar de la raya* means "to overstep the mark"; *rayar en* means "to border on," "to verge on," and so it might conjure up the image of Horacio perched on the ledge, about to leap into the unknown or fall into the section labeled "heaven," or it may lead one's thoughts to Talita in another crucial scene in which she is perched on a plank of wood.

Other elements in the novel lean, often parodically, on Christian and classical mythology. The scene in Paris that ends part 1 (chapter 36) is particularly laden with such associations. In its first two paragraphs there are references to charity, to crusades, to Maga as a Samaritan, to fate, to Orpheus, to Medusa. Lurking in the literary background are works by Dante and Homer, not to mention the Bible. Horacio the middle-class intellectual descends into a foul-smelling underworld of society's drop-outs, there to transgress moral standards and be carried off (crucified?) in the company of two common criminals (sexual perverts). His life in Paris is put to an end and he resurfaces in a world of fair winds, Buenos Aires. Is he resurrected, redeemed? It is striking that during this episode Oliveira ponders on the need to "go back in order to pick up properly, let oneself fall in order perhaps to be able to get up later." There are religious overtones in the names of the people he deals with: the down-and-outs are called Emmanuèle and Céléstin. (Traveler's first name, too, is Manuel.) It is also worth noting that during the scene under the bridge with the *clocharde* Horacio, as if to combine religious and classical strands, remembers the story of Heraclitus, up to his neck in dung in an attempt to cure himself. It is a thought that only a true intellectual could have in such circumstances. There is, in addition, a darkness (probably connoting the darker side of humanity and an absence of the light of reason/enlightenment), even a funereal atmosphere that one finds echoed in other key scenes, particularly the one in which Oliveira kisses Talita—another moment of transgression. Finally, note that all this takes place under a bridge, an image that is ubiquitous in Cortázar's fiction and often linked to the idea of passage to another self or another way of being. As Oliveira is being carried off in the police van, there is a careful and lucid description of the game of hopscotch (too lucid, perhaps, for it to be taken as part of the rambling thoughts of the drunken protagonist) and a clear association of its "heaven" with the Christian one. Oliveira's thoughts, freely associating, introduce the idea of the cross one must bear and of the transgressive child. Perhaps here Cortázar has in mind the overtly Christian agenda that lay behind the quest in one of the books that had influenced him, Marechal's *Adán Buenosayres*. Not that Cortázar's own agenda is Christian; his "heaven," like the heaven (*cielo*) of the hopscotch pattern, is undoudtedly one that is drawn on the earth. Evidently, in this scene Cortázar is revealing the influence of having read Mircea Eliade and Georges Bataille, both of whom are mentioned more than once in *Rayuela*.

The working title of *Rayuela* was different. At the time when he was composing scenes and collecting material Cortázar had been reading about oriental religions, particularly Buddhism, and was obsessed with the idea of the mandala. This form of labyrinth, through which one progresses toward a center, explains the frequent use of that term as a way of referring to Horacio's metaphysical goal. Paris, we are told in chapter 93, is a mandala that has to be worked through without dialectics, a labyrinth in which one will get lost if one relies on pragmatism. To write, Morelli says elsewhere, is to create one's mandala and work through it at the same time. It is well known that *Mandala* was Cortázar's working title, and a very appropriate one it was in the sense that, like that of the reader through *Rayuela,* one's progress through the mandala is personal, not a matter of ritual. But Cortázar decided that *Mandala* was too serious a title for a work that was going to be very playful. There are several points at which Morelli refers to the techniques of Zen and Vedanta. To Cortázar, the appeal of Buddhism was that it offered a totally different way of looking at the world: "What we pursue discursively, philosophically, the Oriental resolves by leaping into it"; "I detest solemn searches. . . . What I like about the masters of Zen is their complete lack of solemnity. The deepest insights sometimes emerge from a gag or a slap in the face. In *Rayuela* there's a great influence of that attitude, I might even say that technique."[15]

A good deal of the humor in *Rayuela* is situational and absurd. Significantly, we find it in key scenes of the novel. In one of the most famous, Oliveira escapes the rain in Paris by going to a piano recital given by a Madame Berthe Trépat; the music, the master of ceremonies, and the pianist herself are farcical and caricaturesque; the meager audience evaporates as the concert becomes ever more awful and finally Oliveira is left alone to face the embarrassment of the demoralized performer. The ridiculousness is counterbalanced by a strong sense of pathos, and Oliveira, despite himself, emits comforting trite formulae in sympathy with the wounded Madame Trépat, like a supportive gesture in response to the hand extended to him, but then the situation once again veers off into farce because Trépat misinterprets his intentions and raises the alarm. Back in the street, his attempt at skillful karma having failed, Oliveira hides his tears in the rain (chapter 23). This is a chapter that has been widely praised by critics, many of whom have pointed out that if read alone it has the self-sufficiency of a short story.

It is interesting, however, to note that self-sufficient episodes such as this and the one to be discussed in a moment left Cortázar dissatisfied in that he felt that he had been a traitor to his aim of undermining the "hypnotic story." In such story-like episodes he saw himself as having given in to the drama and intensity of the moment, whereas his goal had been "to move the action along and halt it exactly at the moment when the reader is captivated and to boot him out of it, so that he would look at the book once again, from outside, and see it from another standpoint."[16]

Another key scene, also laced with the absurd, is the one Cortázar wrote first of all, the scene in Buenos Aires involving the plank, to which I referred briefly above. As the scene opens, for reasons that are never explained Oliveira has been busy straightening out some nails. He calls from his apartment window across to Traveler, who lives opposite, and together they plan to transfer the nails and some mate without going down to ground level and back up again. They extend planks from their windows to form a bridge and persuade Talita to inch her way across under the blazing sun. The operation is risky, absurd, and highly significant. Like the Trépat episode, the bridge episode is about communication, about transition to otherness. If Traveler is Oliveira's double, then Talita can be understood as something more than the woman in the middle (though there are indeed several love triangles in *Rayuela*). Elsewhere in the novel we are offered a passing reference to Talita's real name, Atalia, and it can be used to help explain her role: onomastic invention seems to be at play again, for Thalia was the muse of comedy, and the Spanish verb forms *ata* and *lía* both mean "links," "ties." (While we are on the subject of meaningful names, let us note that, ironically, Traveler is the one who goes nowhere, neither to Paris nor across any symbolic bridge, presumably because he is already "there," is reconciled with life.) The bridge episode (no pun intended) is one of the high spots of the novel, in its own way as accomplished and impressive as the episode dealing with Berthe Trépat, the one about the death of Rocamadour, and not least the final, farcical scene in which Oliveira barricades himself in his room behind his extraordinary defense system.

A word must be said about the contrasting environments against which the Paris and Buenos Aires sections are set. The Paris chapters are full of street names and other pointers that fix the action in space and seem to insist on the role of that city as a physical representation of the maze, or mandala, through which Oliveira is trying to find a way. Paris is referred to at one point as "a huge metaphor"; one should bear in mind the Greek sense of the word "metaphor," which is "means of transition or transfer." Buenos Aires, by contrast, comes across as a vague, almost abstract backdrop, against which various tableaux or set pieces are enacted. The circus and the mental asylum add a carnivalesque impression to the Buenos Aires setting. These contrasts between the two settings may be understood not only as manifestations of different narrative modes but also as representations of different approaches to knowledge. The violent contrast in climate—the action takes place in the depths of winter in Paris and in the height of summer in Buenos Aires—seems to confirm the opposition, one being the counterpart of the other, rather as Traveler can be seen as the counterpart of Oliveira. However, since winter and summer are contemporaneous seasons in Paris and Buenos Aires, whatever is associated with the two may be read as complementary. In other words, once again we have evidence of the affirmation and negation of binary opposition.

Oliveira's search is serious, pretentious, obsessive, and inevitable. "Buscar era mi signo" (Searching was my destiny), he says in chapter 1, and, as we saw in the quotation with which I opened this discussion of *Rayuela*, Morelli maintains that in general man only is in that he searches to be. Oliveira would probably come over as a despicable individual, as an intolerable and outrageous cynic, were it not for his self-deprecating humor that builds a bridge of sympathy with the reader. Another disarming characteristic is the way he laces his search with ironic self-awareness. His deflating use of humor often involves language, such as playing with anagrams and puns, switching syllables, making spoonerisms, or adding an initial letter h to any word that begins with a vowel.

He and Maga sometimes communicate in their invented language, *glíglico* (see chapter 68); though at first sight this language is nonsense, a closer look shows that it is in fact very comprehensible. *Glíglico* is perfectly grammatical Spanish in its morphology and syntax: it uses idiomatic combinations of sounds (and graphic symbols), builds recognizable verbs, nouns, and so forth, and puts these into possible phrase and sentence structures. Where it does break the rules is at word level; many of its words are portmanteau words, built by combining syllables or sound groups from other words. A likely source of inspiration is Lewis Carroll's poem "Jabberwocky." There are possible antecedents among poets of the Latin American avantgarde (Vicente Huidobro, Oliverio Girondo), but we must not forget Cortázar's familiarity with English writers and his admission that it was from them that he had learned the power of irony. It is noticeable that in chapter 18 of *Rayuela* Cortázar quotes, or rather misquotes, a line from Carroll's poem, and he also mentions the poem in interviews.[17] The *glíglico* of *Rayuela* is usually associated with the erotic; the intention is that the invented language should convey what conventional language does not, although it could be argued that *glíglico* conveys exactly the kind of coy, euphemistic quality Cortázar was at pains to avoid. Curiously, Alice, having just heard the recital of "Jabberwocky," makes a comment that seems to suggest precisely those qualities: "Somehow it seems to fill my head with ideas—only I don't know exactly what they are!"[18]

Cortázar said on several occasions that language was the basis for *Rayuela*. Linguistic games are endemic in this novel; they are there as an expression of mistrust of language because it molds our worldview, is based on oppositions, and is inadequate if one wants to achieve authentic communication. Oliveira keeps insisting that words are "*perras negras*" (black bitches). Another way in which Cortázar fosters a consciousness of language (and one that assumes a certain degree of reader sophistication) is by making liberal use of other tongues, reflecting his own familiarity with French, German, and English; he often uses fragments or quotations in languages other than Spanish as a means of varying the tone and guarding against complacency. In this way, pedantry can be avoided; for example, at one point Oliveira says, "*Quod erat demonstrandum, pibe*," appending to the Latin phrase a colloquial Argentine term that is on a par with the American "buddy" or "man."

Language is also the key to breaking away from fossilized forms of literary expression, as is prescribed by Morelli. This explains why, in one of the dispensable chapters (chapter 75), Cortázar parodies "good" writing. The chapter in question begins in an eloquent and polished style, with the text printed in italics; this is abandoned in mid phrase in favor of normal typeface and a complete contrast in tone and content, while Oliveira draws pictures and writes rude words in toothpaste on a mirror in front of him. Gekrepten, submissive and conventional as always, comes in with a sponge to clean up the nasty mess.

A related attack on style is contained in another, much analyzed chapter (chapter 34). One's first impression on reading this is that it has been misprinted, but soon one realizes that it consists of two texts printed on alternate lines, so that by reading every other line it is possible to find coherence. The text that occupies the odd lines is that of a book Maga has been reading, while the text of the even lines consists, at least at the beginning, of Oliveira's criticisms of her and "the things she reads." She has been reading a book by Spain's leading novelist of the nineteenth century, Pérez Galdós, and it is called, significantly, *Lo prohibido* (The forbidden). Earlier, in chapter 31, while Oliveira is rummaging through things on the bedside table, he has come across the Galdós book and has already let us know what he thinks of her reading choices; at the same time he has come across a letter she has written to her dead child, though he has yet to read that when he makes his disparaging comments. From chapter 31 the reader moves straight on to 32, which is the text of Maga's lyrical and moving letter. It is not until seven chapters later that we come to chapter 34, which relocates us back in the scene described in chapter 31 and now gives us details of Oliveira's thoughts as he was leafing through the novel. He expresses scorn for Galdós and several other things besides, and he supposes that after readers have swallowed a few pages of such rubbish it becomes a habit. But chapter 34 subtly progresses toward something more equivocal. The discreteness of the two texts is gradually lost, because the enjambements between odd and even lines begin to acquire a coherence of their own, elements of the Galdós text enter the Oliveira one, first italicized, then without being signaled in any way, until the transitions take place in mid line and Oliveira begins to see some value in the text he so readily dismissed at the start. Have the pages he has read provoked in him exactly the habit he has been despising? Or has his oppositional stance moved in the direction of some kind of constructive reconciliation?

Some defenders of Galdós (who was undoubtedly an excellent novelist) have been quick to take offense at what they see as an unmitigated onslaught on the Spaniard, but it is unlikely that Cortázar is as hostile to Galdós as the initial attitude of Oliveira suggests. One possible observation is that after Oliveira and Maga have separated, the two texts, standing for the two characters Oliveira and Maga, exist in tandem and seem to achieve a degree of coincidence, of shared meaning, until the Maga (Galdós) text ends and Horacio is left alone, book in hand, thinking how he and she are like two points moving about Paris without meeting one another and how their movements follow a meaningless pattern. We might add that that is something reflected in the layout of chapter 34. Maga, quite obviously, is a passive reader. So, too, is another member of the Club de la Serpiente, Perico Romero, a minor character who is caricatured precisely through his language . . . and is also a Spaniard.

Moreover, chapter 34 can be said to be another small-scale imitation of the reading experience of the whole of *Rayuela,* in the sense that one is faced with at least two ways of reading it: all the even lines followed by all the odd ones (or vice versa) or the printed sequence of lines. The technique of alternating and merging texts is probably an attempt to render as simultaneous two experiences (Oliveira's reading though the Galdós text and his thoughts during the process of reading it) that language, by nature, presses one to narrate in sequence. One should also note the amusing effects resulting from the transitions from one text to another.

That *Rayuela* is rarely what one expects is germane. A protean style, an "irrational" structure, a search for meaning (both literary and existential) in which the reader is obliged to engage, all these are things that parallel the protean, irrational search in which Oliveira is engaged. *Rayuela* is not so much read as experienced. Although it does not conform to any formal definition of poetry, it is, as García Canclini puts it, a poetic way of experiencing what it is to be human.[19] It downplays the temporal, its ending is open (formally represented by the reading loop of the *Tablero*'s closing sequence, thematically by Oliveira perched on the ledge and about to jump), it invites the reader to choose a personal approach to reading, and it implies an almost infinite number of possible realizations. It is Oliveira who gives coherence to the text in its first-approach realization; but what I have called the "cronopio approach" finds its coherence in a tacit pact between author and reader. This highly artificial work, which entraps the reader in a search for meaning that is both literary and existential, has led one critic to coin the phrase "ontological fabulation" to describe *Rayuela.*[20] Yet this is a liberatingly humorous book too. If, as some have said, it is the Latin American *Ulysses,* it is Joyce with a liberal dose of Jarry.

"Escribir es dibujar mi mandala y a la vez recorrerlo, inventar la purificación purificándose; tarea de pobre shaman blanco con calzoncillos de nylon," says Cortázar-Morelli in chapter 82 (To write is to trace my mandala and work through it at the same time, to invent purification in the process of purifying oneself; the labor of a poor white shaman who wears nylon underpants). As far as Cortázar was concerned, writing *Rayuela* constituted an act of "superexorcism";[21] on several occasions after its appearance he stated that he had thought that he was addressing the sort of preoccupations with which middle-aged people like himself might identify, but had been surprised at how the book struck a chord with so many younger people. As to the critics, there were some who found *Rayuela* overintellectualized, hermetic, elitist, or otherwise too inaccessible and far removed from the social and economic realities that bore down on the majority of Latin Americans. But the majority hailed it as a major work of literature, and it was promptly canonized. Soon translated into many languages, *Rayuela* brought Cortázar international fame and cast a good deal of reflected light on his short stories, whose sales rose accordingly.

62: Modelo para armar

We have already seen how the title of *Rayuela* is so meaningful in its allusions to several of that novel's salient features: on the thematic front its playful yet serious quest for an ideal state, and on the formal one the jumping style of the reading experience. The title of the third novel published by Cortázar, *62: Modelo para armar* (*62: A Model Kit*), is no less indicative of this work's experimental intent and the fact that it is inspired by thoughts that were articulated in chapter 62 of *Rayuela*. Once again, this is a book that begins with what amounts to a prescriptive authorial note. This one draws the reader's attention to the title's origin, suggesting that one should first consider what chapter 62 of *Rayuela* has to say.

It is a chapter that expounds some of the ideas of Morelli: in it he turns his nose up at the musty idea of psychology as a structuring principle in fiction and ponders the possibility that characters might interact in accordance with other principles. There is also a long footnote that refers to the work of a Swedish scientist who argued that human behavior was the product of chemical processes. Instead of a literature populated by Oedipuses and Rastignacs, Morelli suggests that there could perhaps be an "impersonal" drama, in which the characters' passions only seem to come into play a posteriori. It would be as if the characters were responding to some subliminal force (if not chemistry, then fate: the image of the skein, so ubiquitous in Cortázar's work, suggests that there is some undefined weaver of destinies at work). Thus the characters of this new type of novel would be caught in the flow, and no amount of recourse to concepts such as desire, will, or conviction, no amount of reasoning would account for their behavior: a mysterious, unknowable drive stemming from beyond or above the level of humans would be carrying them along. Were there to be a novel based on these ideas, it would make unsettling and worrisome reading, because one would not be able to understand the actions of its characters in causal terms, nor would looking for their psychological motivation be of use.

62: Modelo para armar is, of course, Cortázar's attempt to write such a novel, and the resulting product is indeed unsettling and worrisome. Whatever its merits, one must admire the author's skill and control in bringing about this complex narrative experiment and not least his preparedness to take on such a challenge. As always, "Il ne faut jamais profiter de l'élan acquis"; rather than succumbing to the temptation of pleasing his readers with a *Rayuela* revisited and taking advantage of that novel's popularity, Cortázar seems here to be courting the ranks of the French *nouveaux romanciers,* something that an early reference to a novel by Michel Butor appears to corroborate.

Reading *62: Modelo para armar*—and interpreting it—is quite problematic, not only because it is a difficult novel, but also because any reading or interpretation is circumscribed by factors that strictly speaking lie outside the confines of the work itself. Any act of reading is, of course, undertaken against a background of past readings and often against one that includes previous works by the same author; there is no such thing as an "innocent" reader. But in the case of *62: Modelo para armar,* the "coloring" of our reading is of a rather special and deliberate kind. Readers are more or less instructed to read in the light of chapter 62 in *Rayuela,* which itself extends a frame of reference that encompasses all of Morelli's ideas, if not the whole of that earlier novel. Like *Rayuela, 62: Modelo para armar* embodies a degree of prescriptivity that risks countermanding, or at least conflicting with, the stated aims. Though in no way instructed to do so, one is further induced, almost ineluctably, to take into account other texts in which Cortázar talks about *62: Modelo para armar.* For readers at all familiar with Cortázar it is a work that can hardly be read as it stands, on its own terms, without "addenda." By "addenda" I mean certain interview material and two other texts that Cortázar published at about the same time in a miscellany titled *Último round* (1969).

Once *62: Modelo para armar* was finished, Cortázar felt that he had only partially realized his goal and that he had made compromises along the way. He believed, however, that the technical problems that he had had in writing this novel were not reflected in the end result and that it was "fairly easy reading."[22] Few readers would agree that reading *62: Modelo para armar* is easy. While on the face of it this novel does not pose great formal or linguistic challenges—one begins at the beginning, ends at the end, for example—confusion in the minds of the readers is undoubtedly concomitant with the author's unusual enterprise. It makes for a good deal of difficulty, especially during the first part of the book, although its opening pages can be read as programmatic. In general, in *62: Modelo para armar* actions occur, but one does not see why; the characters have to be accepted at face value, in incomplete sketches; they relate to each other in ways that are not clear, and the normal limits of time and space are not respected. Relief from confusion comes after some thirty or forty pages, but it is only partial relief. One might be tempted to suppose that these characters and actions are dancing to the tune of a perverse demiurge who is withholding information from his readers in a demonstration of authorial power. Yet, if one is to believe Cortázar, he had no interest in doing that; what he was interested in was starting from a hypothesis and seeing where it led him; in a sense he becomes a player in "the game," not its referee. Cortázar is quite emphatic in response to González Bermejo, denying that he ever had a detailed plan of action, and claiming (not for the first time) that this work took shape as he wrote it, surprising and puzzling him.[23]

Perhaps Cortázar sensed the misunderstanding and frustration that *62: Modelo para armar* was likely to generate among its readers. He had had great difficulty in writing it and had almost given up on the attempt to follow his self-imposed "rules of the game," which at times had seemed to him to be impossible to follow. He had been encouraged to continue by his chance reading of other literary works, by authors such as Felisberto Hernández, Aragon, Merleau-Ponty, and Rimbaud, which had seemed to Cortázar to suggest patterns and correspondences in spite of the fact that he had had no plan in choosing to read those works. It is his unplanned reading of works by the authors that I have just mentioned, their influence on Cortázar, and the process of writing *62: Modelo para armar* that is the subject of "La muñeca rota" (The broken doll). That text, in *Último round,* is accompanied by parodic filmstrip images of a doll in various stages of undress. In the novel, one driving force is a Monsieur Ochs—possibly a literary relative of Baron Ochs in Strauss's opera *Der Rosenkavalier*—an old man with a subversive sense of humor who manufactures dolls in whose bellies he secretes a variety of things, sometimes money, sometimes obscene objects, with predictably scandalous results.

The second piece that is included in *Último round* contributes to a better understanding of the underlying principles of composition. In "Cristal con una rosa dentro" (Glass with a rose inside) Cortázar describes how in moments of "distraction" he senses that a series of apparently unrelated perceptions, such as hearing a door slam shut, seeing someone smile, remembering an alley in a southern French town, and noticing a rose in a glass suddenly enter into a system of relations that has nothing to do with any normal, rational, or causal order. Cortázar describes such revelatory experiences as "blinding" and "unrepeatable"; he also says that they are not the result of any conscious, willed process, but that they come upon him unannounced. The perceptual "slippage" entailed is somewhat like the experience of *déjà vu.* Brief as it is, then, "Cristal con una rosa dentro" is one of the clearest accounts that the author gives of the phenomenon he calls the *figura. 62: Modelo para armar* is the apotheosis of the concept of the *figura.*

It is exactly such a moment of fresh perception (in fact, one experienced in real life by Cortázar) that opens *62: Modelo para armar.* The first words of the novel are a quotation: "Quisiera un castillo sangriento" (I should like a bloody castle). Those familiar with Cortázar's previous novels are immediately reminded of the beginning strategy of *Los premios,* where the opening quotation was a literary one that ironically used some words that another writer had asserted could never open a novel. In *62: Modelo para armar,* however, the opening quotation is not ironic so much as polysemic. As at the start of *Los premios,* the initial narrator of *62: Modelo para armar* is sitting in a restaurant. The words of the opening quotation are his mental translation of words uttered in French by another diner. Spoken by a customer in a restaurant, there is no doubt that "Je voudrais un château saignant" is simply a request for a Chateaubriand steak, done "rare." Pondering on the suggestiveness of the phrase, however, the narrator tells us that as he sat in the restaurant he could not have known (any more than the reader can, at this stage in the novel) how "el desplazamiento del sentido de la frase iba a coagular de golpe otras cosas ya pasadas o presentes de esa noche" (10; the displacement of the meaning of that sentence would suddenly coagulate other past or present things of that night). The use of the word "coagulate" is highly significant: it carries the mind back to the image of blood. The narrator goes on to mention an unidentified countess and repeatedly refers to the wine he is drinking, a Sylvaner. These are early hints at one of the principal associative forces—no doubt Persio would have called them constellations—that underpins the novel: the idea of vampirism. Hence the image of a bloody castle, the reference to the countess (by implication, Countess Bathory), a wine that is loosely suggestive of Transylvania, the fact that a character who seems to be associated with her is living on Blutgasse (Blood Lane), and the frequent contemplation of necks during the course of the book.

But the reader can scarcely draw such conclusions until well into the novel. For much of the time it is difficult to see quite what the relationships between the various characters are; they appear and disappear without explanation and without regard to chronology; events take place for no apparent reason; indeed (despite his protestations of ignorance as to what was going to transpire) one has the feeling that Cortázar is willfully refusing to give the reader helpful information. It is as if the author were postulating characters and actions that float freely in different spaces and temporal frameworks, interrelating in an aleatory, dreamlike fashion, coinciding on a level and in ways that one cannot adequately access. If, on one level, the novel is set in real-world scenarios like Paris, London, and Vienna, on another it is set in two contrasting conceptual spaces referred to as *la zona* (the zone) and *la ciudad* (the city). Neither of these last is very clearly defined: the *zona* appears to relate loosely to the real world, but the *ciudad* lies beyond any physical reality, representing another, more obscure, and perhaps more meaningful mode of existence, though it is also a labyrinthine, dark, and disturbing one, which brings echoes of the descents evoked in the previous novels. A nightmarish, yet intriguing, poem on pages 34–39 explores the notion of the *ciudad*. In an interview, Cortázar also explained that for years he had entered such a city in his dreams, that entering it always involved descent, and that the city did not correspond with any city in the real world, though parts of it might suggest cities he knew; he added that he always knew when he had entered *la ciudad* because he would sense its special atmosphere.[24]

A related complication, stemming from Cortázar's idiosyncratic concept of character, is the *paredro*. In *62: Modelo para armar* there are a number of plausibly real (though hardly "rounded") characters, but all but one of them (Feuille Morte) may also be represented by what may be described as a kind of abstraction, designated by the invented term *paredro*. In one of the novel's most self-referential passages we read:

> La atribución de la dignidad de paredro era fluctuante y dependía de la decisión momentánea de cada cual sin que nadie pudiese saber con certeza cuándo era o no el paredro de otros presentes o ausentes en la zona, o si lo había sido y acababa de dejar de serlo. La condición de paredro parecía consistir, sobre todo, en que ciertas cosas que hacíamos y decíamos eran siempre dichas o hechas por mi paredro, no tanto para evadir responsabilidades sino más bien como si en el fondo mi paredro fuese una forma de pudor (The honor of the title of *paredro* was granted on a fluctuating basis, and it depended on a decision of the moment made by each person, with no-one being quite sure when he was or wasn't the *paredro* of others who were or weren't there in the zone, or whether he had been or had just stopped being. Being a *paredro* seemed to depend, above all, on certain things that we did or said being said or done by *my paredo*, not just to avoid responsibility but rather because at bottom *my paredro* was an expression of modesty). (29)

A little later, the *paredro* is said to be a silent witness to the "vitality of *la ciudad* in us." The link between these two slippery concepts has also been traced earlier by Juan when he explains that the *ciudad* could come about ("podía darse") anywhere, at any time, for anyone: "We had all wandered through the city, always without planning to do so. . . . There was no way of explaining the *ciudad*, it just was; it had emerged on some occasion during conversation in the *zona,* and although *my paredro* had been the first to bring news of the *ciudad,* being there or not almost became a matter of routine for all of us, except Feuille Morte" (23–24). But the identity of the *paredro* is even more chameleonlike than has previously been suggested: at times he is a kind of other self for the characters, at times a protective figure, at times a conscience, at times a governing force; at one point the *paredro* is described as a *comodín,* a wild card.

Further complications in *62: Modelo para armar* have to do with the narrative mode. The narrative shifts quite frequently from third to first person (characters narrate and "are narrated" in almost the same breath, sometimes seeming to talk schizophrenically about themselves); in addition, the perspective shifts from character to character, so that the reader must be constantly on the alert. The narrative changes involved are somewhat like those Cortázar used to such good effect in "La señorita Cora" (1966) and would carry further in "Ud. se tendió a tu lado" (1977).

Aware that for his readers this was going to be heavy going and potentially very mechanical, Cortázar provided various forms of light relief. He inserted two absurd characters named Calac and Polanco, fellow Argentines who are like Shakespearean fools, if not inspired by the works of Edward Lear or Lewis Carroll. The episodes involving Calac and Polanco, who sometimes bicker like another "odd couple," are often hilarious; for example, one is an inventor, who succeeds in turning a lawnmower into a boat, in which the two of them and the *paredro* set out on an heroic voyage that leaves them "marooned" on an island that is only a few yards from the mainland and set in water that is waist-deep. Yet these two characters have their serious side. Calac, for example, is a writer who takes notes on what is happening and seems to be the "author" of the book, a Cortázar stand-in; the fact that Calac's name is a palindrome only reinforces the equation, given that word games are dear to Cortázar, who explains: "Although it doesn't say so in the book, Calac is an extremely clear-thinking man . . . the only one who manages to see how the *figuras* are playing out. . . . I'm not sure the reader realizes that Calac is the author of *62: Modelo para armar.*"[25]

The author is also projected in Juan, who has a translator's job like Cortázar's, who narrates a good part of the time, and is sometimes quite self-conscious in that capacity. It is Juan who is in the restaurant listening to the opening words that Cortázar once heard, it is Juan who promises that clarification of the concept of *la ciudad* (a concept with which Cortázar had lived for decades before writing *62: Modelo para armar*) will be forthcoming ("In due course the matter of the *ciudad* will be addressed . . . there is even a poem that may or may not be quoted") (29), it is Juan who self-consciously passes the narrative reins to his lover, appropriately named Tell ("Cuéntame, Tell") (68; Tell me, Tell), and finally it is Juan who is most intrigued by Hélène, the character who most fascinated Cortázar. However, Juan never quite achieves the status of protagonist, as does Oliveira in *Rayuela*. In fact, Juan and Hélène disappear from view at times, and other characters occupy center stage.

Difficult though they are, most critics have agreed that the opening pages, during which Juan sits pondering in the restaurant, are key passages. In those pages Juan refers to most of the elements around which the novel's web of associations takes shape, and, what is more important, he constructs an idea of the ideal reader, who will discover the associative strands that hold its various elements together. Juan, the professional translator, is a "seasoned interpreter" (11), by his own admission he is captive to a "useless desire to understand" (12), and he is engaged in "that old human chestnut, deciphering" (12). Furthermore, he is aware that trying to relate all this to anyone else, in the vain hope that it will all acquire some sense, will involve erecting a smoke screen of analysis and words (12–13). And thus it is that the narrative by and about Juan in these initial pages advances the elements around which meaning is to be constructed and at the same time specifies how that meaning is to be constructed. In other words, the author, while on the one hand talking of his readers' discovering patterns together with him, is in fact almost saying how they should go about it; he postulates an ideal reader who will see the associative patterns that Cortázar sees (assemble the kit, discover the *figuras*), a reader who by implication shares Cortázar's culture. As Kerr puts it: "Juan's episode at the Polidor thus has as much heuristic as hermeneutic value"; it is a text that "tells its readers how difficult it is to read but also ('secretly') plots out a reading strategy."[26]

If the purpose of *62: Modelo para armar* is heuristic, then this is not the place to attempt to map out in detail all the associative patterns in the novel; some indications must suffice. Steven Boldy has demonstrated how certain stories or myths, to which the text quite clearly, though none too systematically, alludes, can be said to underlie some *figuras,* stories such as those of Parsifal, Acteon and Diana, and, as has already been suggested, the Countess Erzebeth Bathory. The most overarching of several loosely related and somewhat hazy plot lines, introduced quite early on, concerns a sculptor who is in search of some strange material from which to fashion a statue that has been commissioned by a French town. He plans the statue as an irreverently parodic image of Vercingetorix, in which the figure is supporting the pedestal, rather than vice versa; this work is ceremoniously unveiled near the end of the novel. Marrast, the sculptor, is also responsible for more (perhaps ironic) absurdity: in London, he entices members of a group called Neurotics Anonymous to converge on the Courtauld Art Museum in a wild goose chase to find out why the man in a certain portrait is holding a particular species of plant.[27] Another structuring element in *62: Modelo para armar* is color symbolism: green, for example, tends to connote the erotic and often the sinister or distasteful. Another is the image of the doll, broken, violated, and deprived of innocence, and in those respects indicative of the interactions of several of the characters, while from another angle it is symbolic of their dehumanized, puppetlike status. (The characters are likened to cards being shuffled by an unknown hand or to pieces in a kaleidoscope. They themselves are dehumanizing: for example, when Austin, a naïve youth, is incorporated into their ranks, he is said to be like a dog or a novel that helps to furnish the emptiness of their lives.)

A network of love interests may also be said to give some cohesiveness to the novel. The many relationships that exist between the men and women portrayed in it are almost all unfulfilling, and some are even abusive. People are generally involved in relationships other than the ones to which they aspire, and unrequited (in one or two cases unrevealed) love is the norm: A loves B who loves C who loves D, though there are qualified signs of optimism in the union of the Arcadian couple, Austin and Celia. Punning on the novel's title, one critical study of *62: Modelo para armar* is titled "Modelos para a(r)mar" (A model [love] kit).[28]

As I have already suggested, the real value of *62: Modelo para armar* is not to be found in such matters, neither in plot nor in human relationships, nor in the various searches in which the characters of the novel are engaged, but in the search being carried out by the reader of the novel, in the process of assembling the pieces, in the orchestration. Morelli can be called upon once again in support of this assertion; in chapter 109 of *Rayuela,* we read:

> Los puentes entre una y otra instancia de esas vidas tan vagas y poco caracterizadas, debería presumirlos o inventarlos el lector. . . . El libro debía ser como esos dibujos que proponen los psicólogos de la Gestalt, y así ciertas líneas inducirían al observador a trazar imaginativamente las que cerraban la figura. Pero a veces las líneas ausentes eran las más importantes, las únicas que realmente contaban. (The bridges between one moment and another in those vague and poorly characterized lives had to be postulated or invented by the reader. . . . The book had to be like those patterns suggested by Gestalt psychologists, so that certain lines would induce the observer to trace others in his imagination and thus complete the *figura.* But sometimes the missing lines were the most important, the only ones that really counted.)

Any meaning and satisfaction that may be found in reading this novel stem from a process of discovery of whatever structures the behavior of its characters; readers and critics must try to achieve an awareness, like Calac's, of the *figuras* that underpin *62: Modelo para armar.* Surely it is for that reason that Cortázar puts the closing words of the book in the mouth of Feuille Morte (perhaps not so much "Dead Leaf" as "Lifeless Page"?), the one character who has no depth, no *paredro,* no access to the *ciudad,* no love relationship, who has played no part in the action other than that of being around and protected by the others. At the end of the novel she murmurs, "Bisbis," as she always does, like a simpleton uncomprehendingly asking for a repeat performance.

With regard to the process of decipherment, a comment made by Cortázar in conversation with Prego seems relevant. He mentions the fact that one critic has argued that the Polidor Restaurant, in which the action begins, must be so named in order to push the reader in the direction of Byron and Shelley, who had an Italian friend called Polidori (another link with vampirism). On the contrary, says Cortázar, he had no such thing in mind; furthermore, he states that a Polidor Restaurant really does exist, and he gives its address.[29] But most interesting is his following comment that "imaginative critics discover a number of constellations, of symmetries . . . many of which must be accurate."[30]

62: Modelo para armar is above all a writerly undertaking, the most esoteric of Cortázar's novels, the least accessible, the most seamless, a novel that is all but bereft of the human, ethical, and metaphysical dimensions that so enrich *Rayuela.* For that reason, and despite its evident development from *Rayuela,* it may be regarded as a rarefied form of regression to the aestheticism of the days prior to "El perseguidor." It stands in rather stark contrast to Cortázar's next novel, *Libro de Manuel,* which is discussed in chapter 7. Compared with the critical onslaught on *Rayuela, 62: Modelo para armar* has received rather little attention, which is probably evidence of its inherent difficulty. I would argue, however, that the true antecedent of *62: Modelo para armar* is not *Rayuela* but *Los premios* and that the comparable opening strategies of *62: Modelo para armar* and *Los premios* turn out to be emblematic of that relationship. Whereas in the earlier novel Persio's monologues sat awkwardly in contrast with a narrative that otherwise was easy to read, linear, transparent, and reassuringly narrated by an omniscient third person, in *62: Modelo para armar* the Persio character has disappeared, but his philosophy, now in a more refined form, is dictating the very fabric of the work, and his search has been displaced to the reader. Among Cortázar's novels, *62: Modelo para armar* is the one that shares the closest affinities with the sometimes sterile, but invariably clever, experiments of the authors of the *nouveau roman.* It is an extraordinary and ambitious undertaking, the most exclusive of his novels in the sense that it demands a determined and very sophisticated reader, and it is a work that cries out (though "bisbis" in Spanish is more like a whisper) for an encore, a second reading.

CHAPTER 6

The Brawl Outside

Literature and Politics

The Cuban Revolution and Cortázar's subsequent visit to the island, which on several occasions he referred to as a "cathartic experience," amounted to a turning point in his life. Thereafter, as we saw in chapter 2, because of his political activities Cortázar became an increasingly prominent and problematic figure; on the one hand, he came to be viewed as a *persona non grata* by some people on the Right, and on the other hand, as a creative writer he came under pressure from the Left to convey political messages that were both explicit and accessible to unsophisticated readers. Increasingly, Cortázar gave speeches and wrote letters and essays that openly addressed political matters. But he remained anxious to preserve the artistic integrity of his creative work.

There is a page in *Último round* (whose first edition dates from 1969) on which the image of a U.S. dollar appears beside a very brief report by a United Nations agency stating that in 1959 the United States had gleaned 775 million dollars profit from private investments in Latin America and had reinvested only a small fraction of that sum. This report is followed by an equally brief prose-poem that asserts that a writer should simply be led by the dictates of his vocation and leave economics to the experts (*Último round,* "upper floor," 75). All the same, after "Reunión," his "Cuban" story of the mid-sixties for which he had drawn on the writings of Che Guevara, Cortázar made several more attempts at bringing sociopolitical issues into his creative literature, always hoping to find ways of resolving the tension between his political commitment and his aesthetic one. Not surprisingly, the way critics have assessed this creative "political" literature has often reflected their own political or aesthetic leanings; most would agree, however, that the "new" Cortázar engaged in some interesting experiments and that he respected his much-reiterated benchmark that a writer should never rest on his laurels.

Although the year of triumph for the Cuban Revolution appeals as a historically precise moment of change, in order properly to understand Cortázar's personal evolution it is more helpful to think in terms of two phases in his life, which I shall call the Argentine and the French, corresponding to the periods before and after his displacement to France. From the Argentine phase we have works such as the story "Las puertas del cielo" and the novel *El examen* (published posthumously and discussed at some length in chapter 8), works that evoke the mindset of a middle-class intellectual who, like many who lived through the rise of Perón, felt some distaste for the invasion of the capital by proletarian hordes and found themselves marginalized by the processes of change. The Cortázar of the Argentine phase, while not politically unaware, was certainly not politically committed or active. As Aurora Bernárdez, his first wife, put it after his death, during the forties Cortázar had been "a long way from any form of militancy."[1]

We also have the benefit of Cortázar's own reflections about that early period. These were recorded in interviews during the seventies and eighties, by which time he certainly was politically active. Looking back, he told González Bermejo that in Argentina he had lived in a solitary world composed largely of teaching and reading.[2] His political consciousness, such as it was, had not interfered with his other activities: he had, for example, been sympathetic to the Republican cause in the Spanish civil war of the thirties, he had joined the ranks of those who were offended by the rise of fascism in Europe, and he was openly opposed to Perón, but he characterized his behavior at that time as "oposición de café," armchair opposition, no more than indignant talk in cafés. It was true that he had resigned his post at the Universidad de Cuyo, but this had been a self-protective act of withdrawal as much as one of protest. An eloquent measure of the attitude that Cortázar had shared with his fellow intellectuals as they faced the rise of Perón is this: he says that they had found the loudspeakers that were proclaiming the greatness of the new leader from the street corners in those days offensive, not because they were bothered by the politics of it all, but because the noise interfered with listening to the latest quartet by Alban Berg. In the later interviews with Prego Cortázar sums up that he was "decidedly indifferent to political circumstances."[3] Surely the disparaging tone of Cortázar's recollections reflects the fact that by the time he engaged in them he had long since left the armchair and had fully entered the fray.

In discussing "Casa tomada," the first story for which he was noticed, I noted that an interpretation of it as political allegory was possible. Similarly, other stories of the early period have been pounced upon by critics eager to read them as veiled allusions to the dominant political and social order in the Argentina of Perón; examples are "La banda" and "Las Ménades." Cortázar himself denied that he had ever had any conscious political intention in writing these early stories but accepted the legitimacy of these critics' readings. There had perhaps been an unconscious agenda at work. Except at this level of possible allegory, political awareness in Cortázar's works is scarcely noticeable until the appearance in 1966 of the stories of *Todos los fuegos el fuego,* and even then it is confined to one of the eight stories in that collection, "Reunión."

"Reunión" is based on certain passages from *Pasajes de la guerra revolucionaria* (translated as *Reminiscences of the Cuban Revolutionary War*), an account of the revolutionary campaign in Cuba, which had been published by Ernesto "Che" Guevara. As his nickname implies, Guevara was also an Argentine. A man from a comfortable background who had qualified as a physician, Guevara turned into a radical when the Central Intelligence Agency backed the overthrow of a democratically elected government in Guatemala during the mid-fifties. He later met Fidel Castro, helped plan the Cuban Revolution, and fought alongside the rebels against the Batista dictatorship. Che Guevara was one of the driving intellectual powers behind the revolution, and during the sixties he achieved the status of an icon, in that his image, bearded and sporting a beret, became recognizable to people the world over.

Cortázar's plundering of Guevara's book is very evident: it is easy to identify passages from *Pasajes de la guerra revolucionaria* that have been carefully rewritten and adapted by Cortázar. Superficially, it appears that Cortázar is offering an alternative account of how a boatload of revolutionaries arrive on the Cuban coast from Mexico, are attacked by the enemy, and become splintered into groups that then struggle to reunite in the Sierra Maestra. When, much decimated, they finally achieve this in Cortázar's story, the dialectal differences that are apparent in the narrator's meeting with Luis prove that the former is Che and the latter Fidel. Not that this identification was at all difficult to deduce quite early in the story. When Luis, the true leader, is first mentioned, we are told quite openly that that name is not his real one; and as for the narrator, he is a doctor and an asthmatic, as was Che Guevara. There are many references to the campaign as a romantic quest for a final goal, but there is also a sense that if that goal is achieved, the real struggle will then begin. The articulation of this idea at one point (539) is immediately followed by the narrator's (Che's) account of a vision in which he has seen Luis beside a tree, trying to pass a mask of his own face to the disciples there with him, who one by one refuse to take it. There are Christian overtones here, and many more elsewhere in "Reunión." For example, other followers of Luis (Fidel) are called (by Cortázar) Pablo (Paul) and Lucas (Luke). The name Fidel itself evokes the idea of faith. And when Guevara's group of men is making its final *ascent* to meet him on the hill, Paul comments that it is going to be like going to church.[4] "We even have a harmonium," one quips, referring to the wheezing *passacaglia* being sounded by the asthmatic Guevara (546). This last is one of many musical allusions in "Reunión," all of them associated with the narrator/Guevara. Even though music generally plays so important a part in the works of Cortázar, here it is as if he were taking a leaf out of the book of Alejo Carpentier, the well-known Cuban writer, who is known for basing his books on historically verifiable events and for using music in them as a constant frame of reference, if not as a structuring device. In "Reunión" Cortázar makes Guevara recall Mozart's *Hunt* quartet and by means of this device is able to describe the revolutionary campaign in terms of allegros and adagios: the quartet progresses from the dramatic allegro of the hunt to a calm adagio. Further, it is compared to the tree under which Guevara sits as he remembers it: the main subject is the trunk, the theme struck up by an errant violin, a branch. Elsewhere Fidel is juxtaposed with a tree. Moreover, at the very beginning of "Reunión" Cortázar quotes from the real Guevara's book, and in that quotation there is a reference to a protagonist leaning against a tree trunk and preparing to put a dignified end to his life. All of these things—the quasi-religious nature of the journey, the godlike status of Luis/Fidel, the quest for a utopian order—run parallel with, are qualified by, are perhaps reconciled with the aesthetic ideal implied by Mozart's *Hunt* quartet, by the striving toward satisfactory artistic form, toward a satisfactory resolution.

As "Reunión" ends, Luis is pictured talking to the narrator about the state of the revolutionary campaign. Luis is said to be "alien to [Guevara's] fantasizing," as if that comment were a hint that Fidel does not understand the implications of the new order that "Guevara" has in mind (I put Guevara's name in quotation marks, since by this stage it is clear that Cortázar has usurped Guevara's role). At the conclusion of the story "Guevara" is looking at an unidentified star (in the east?), but he is sure that it is neither Mars nor Mercury (neither conflict nor commerce nor, perhaps, the messenger). To sum up, "Reunión," although superficially realist in manner, works primarily through allegory. On the one hand it seems to constitute a declaration of faith in the Cuban Revolution on the part of Cortázar, his commitment to leaving behind, as did Guevara, the middle-class complacencies that are so eloquently enumerated (544); on the other hand "Reunión" is Cortázar's appropriation and adaptation not only of Guevara's original text, but also of his ideal of the "new man."[5]

Chronologically, the next piece of creative political literature, and by far the most consequential ever to come from Cortázar's pen, was *Libro de Manuel* (*A Manual for Manuel*), the fourth novel published during his lifetime. It is because of its political significance, both in terms of its "message" and in terms of the furor that it provoked, that *Libro de Manuel* is being dealt with in the present chapter, rather than together with the other novels published during the author's lifetime. Though by no means abandoning the introspectiveness of earlier works, *Libro de Manuel* is a response to Cortázar's personal wish, and especially to the pressures placed upon him, to pull back from the hermeticism that had characterized *62: Modelo para armar.*[6]

As usual, in *Libro de Manuel* Cortázar succumbs to the temptation of giving his readers an orientation at the start, but the orientation that he provides focuses far less on the nuts and bolts of his work and the business of reading it than it does on the intellectual and political background against which *Libro de Manuel* was composed. In its preface Cortázar warns that champions of social realism in literature are likely to find his book too fantastic and that those who favor literature for its own sake are likely to be disturbed by his deliberate "conspiracy" with contemporary historical issues. For years, he says, he has on the one hand written essays and commentaries about social and political problems in Latin America and, on the other, written novels and stories in which such problems play no part, or at most a marginal one. Now, he declares, the two are about to converge: "Hoy y aquí las aguas se han juntado, pero su conciliación no ha tenido nada de fácil, como acaso lo muestre el confuso y atormentado itinerario de algún personaje" (10; Here and now the waters come together, but reconciling them with each other has not been at all easy, as may perhaps be deduced from the confused and tormented journey of one of the characters). The character in question has had a dream that was once Cortázar's dream, and that dream has become part of the novel. Though Cortázar does not say so in *Libro de Manuel,* the character he is referring to is Andrés Fava. He does say so in a letter written in 1974 to Ana María Hernández; expressing his regret that the Andrés of his "first" novel, *El examen,* had not come to light because that novel had not been published, he writes that "Andrés (*andros,* "man") represents me in a very deep sense in both cases, and that is why on the one occasion when his surname is given I automatically opted for giving the full name from the previous novel."[7]

Once again, the plot of *Libro de Manuel* is sketchy. It deals with a group of revolutionaries, mostly South Americans, who are based in Paris; they plan to abduct a VIP and as ransom demand the freeing of some political detainees. This plan and its enactment and consequences only occupy the second half of the novel. Prior to that, the group members carry out a number of iconoclastic *microagitaciones* (minidisturbances). These are amusing and they disrupt everyday life, but they have little to do with politics: for example, one member of the group insists on eating while standing up in an elegant restaurant, another delays the bus service by giving a long speech of profuse thanks to the driver before leaving the bus, and in another instance an elaborate ruse is hatched in order to bring a "turquoise penguin" through customs into France from South America, thanks to French members of the group posing as an official welcoming delegation from the Vincennes zoo. Collectively, the subversive activities of the group are dubbed "La Joda." One of the virtues of the published English translation of *Libro de Manuel* is its rendering of this word as "The Screwery," for it fairly reflects the connotations of the Spanish verb *joder,* on which Cortázar has based this invented name. These connotations can range from innocuous to offensive, and in some dialects can be sexual; in Argentina the verb *joder* means to annoy, or to play the fool.

No less apt, in fact probably an improvement on the original, is the English translation's rendition of the book's title as *A Manual for Manuel,* because, as a corollary to the activities of the Screwery, a book (manual) is being compiled for the infant son of two of its members, Patricio and Susana. This book is a catalog of press cuttings that for the most part detail political and economic abuse and repression. Manuel (and here, surely, his name is significant: he is Emmanuel, the Messiah) is the symbol of a new generation (Cortázar's rather personal adaptation of Guevara's "new man"), and he will carry his manual with him into the future. But we are told that Manuel's book also contains pleasant extracts: "Susana gathers together cuttings that she sticks in pedagogically, that is, alternating between the useful and the agreeable, so that, when the time comes, Manuel can read the album and switch between lessons and playtime, though who knows which is the lesson and which is the play and what Manuel's world will be like" (241). Here the talk of a marriage between the instructive and the ludic is applied to the book-within-the-book, but it is as apposite with regard to the parent work. One of the most vital aspects of *Libro de Manuel* is Cortázar's determination to bring injustice to light and champion political freedom, but he is also adamant that other freedoms must be protected or pursued at the same time, and one such is the freedom to play.

The press cuttings are the main device by which Cortázar varies the pace and appearance of his novel; they are reproduced in facsimile, sometimes with the text snaking around them, and some are also fully integrated into the main text in translation. In order to achieve their integration, Cortázar yet again makes a translator figure out of one of his characters, Manuel's mother, Susana. These characteristics contribute significantly to making *Libro de Manuel* a book that is fragmented and varied in style, in marked contrast with the seamlessness of *62: Modelo para armar.* As we have seen, many of the press cuttings relate to political matters, so they provide a political context that implicitly justifies the actions of the Joda. However, not all the cuttings are focused on political issues, and moreover they enter the book in an almost aleatory manner, as if to reflect whatever happened to come to the author's attention as he was in the process of writing the book.

Libro de Manuel has many sections, all unnumbered. They progress in a series of cinemalike cuts from scene to scene; the information in them comes in relatively digestible doses, and as a result readers have few of the orientational problems they have to face with *62: Modelo para armar.* The reading of *Libro de Manuel* is (presumably) linear, and such contrasts, contradictions, and suprises as it entails are far more muted and less challenging than are those of *Rayuela.* But all this is not to claim for *Libro de Manuel* the same degree of readability as one finds in *Los premios; Libro de Manuel,* contrary to the demands of some of Cortázar's left-wing critics, is not a novel for easy mass consumption.

The characters in the book may be grouped into the revolutionaries proper (Marcos, Gómez, Heredia, Verneuil, and so on) and those on the periphery, whom Cortázar explores in greater depth. One of these last is Lonstein, an Argentine Jew who "rabbinizes" or "cabalizes" his way through the book, playing with language, obsessed by a mushroom he is cultivating at home, and given to digressions on the virtues of masturbation.[8] Lonstein acts as a foil for another character known only as "el que te dije" (you know who), who seems to stand for Cortázar. When "el que te dije" is first introduced (26), there are references to pressures brought to bear on him by the more single-minded members of the revolutionary group and to the mysterious origins of the creative impulse (the aroma of jasmine in a garden in Buenos Aires, his grandmother laying a tablecloth—images that lead one's thoughts back to the boy Cortázar as reflected in "Los venenos"). "El que te dije" is a man who, when he first appears, is sensing the onset of a story that is taking shape and acquiring its own impulse in precisely the manner that Cortázar has described in interviews: a confluence of sensations and images, whether real or imaginary, past or present, will come to assume roles in the ensuing narrative, "while 'el que te dije' turns his back and his right index finger strikes the key" (27). "El que te dije," then, is clearly a representation of Cortázar as writer, and his situation here reflects the author's frequent assertions that he does not know quite where his writing is going and that it carries him along as if it had a life of its own. But there is also the second alter ego here in the person of Andrés, a character who represents the author's blend of warring metaphysical, cultural, and political concerns. Andrés, somewhat like Oliveira, is a man trapped by the habitual need to explain, a man who is trying to stretch himself and move toward something new. He listens to Stockhausen even though he is more at home with the traditional forms of classical music. As he sits between the speakers of his stereo, self-analytically, Andrés sees himself as the old man and the new coming together, placed strategically in a third position between the opposing poles of the stereo. There is a further metaphorical lesson to be had from this experience, and it is this: Stockhausen makes for difficult listening; like any artist he must have been concerned about building bridges to his audience, yet he too is clearly striving for something new. In relation to this, Andrés reflects that "fossilized socialist dogma" demands nothing less than a "total bridge," in other words, that writers be easily readable.

As if he were Stockhausen's fellow traveler, Andrés is confronting the old man with the new; he is striving for a worldview that will encompass art and politics, and that is "by no means a happy confrontation" (29). Andrés is described by Susana as yet another Argentine who is in Paris for reasons that are not clear (again, very much like Oliveira, who during the episode with Berthe Trépat was at a loss to explain what he was doing in Paris). Susana says that Andrés is someone who listens to a lot of avantgarde music, reads widely, and is waiting for the time to come, though she cannot say of what (31). (In these last there are echoes of some words used to describe Felipe, the boy in *Los premios.*

Andrés is also positioned in a love triangle. One of his lovers is Ludmilla, a character presumed by some critics to have been based on Cortázar's partner at the time, Ugné Karvelis. Nicknamed "Ludlud" by Andrés, as if to emphasize her ludic, free-spirited personality, Ludmilla soon strikes up a new relationship with one of the leading revolutionaries, Marcos, and in parallel she becomes involved in the schemes of La Joda. The other lover, Francine, is more conventional, bourgeoise, and bookish (even to the extent of working in a bookshop); she is not involved in politics. The trajectory of Andrés, the self-analytical intellectual and aesthete, in some ways echoes that of Oliveira. Andrés sees renewal as an all-embracing process, one that entails descent and self-loathing as a prelude. Rather as Oliveira descended into the demimonde of the Paris *clochards,* Andrés takes Francine to a strip club. Afterward he leads her to a hotel, on the grounds that there they can be free from the normalcy of their homes. The established patterns must be broken, the taboos must go, and so at the hotel Andrés is impelled to sodomize Francine, in an act of transgression that is like Oliveira's under the bridge in *Rayuela,* but goes a step further. Apart from its violent transgression of social norms, it is also transgression in a more literal sense: a crossing over. Symbolically, the scene takes place on a balcony overlooking a cemetery, providing a suggestion of a precipitous fall, a premonition of death, and an invitation to Francine to look beyond her own bourgeois life. Eros faces Thanatos. It may also be that the cemetery represents a negative alternative to human commitment.[9]

An aside is in order. The sexual act narrated here was almost excised by Cortázar when he was reading the proofs for *Libro de Manuel,* because he found that rereading the episode made him feel very uncomfortable. However, he decided to let it stand since he felt that to eliminate it at that stage would be both cowardly and hypocritical. He recognized that quite often there was a sadistic dimension to the erotic episodes in his literature, but argued that there was plenty of evidence, thanks to Baudelaire and Freud in particular, that the erotic and the sadistic were always closely related to each other, whether on a conscious or unconscious level.[10] Cortázar also drew attention to the need to find ways around the taboos that stifle the expression of the erotic in Spanish, a subject he also dealt with at some length in *Último round*.

Lest the sodomizing of Francine be dismissed as merely perverse and distasteful, I invite the reader to consult the interesting analysis of it carried out by Margery Safir.[11] Cortázar's own analysis of the episode can be read in *Cortázar por Cortázar*.[12] His explanation is as follows. Andrés has abused Francine, because she was unwilling to engage in the act; realizing this afterward, he grows full of remorse, but she absolves him (I choose the Catholic metaphor deliberately) because she comes to understand that she has been prisoner of certain religious and moral taboos. Cortázar viewed that scene as ritualistic, as a form of exorcism, an ultimate violation that would open up the way to something new; he saw Andrés as being motivated by a wish to liberate both of them.[13] Significantly, however, Cortázar has the most open-minded of the revolutionaries articulate the aim with the greatest clarity and conciseness: "Everything has to be reinvented . . . there's no reason why love should be an exception" (237.)

A little later in the novel, hurt but not humiliated, Francine asks Andrés what the experience has done for him, to which he replies that he doesn't understand what it all means but knows that the "mancha negra" (black blotch), is still there. This image, which is frequently used, appears to represent the need that weighs upon Andrés to progress toward something that is elusively, undefinably new. In a sense, Andrés "finds himself" at the end of the book. Following a "rabbinical" map provided by Lonstein, in a dreamlike sequence he approaches the kidnappers' hideout (and in doing so facilitates their discovery by the authorities). Andrés's labyrinthine progress, plotted by a man whose name reminds one suspiciously of the Lönrot of Borges's rabbinical whodunit "La muerte y la brújula" ("Death and the Compass"), is only one of a cluster of literary and cinematic allusions throughout the climactic pages of *Libro de Manuel*. Andrés is both actor and observer. He knows that he is caught at an "Oedipal" crossroads, is engaged on a "viaje iniciático" (journey of initiation), is another Siegfried. He is awakened from this surreal and erudite reverie by (rather too predictably) a Cuban.

Yet at this point, just when it seems that Andrés is being brought firmly back to earth, Cortázar reminds us that a fiction is at work. "El que te dije," the chronicler of what has been happening, now comments that the events just related serve as a wake-up call for him, too; like an author who is faced with a rebellious character, he protests ironically that all that he needed was for Andrés to turn up in the internal drama (in practical terms, join the political fray, step into the inner circle of characters made up of the revolutionaries proper) and that he ("el que te dije") doesn't know how to finish the book. He makes a final attempt at controlled narration of the dramatic events that now seem to be occurring too rapidly or simultaneously to capture on paper; during that attempt he exhausts a whole armory of literary parallels and biblical parody, also taking a little self-referential time to point out that he is doing so. At this juncture, "el que te dije" steps down. And so the narrative baton passes on to a less detached narrator, Andrés (333), who finds himself, finds a role, in the process: Andrés has both entered the political arena and assumed responsibility as writer.

Andrés now attempts to put the materials left by "el que te dije" into some coherent order. Lonstein, however, pours scorn on the whole enterprise. Why, he demands, is Andrés so determined to see the matter through to completion? Andrés replies that some things have happened to him, and others to the other characters, and that, for want of a better term, there has been a "convergence." He acknowledges that Gómez and Verneuil ("fictitious" characters, anyway) are now being written out of the story, but he claims that what is being left for the edification of Manuel's generation is what really matters.

There follows the most powerful of the pieces of political evidence amassed by "el que te dije," which runs to several pages and provides two types of personal testimony: on the one hand a number of victims recount the horrors of torture, and on the other U.S. personnel reveal exactly how and where they were trained in its techniques. Even here, there is a hint of lightheartedness, of the continuing presence of the erotic, for one of the American witnesses, from Nebraska, goes by the name of Chuck Onan. Is this only an (extraordinary) example of the happy sort of "figural" coincidence that so haunted and delighted Cortázar or is it possibly a sign that, for all its photocopied appearance of authenticity, this testimony may conceivably be suspect, even fabricated? After all, the trustworthiness of all media reports, as Cortázar has shown in this book and elsewhere, is open to suspicion. And is it a coincidence that in the penultimate section of *Libro de Manuel* Andrés reasserts his commitment to fun, to art, and to individuality, admitting to Patricio that he has slipped one or two cartoons and bits of entertaining news in among the distressing material? When asked whether in future he will be giving listening to Joni Mitchell a higher priority than working as compiler of Manuel's manual, he replies : "I don't know . . . it may be that way round or the other way, but it will always be both things" (353).

On the final page of *Libro de Manuel* Lonstein, who works in a morgue, encounters an old friend lying dead on the slab in front of him. At this point, the reader's mind goes naturally to the cases of torture just reported, but also to the presumed outcome of the Joda's encounter with the authorities. Circumstances favor the possibility that the dead man is Marcos, the leader of the group, but once again, Cortázar's ending is ambiguous. The confidential tone of the thoughts of Lonstein as he tends to the body suggests that the dead friend may well be Andrés or "el que te dije"; if so, this would confirm the implication that the writer/intellectual has made the ultimate commitment. Lonstein pays homage to his friend, but in his closing thoughts he expresses the fear that people might brush it all aside as fiction.[14]

Although some, Cortázar included, have expressed reservations about the end of *Libro de Manuel,* its last forty-odd pages are something of a *tour de force.* The same cannot be claimed for the bulk of the novel. Too often one has the feeling of reading Cortázar-by-the-yard (as he might have phrased it), sometimes the writing is mannered and repetitive, and Argentine colloquial usage is overexploited. It must also be recognized that *Libro de Manuel* suffers from a certain amount of dead weight. Some of the issues addressed have been addressed by Cortázar more effectively, and more concisely, elsewhere. Some of the interpolated material quite simply is not interesting. The interplay of the authorial figures of Andrés and "el que te dije" is novel, though both figures are cloned from earlier Cortázar characters. Also interesting is the figure of Lonstein, the eccentric linguistic experimenter and confidant. Many stock Cortázar features put in an appearance in *Libro de Manuel,* such as cords, skeins, the *métro,* the idea of the loss of innocence, and games with language. Apart from Lonstein's linguistic inventions there are, for instance, transliterations of foreign terms such as "veltanshaun" (*Weltanschauung*), "comilfó" (*comme il faut*), and "baideuéi" (by the way). The protectors of the VIP (and his consort, the VIPA) are *hormigas* (ants) while the more inflexible revolutionaries are referred to as "hormigas del buen lado" (ants on the side of the good guys). Language, too, has its "ants" in the form of trite or euphemistic expressions that require replacement.

Libro de Manuel is laudable for its attempt at dealing with the difficult issues with which Cortázar was faced at the time when he wrote it, but it is the most flawed of the novels published during his lifetime; the author knew it, and in the *A fondo* television interview referred to the novel as "my worst book." One interesting aspect of it, however, is the controversy it sparked in a number of quarters. In the first place, it will be evident from what I have said so far that, although far less esoteric than *62: Modelo para armar* and quite insistent about certain sociopolitical matters, *Libro de Manuel* is not the sort of easy novel (the "total bridge") that was likely to satisfy the critics who had been arguing that Cortázar was too elitist a writer. Moreover, his continuing focus on the personal, his insistence on individual freedom, and his blunt references to revolutionary movements that had, in his view, grown stagnant and repressive were not calculated to endear him to revolutionary fanatics.

In reference to the risks of anchylosis among revolutionaries Cortázar writes that there is a world of difference between theory and practice, between operating in the street and operating the tiller. Why, he asks, move from a language defined by life to a life defined by language, to the puritanical rhetoric of revolutionary government? Sometimes, he says, it is as though the "hombre nuevo" (and let us not forget that the concept of the "new man" was Che Guevara's and intimately linked to the Cuban Revolution) reverts to the old self as soon as he sees a miniskirt or a film by Andy Warhol (81). While Marcos is described by "el que te dije" as someone who is capable of seeing things from different perspectives (166), other members of the Joda are monolithic, "resolutely oriented toward the Screwery," and they are lacking in a sense of fun and beauty.

Libro de Manuel drew immediate fire from Right and Left. It suffered a barrage of criticism, particularly from Latin Americans, some of them unthinkingly aggressive and some more tempered in their argument that the "convergence" had not taken place, that Cortázar had not delivered on his promise of the waters coming together. Critics outside Latin America were intrigued, but generally gave *Libro de Manuel* a lukewarm reception. Boldy, for example, writes that "the repetition of structure and character types from earlier works is mechanical; the language is often stereotyped Cortázarese bordering dangerously on rhetoric," but he concedes that "it is nevertheless a brave and honest book."[15] One problem is that it is hard to avoid comparing *Libro de Manuel* unfavorably with the more accomplished *Rayuela*. Just as Cortázar's exploration of the issues that troubled him personally was carried out in *Rayuela* through Oliveira and Morelli, in *Libro de Manuel* it is conducted through Andrés, "el que te dije," and to some extent Lonstein. There are also some respects, as we have begun to see, in which *Libro de Manuel* harks back to *El examen.*

In early 1973 Cortázar had come back to Argentina for the first time in eight years, for the publication of *Libro de Manuel;* he had traveled there by train from Chile, where he had visited his friend, Chile's president, Salvador Allende, and the two of them had been celebrating Allende's victory with cigars provided by Fidel Castro. Elections were also about to take place in Argentina and in France. Argentina was entering a period of change, which made Cortázar cautiously optimistic, leading him to talk of a "new" Peronism that had little in common with the variety he had opposed about twenty-five years earlier. But any such optimism was ill-fated. A new wave of coups swept through Latin America, affecting both Argentina and Chile. Argentina, from 1976, found itself caught up in the "Dirty War," during which military governments caused their opponents to "disappear." In Chile, Pinochet overthrew Allende, who died in the process, and many Chileans had to flee the country, while many who stayed were tortured.

The fire of controversy surrounding *Libro de Manuel* was rekindled in 1974, when it won the Prix Médicis, awarded annually in France for the best foreign novel. In a symbolic and very public gesture, Cortázar donated the (modest) prize money to the Chilean resistance movement. The award of the Prix Médicis, and Cortázar's donation of it, increased his already considerable visibility. When interviewed on French television for a series called *Apostrophes* he said that in his view the combative part of *Libro de Manuel* was not to be found in the story, which was essentially rather commonplace, but in the critique of taboos and inhibitions that allow people to think they are revolutionary, even to the point of being ready to lay down their lives, when the truth is that they are trapped in ways of thinking and expressing themselves that belong to the enemy.

Some sense of the reactions that all this provoked can be had by reviewing an exchange that took place in 1974 via the pages of the Argentine newspaper *La Opinión,* about a year and a half after the novel's publication. On 26 November 1974, *La Opinión* published a note by Osvaldo Tcherkaski, a reporter for *France Presse,* denouncing the donation of the prize money as evidence of a modish French interest in Latin American guerrilla movements. He also drew attention to Cortázar's many years away from Argentina, claiming that they falsified his view of the situation. Counterprotests and more criticism piled up until *La Opinión* determined to try to put some order into the debate by contacting Cortázar and inviting his comments on what it held were new perspectives on an old controversy.[16]

It was put to Cortázar that (a) the language of *Libro de Manuel* was elitist and aimed at intellectual enlightenment rather than at establishing a bridge to the Latin American reader, to whom the book would seem like exotic food; (b) in Latin America it was difficult to see how a revolutionary could stay so far away from the line of fire and prefer to speak out through his books and by signing his name to manifestos that had little or no effect in Argentina. No one was demanding that Cortázar live there: it was simply that, given that he had declared himself to be a revolutionary, he was expected to show total commitment; (c) his contact with Latin America had become purely intellectual, and 'what the eye doesn't see the heart doesn't grieve for'; (d) the donation of the prize money was viewed with suspicion. All acts of charity, especially when they came from the Left, smacked of a need to clear one's conscience; and (e) being a revolutionary in Paris seemed to be a comfortable and convenient solution for someone whose exile was never earned (Cortázar's, it was noted, had begun as a cultural journey, rather than a political one, in 1952), and the Médicis Prize was evidence of metropolitan interest in fashionable revolutions, which caused a stir over there but had no effect in Argentina. *La Opinión* went on to say that these views, expressed by Argentine writers and critics, would appear in an imminent issue; it invited Cortázar to respond to them.

He did so, protesting that the digest of opinions he had been sent was anonymous and that it was all he had to go on, and arguing that the only proper way to proceed would be for the paper to reproduce the text of the telex verbatim along with his replies, which in essence, and point for point, were these: (a) that three editions of "exotic food" were hard on the Argentine digestive system but their "elitist language" proved that Argentine writers and readers were aiming high and that the elites were growing less and less noticeable; (b) that any writer worth his salt lived for and through his writing, in which everything converged. As for the "firing line," it was a matter of each person deciding where his personal one lay; (c) that "I could say the same to you, Sir: you are not seeing me with your eyes, and you're not batting an eyelid"; (d) that he refrained from commenting on the person who had thought "charitable" an act that was consistent with so much of Cortázar's past behavior; and (e) that he found the last opinion listed particularly muddleheaded and tendentious. He had come to France because he felt like it. As for the prize, it was clear that the jury, given who they were, had been interested in literature. Finally, people in France were less interested in "fashionable" revolution than in fashionable clothes.

The issue of *La Opinión* duly appeared on 8 December 1974, including the material already described, together with articles by a number of people, under the predictable banner of "The Responsibility of Latin American Intellectuals." Among those writing the articles, María Rosa Oliver's contribution is loosely structured; in it she says that whenever she hears an attack on Cortázar based on his absence in Europe she remembers that the best book about the Argentine countryside was written by a man who had left it forty years before he wrote that book (Guillermo Enrique Hudson's *Far Away and Long Ago*). She calls attention to the authentically Argentine nature of some Cortázar stories and of the characters in *Los premios;* and she does not doubt Cortázar's motives in giving the prize money away.

In a far more dense and suggestive contribution, Ricardo Piglia (another noted novelist, of a younger generation) writes that there is a constant toing and froing in Cortázar between the popular and the avantgarde, and he says that Cortázar is like an explorer trying to leave his mark in a capitalist jungle; he sees Cortázar, the writer of collage books, as an inveterate collector, who in *Libro de Manuel* is aestheticizing political issues, using them as he uses so many diverse materials and references. Cortázar, according to Piglia, is a liberal and a romantic, whose anarchic metaphysics is based on the intellectual gurus of the 1968 movement in Paris (Marx and Freud, with a dose of Marcuse). He is also a man who does not understand politics. Piglia says that *Yo, el Supremo,* the most celebrated work of the Paraguayan writer Augusto Roa Bastos, is an admirable example of what a political novel can be, but claims that the reason why it is so successful is that its approach is the obverse of Cortázar's.

Aníbal Ford believes that Cortázar's early works have a greater political charge than does *Libro de Manuel*. Ford regards Cortázar's claim that he has brought the two sides together in *Libro de Manuel* as both "ingenuous and mechanistic," saying that merely reproducing press cuttings about atrocities does not make for a powerful denunciation of such atrocities. But Ford also recognizes that fundamentally Cortázar is trying to explain and justify his own trajectory, his personal aspirations toward a variety of socialism that embraces love, joy, and playfulness; in that, says Ford, lies his originality and the explanation of his failure. The aestheticist inspired by surrealism and romanticism has evolved into a European humanist inspired by the intelligentsia of the Paris of May 1968, and therefore Cortázar has little in common with movements that have sprung from the working class in Latin America. Ford goes on to say that Latin Americans in Paris generally show clear signs of cultural dependence. As regards the prize, Ford regards the donation of it as laudable, but not the publicity that it has attracted; that, he finds patronizing.

Everything in the tone and content of Ernesto Goldar's contribution is critical of Cortázar. Goldar accuses him of being part of a commercial and academic machine, pandering to the self-indulgence of the middle class, and conveniently arriving back in Argentina for the launch of *Libro de Manuel* at a time when the political climate was much better than it had been. Goldar is cynical about the prize and its donation to the Chilean Resistance, saying that Cortázar has always been a "committed" writer, committed to racial and anti-working-class sentiment. (Goldar adduces "Las puertas del cielo" as evidence.) He will not forgive Cortázar for having been associated, two decades earlier, with that "dusty" literary magazine *Sur*, and he refers to *La vuelta al día en ochenta mundos* as a book "for the delight of the dilettante." Goldar makes several other comments that I find too confusing to summarize, and he ends by talking of "ideological colonization" and cultural dependence. The best he can say about the Médicis Prize is that it must have been a way for Cortázar to clear his guilty conscience.

Haroldo Conti (whose fate, incidentally, was to be "disappeared") says that the very fact that the debate is taking place is proof of the effectiveness of Cortázar's donation. He doubts that being away from Argentina makes effective participation in the political process impossible any more than being in Argentina guarantees it. Having personally come to know Cortázar, he bears witness to the writer's sincerity and sensitivity regarding problems in Latin America. Poignantly, Conti concludes that "cuando enmudezcan todas las voces, habrá todavía una, salvada por la distancia, que señale y condene, que denuncie y ayude, que movilice y congregue" (when all the voices are silenced, there will still be one, protected by distance, to draw attention and condemn, to denounce and support, to mobilize and create solidarity).

The final contribution to the special issue of *La Opinión* is by Jorge

Abelardo Ramos, who writes despite not having read *Libro de Manuel*. He says that he prefers the new Cortázar to the Cortázar who was on the fringes of the bourgeois circle associated with *Sur*. He contrasts Cortázar's behavior with the indifference of Borges to the plight of fellow humans. Cortázar, who is away, is more feelingly Argentine than Borges, who is present in Buenos Aires. If Cortázar has sinned, says Ramos ironically, then he has committed the sins that everyone is tempted to commit in Paris, and many are jealous of him because of it. What should be the subject of criticism is his work, not where it was written.

So much for the contributions to the special issue of *La Opinión*. The hostile reception of *Libro de Manuel* is also discussed in Cortázar's interview with González Bermejo. There Cortázar comments that the reaction that he had foreseen in his book's prologue came about exactly as anticipated. He refers to a review published in a leading Argentine daily, *La Nación,* which amounted to "a sort of extended lament for the literary passing of someone who, so long as he was writing pure literature had been satisfying the desires and aspirations of the social class to which he belonged, but who now had turned to introducing politics and history into his books and, as anyone could see, was betraying his glorious past."[17] As predicted, the reaction from the other extreme had been that *Libro de Manuel* was frivolous and displayed a lack of solidarity. Cortázar says that he brushed aside the right-wing reaction, but had been saddened by that of the left. Some readers and critics had understood that *Libro de Manuel* involved, as González Bermejo aptly puts it, "an attempt to demystify a whole monastic revolutionary way of thinking," and they assessed the book on those terms. Others had refused to understand what Cortázar was trying to do. The attacks on Cortázar were not easy for him to forget. In a speech Cortázar gave in Mexico he said: "At the time when I wrote *Libro de Manuel* I had to put up with the worst and bitterest of attacks from many people who were my comrades in arms, who felt that my denunciation through literature of the bloody regime of General Lanusse in Argentina lacked the seriousness and documentation of their pamphlets and articles."[18] In the interview with Prego Cortázar explains that part of his purpose in writing *Libro de Manuel* had been to pose a friendly challenge to guerrillas, to free up, or perhaps lighten up (characteristically, the verb that Cortázar uses is *desquitinizar* [to de-chitin-ize]) the tentative beginnings of revolutionary change in Argentina.[19] He had personally become acquainted with some of the exiled revolutionaries working in Paris and had been frightened by their dramatic and humorless attitude: "I realized that those people, despite all their merits, despite all their courage, despite all the reasons they had to justify carrying out their action, if they managed to see it through to the end . . . the revolution that they would bring about was not going to be *my* Revolution."[20]

Cortázar capitalizes the *R* to highlight the all-embracing nature of his concept of revolution, which he sees as ongoing, flexible, "chameleon-like"; he contrasts that with the process of "chitinization," the tendency toward rigidity, that has been observable in so many revolutionary movements (including the Cuban one). His view was that revolutions that began by being open, inventive, and free, and in sympathy with experiment and innovation in the arts, had a distressing tendency to become institutionalized and restrictive.

In 1977 Cortázar published the collection of stories titled *Alguien que anda por ahí* (Someone walking around). This was published in Mexico and Madrid, the Argentine authorities having taken exception to two of the stories therein. Cortázar explained that the publication of his last book of stories in Argentina was banned by the military junta, who were only prepared to authorize it if he agreed to remove two tales that they thought would be harmful to them. One of the stories concerned referred indirectly to the physical disappearance of people in Argentina and the other had to do with the destruction of the Christian community established by the Nicaraguan poet, Ernesto Cardenal, on the island of Solentiname.[21]

In "Segunda vez" (Second time around) María Elena befriends Carlos, whom she meets when she obeys an unexplained summons to the offices of an anonymous, flagless government agency located in an out-of-the-way place. As she sits in the waiting room, other visitors are called into the inner office one by one, to reappear later, visibly relieved at their release. One of them comments that life is like a waiting room. Carlos is called in before María Elena. She is then called in before he has come out. Once inside, she is told to do some meaningless, routine filling out of forms and has to respond to spoken questions that reiterate the same material. When she returns to the waiting room, it is empty; she waits for some time, and still Carlos does not come out. Puzzled, she recalls that there was only one way into the inner office but reasons that he must have gone through another door, hidden by posters. But then she remembers that this was Carlos's second time there. So the reader is left with the thought that on her second visit she too will come out on the other side, but it is not another side that promises some form of self-knowledge, as is so often the case with such transitions in Cortázar; the implication here is far more sinister. The story opens and closes with passages that frame the action described above; these passages present the thoughts of the faceless bureaucrats who await the innocents who have been summoned and deal with them according to a well-oiled procedure, following orders from above. These bureaucrats accept no personal responsibility for their actions and are more concerned with when the coffee will arrive.

Certain street names and proper names strongly suggest Buenos Aires to anyone familiar with that city, but other readers should be forgiven for missing the Argentine association. Indeed, in view of the author's long-standing tendency to write universalizing stories about people caught up in designs that they can neither understand nor influence, it would be quite possible to read this story as geographically unspecific, even as a story that has nothing to do with politics.

This is in marked contrast to "Apocalipsis de Solentiname" (Apocalypse at Solentiname), whose geographical setting is absolutely specific and whose references to the sociopolitical woes of Latin America are quite explicit. Here, Cortázar is the protagonist and makes no attempt to hide behind a fictional alter ego. The story begins with his arrival in Costa Rica en route to Nicaragua and to Cardenal's community on the island of Solentiname; thence he goes to Cuba, where this story was in fact written. At a press conference in Nicaragua he is faced with "the usual business," namely questions about why he lives in France, why the Antonioni film *Blow Up* turned out to be so different from "Las babas del diablo" (the story that inspired it), whether writers should be politically committed, and whether his own work is not too unapproachable for the common man. A weary Cortázar wryly adds that he expects to have to answer the same questions as he leaves this world for the next. These preliminaries serve to herald a political story. The reference to "Las babas del diablo," in which photography was so important, further hints that photography will also play a central role in "Apocalipsis de Solentiname." More preliminaries ensue, during which polaroid photos are taken and Cortázar expresses his wonder at how the images can change before one's eyes, joking that one day a family photo will come out as Napoleon on horseback. In this way the reader is given a foretaste of a crucial theme in the story: the tension between image and reality. The whole story is in fact structured around a series of visual images that begin when Cortázar arrives in Solentiname and is intrigued by some naïve paintings done by local peasants, paintings that reveal their closeness to the world they are portraying, their "mirada limpia del que describe su entorno" (clear vision of people who are describing the world they live in). Ernesto Cardenal explains that these are paintings that members of his community sell to make ends meet. As sleep gets the better of Cortázar and his friends, the author gives his readers another hint of where he is heading: he dwells on the impression left by one particularly striking painting that has a sky full of stars and one cloud, driven into the corner of the frame, "already escaping the awesome canvas" (156). The next day, Cortázar attends mass and is struck by the way the peasants identify personally with the text of the day because the episode it relates, dealing with Christ's arrest in the garden, reflects their own vulnerability. At this point Cortázar expatiates openly about the threats to ordinary people in many parts of Latin America; he singles out—in addition to Nicaragua—El Salvador, the Dominican Republic,

Argentina, Bolivia, Chile, Colombia, Paraguay, and Brazil. Back in the communal hall and fascinated once again by the naïve paintings, Cortázar takes photos of them, making sure that each occupies the whole frame; it turns out that the number of paintings matches the available number of exposures on the film. These details are important, since they signify the elimination of context, and in doing so they constitute yet another hint as to the story's outcome.

Cortázar continues his journey to Cuba and then returns to Paris, readjusting to the routines of his life there. Once his slides have been developed, he settles down to look at them, reminding himself that they are only representations (and in the case of those of the paintings, representations of representations) of life. First he sees the slides of the community, which prompts him to reflect on how it is "surrounded by henchmen" (58); then suddenly he is faced with the image of a child slumping forward, shot through the head. Although he tries to tell himself that someone has confused his slides with others when developing them, Cortázar now finds himself swept through a series of images of acts of violent repression in Latin America. The images end as his friend Claudine arrives at his apartment. He sits her in the very chair that he has just been using (ostensibly imposing on her the same point of view), and while she looks at the slides, he slips away to the bathroom to recover. When at last he returns, he finds her composed and calm, and she tells him how she loves the naïve paintings. He refrains from telling her what images the slides have brought him, but is tempted to ask her whether she has seen one of Napoleon on horseback. Other stories in *Alguien que anda por ahí,* including the title story, have political implications, but none is as powerful as "Apocalipsis de Solentiname."

Most of Cortázar's political stories, however, are cast in a realist mold. An effective example is "La noche de Mantequilla," whose title, despite its apparently surreal quality (literally, "The night of Butter"), has a banal explanation. "Mantequilla" is the nickname of one of the boxers who fought in a world middleweight title fight that took place in Paris. The fight was between the Argentine champion Carlos Monzón and the Mexican challenger, José Nápoles. The fight is watched by a man called Estévez, who is using it as an elaborate cover under which to pass material to a political accomplice. The boxing match comes to a conclusion that seems both predictable and inevitable: Mantequilla retires from the fight and the two fighters embrace, never again to engage one another in the ring. The undercover "game" that Estévez has been involved in is also over. He has made contact, but it turns out that it was with the wrong man; all the while his actions have been monitored by his comrades, though they have been powerless to prevent his mistake. Since the enemy has already detained the true accomplice and tortured the details of their plans out of him, Estévez now represents a security risk, and so they must take him to the country to be shot.

Estévez thinks back to how his false contact had been supporting the losing boxer, the poor fellow with the beaten face who had held out his hand and said it had been a pleasure. Just as Estévez himself did, being another loser. It has been the loser's night, "La noche de Mantequilla." Though effective as a story, the political implications of this tale are none too specific.

Two highly effective stories from *Queremos tanto a Glenda* (1980) deserve discussion here, "Recortes de prensa" and "Graffiti." "Recortes de prensa" (Press cuttings) is based, somewhat like "Reunión," on a text that has independently verifiable status: a press cutting from a 1978 issue of the respected Spanish daily *El País* in which Argentine nationals from the same family make formal statements regarding the horrific abduction, torture, and murder of other family members. The narrator, a woman called Noemí (Naomi, in its Anglicized form), is a writer and has been invited by a friend who is a sculptor working in Paris to provide some text to accompany a series of his sculptures, whose theme is man's inhumanity to man. She comments that the two of them know something about that subject, because both of them are Argentine. She says that she is pleased at the unsystematic way he has approached his work and notes that sometimes one has to study it quite closely to see how the theme is in evidence. Even torture, that basest form of human abuse, is treated without resorting to the "questionable detail that characterizes so many posters, texts, and films" (361). She tells the sculptor that if she is going to provide a text to accompany his works, that text must have its own artistic integrity, and she emphasizes this point by adding, "I shall never let myself be carried away by the facileness that is far too common in this sort of thing." The sculptor replies that that decision is up to her. He also wonders if the way they are inclined to edit and adapt awful memories is not just a form of self-defense. Noemí then hands him the press cutting. Its documentary, legalistic style contrasts starkly with the oblique form of expression used by Noemí and her friend. When he has read most of the press cutting, he comments that he spends months churning out "this shit" (referring to his sculptures) while Noemí writes books and the woman in the newspaper denounces atrocities, and that they go to conferences to protest and deceive themselves into thinking that things are changing for the better. Here he is in Paris, busily arguing with his publisher about what kind of paper should be used for a book of photographs of his work; Noemí is in the middle of writing a story about the psychological trauma of an adolescent girl; and meanwhile, over there, bodies are being dismembered and shoveled into mass graves. "Nunca estuvimos ni nunca estaremos allí" (We were never there, and we never shall be) (364). Significantly, these qualms are said by Noemí to be a form or self-torture.

Cortázar quite often uses female narrators, but rarely is his presence in them so obvious as it is in this instance. The reference to a text to accompany art works could be an allusion to any of several pieces that Cortázar wrote in response to the work of painters, for example the story "Graffiti," which first appeared in a catalog for an exhibition of canvases by the Catalan painter Antoni Tàpies (who, like the sculptor in "Recortes de prensa" is in many ways a painter of protest, but not a facile propagandist). The reference to a story about a troubled adolescent girl may well be to Cortázar's "Ud. se tendió a tu lado" (*Alguien que anda por ahí*). If so, the change of sex involved in that last reference provides a fitting parallel to the one that turns Cortázar into Noemí. Moreover, the concerns expressed by the Paris artists are exactly those which troubled Cortázar, and the refusal to give in to easy propaganda is also his. Noemí, however, is not a name that Cortázar has idly chosen, because it is associated with the evidently Jewish names of the family members in the other text, the cutting from *El País*. Furthermore, at one point the sculptor interrupts his perusal of that text to comment that the way in which the authorities are said to have fed their victims seasonal delicacies immediately prior to killing them on Christmas Day recalls the tales of candy being given out prior to herding children into the gas chambers at Auschwitz. Finally, there is another conspicuous reference to anti-Semitism: when arresting a member of the persecuted family, an officer is reported to have expressed outrage that "any Jewish son of a bitch" should have dared to start proceedings against the Argentine army (363). As far as correspondences with the biblical Naomi are concerned, she may be said to change territories and undergo personal change, perhaps a form of conversion, in ways that are echoed in Cortázar's Noemí.

Noemí leaves the sculptor's home. For reasons that are not clear to her, but which the reader understands as symbolic, Noemí crosses the street. There she discovers a little girl, who, frightened and in tears, tells her that her father is "doing things" to her mother. Despite her reluctance to become involved in other people's business, she allows the girl to lead her (symbolically, again) across a threshold, through a garden, and into a gloomy building. There Noemí encounters the mother manacled to a bed, being tortured with cigarette burns by the father. The actions that follow, stemming from horror and rage, are more oneiric than realistic in the way they are narrated: "What happened next I might have seen in a film or read in a book. I was there and yet I wasn't." Having knocked the man out, Noemí frees the mother, and together they tie him to the bed and resume the torture. Now it is a case of the mother "doing things" to the father. There is a hint that the women are like the Maenads: "women of the tribe who string his life out horrendously with spasms and shrieks, killing him but not killing him, and with such refinement" (367). And so Noemí comes to a realization that though she had thought herself to be on the "good side," she is capable of going over to the bad one; she has recognized the monster within her (as

Cortázar advocated long before, in *Los reyes*). Then she turns her back on the horrible. She goes back to work, calls the sculptor to tell him breathlessly what has happened, and promises to fax the requested text, the written version of what has just been delivered orally. A couple of days later she is surprised to be handed another press cutting by the sculptor, who tells her that in another newspaper, *France-Soir,* he has read an account of her story: a little girl has been lost, not in Paris but in Marseille, a man has been found tortured to death, and his lover is under suspicion. Thereafter, in search of the truth, Noemí rushes back to where she has encountered the little girl.

Like *Rayuela* and *Libro de Manuel,* "Recortes de prensa" takes its protagonist (by association, Cortázar) on an infernal journey, an especially dreamlike one in the case of the last two works mentioned. In "Recortes de prensa" Noemí descends, crosses over, into action, but she also appears to return, to the comfortable, insulating Paris where she began her story. Even the French horrors seem to have been enacted at a distance. In the end, her involvement is reduced to a matter of imagination. Before beginning the story proper, Cortázar alerts his reader to the fact that the first press cutting is authentic, whereas the second (the one from *France-Soir*) is fictional. Supposedly cut by the other artist from that newspaper, it is also inadvertently mutilated by him, cut once more, before he gives it to Noemí.

Cortázar seems here to be expressing skepticism about the very sources of information: texts are versions of the truth, and they are subject to modification and manipulation, whether conscious or inadvertent. Beyond that, surely there is an implied questioning of the use of press cuttings in his own work, especially *Libro de Manuel.* And yet the power of the nonfictional press cutting remains so strong that one is left with a sense almost of guilt, of compliant and self-indulgent fiddling while Rome burns.

As mentioned earlier, Cortázar wrote a number of pieces to accompany the works of friends who were fellow artists, especially painters. "Graffiti" began life in a catalog for an exhibition that took place in Barcelona and in Paris, at the Maeght Gallery, in the late seventies.[22] A few details about the biography and techniques of Tàpies contribute to one's appreciation of Cortázar's story and explain its inclusion in the catalog. Tàpies works with mixed media, such as wood, sand, and cloth, and he often emphasizes the inherent qualities of these materials. Frequent images in his work include doors, crosses, and walls, which are sometimes daubed with esoteric graffiti. (It has become common for Spanish critics to refer to "las tapias de Tàpies," playing on the fact that his name, in Catalan, means "walls"—*tapias* in Spanish.) Tàpies lived through the years of the dictatorship of General Franco in Spain, a period during which Catalan culture went underground and the language was officially banned. At one point,

Tàpies was imprisoned for his opposition to Franco. A particularly relevant example of his work would seem to be *The Catalan Spirit,* dating from 1971. It would, however, be wrong to leave the impression that Tàpies is a political artist. Although signs of protest are very evident in some of his work, much of it has a mystic, almost religious quality. Since the death of Franco in the early seventies Tàpies (and all things Catalan) have flourished. He is now recognized worldwide as one of Spain's leading artists of the century.

In "Graffiti" an anonymous narrator tells of the activities of someone who has been daubing public walls with graffiti in a city whose authorities are intolerant even of the innocent doodlings of a child. Graffiti that first seem to be merely playful, or at most anarchic, soon acquire a subversive air: the graffiti are not just unsightly, they are something that threatens authority's sway. The actions of the painter of these graffiti are not described in the third person, but instead the painter is addressed directly by the narrator, who uses the second person; in other words, the painter becomes a "narratee" within the narrative, not external to it. A "dialogue," carried out through the graffiti, develops between the narratee and another painter, who is a woman. These graffiti are all abstract, with one exception: the use on one occasion of the phrase "A mí también me duele" (It pains me, too) (*Cuentos completos,* 1: 397). This is a transparently meaningful phrase, which is very promptly erased by the authorities. As the risks run by the graffiti artists increase, a love interest develops; the closest they come to meeting each other in person, however, is when the man glimpses the woman being apprehended and taken to prison. The remaining artist, the narratee, has plenty of time to imagine what must have become of her and to reflect on the general human tendency to turn one's back on the realities of torture and oppression. After some time, he returns to the garage wall where she was detained. Now completely free of graffiti, it does not sport even a thing as harmless as a child's drawing of a flower. The man defiantly paints a passionate protest on it: "un grito verde, una roja llamarada de reconocimiento y de amor . . . un óvalo que era también tu boca y la suya y la esperanza" (a green cry, a red call of recognition and love . . . an oval that was also your mouth and hers and hope) (399). This message escapes erasure for longer than usual, because it transpires that protests are spreading through the city and the authorities are being kept busy elsewhere. When the artist returns and discovers, to his surprise, that his latest painting is still there, he notices that a small reply has appeared in the top left corner of it, an orange oval with purple patches that seems to suggest a battered face. Yet it is a sign of hope and encouragement to continue the campaign. In a moving conclusion, Cortázar now reveals that all along the narrator has been the woman artist; in other words, the dialogue between narrator and narratee has been the corollary, in words, of the one they carried out via the graffiti. The revelation of the narrator's identity constitutes a final twist that is similar to the one used in "Reunión con un círculo rojo," but its effect, in the more anonymous, concise, and lyrical context of "Graffiti," is much more powerful. That, at least, would seem to be the most obvious reading of "Graffiti." However, the reader progressing through this story has been led to make shifting assumptions regarding exactly who is narrating and to whom. Those aware of common tricks of the trade among contemporary authors will not have been surprised, for example, to have spent an initial moment when the narratee "you" seemed to imply themselves, quickly to discover that this was a red herring. Or consider the conclusion of the story: the ambiguity of the narrator's "Ya sé, ya sé" (I know, I know) hints also at the possibility that the "I" is the author (a self-reflexive reading), or indeed that it represents the manipulative powers of authority (an "enhanced" political reading). Certainly there are areas of knowledge about and between the correspondents that do not seem to have come to light via the exchange of graffiti.[23]

Three other stories, included in *Unreasonable Hours,* also deserve comment here. "Pesadillas" ("Nightmares") is a title that refers to several forms of "nightmare" that make themselves felt in the story concerned. Family members visit the bedside of a girl, Mecha, who is in a coma. The family is living this nightmare but also a wider one, namely, the society in which they live, because it is restrictive and controlling: sirens and gunshots are sometimes heard in the distance. The reader learns nothing about the cause of Mecha's coma or the reasons for the civil oppression, but may suspect that the two are related; in fact, the text seems to confirm this at one point (482). Mecha's brother, a student, is apparently involved in some form of protest activity, and before the story is over, he will disappear. However, at the same time Mecha stirs, restless like the society itself. It is as if her awakening symbolizes the awakening of a society that has been trying to turn a blind eye to the realities of modern oppression, hiding its head in the sands of the routine and trivial; witness, for example, the ironic comment in praise of a television quiz show contestant who is said to know so much about ancient history that one would think she were living in the age of Julius Caesar (486). Mecha's awakening, shuddering and spasmodic as it is, signifies not only awareness of the horrors of everyday life, but also hope for the future. The reality to which she awakes may be harsh, but the final words of the story assert that life is sweet. Quite plausibly, Mecha can be read as a symbol of Argentina. Her awakening lights the way toward something better: *mecha* is Spanish for fuse or wick. Finally, one may note that her brother's main associate is called Lucero (Star), a word that is also associated with light (*luz*).

Somewhat more oblique, though its political overtones become explicit enough at the end, is "La escuela de noche" (Night school). In this story two friends at a boys' school break into the building at night to discover that a strange masque is in progress, with some students in drag dancing with others. The two who have broken in start to become drawn into the proceedings, and after they have been made to submit to a perverse, if not cruel, initiation ceremony, things come to a climax with the incantation by members of the group of a Nazi-like creed. One of the visitors becomes integrated into this group, while the other manages to escape into the night. In the light of day, the escapee wishes he could denounce what he has witnessed, but he is persuaded or threatened to keep quiet for his own good. As the story concludes, we understand that it will only be a matter of time before those in power call upon the militaristic training that the night school has been imparting "for the good of the fatherland" (469).

The last story on which I shall comment in this chapter is called "Satarsa." It will be recalled that an early story, "Lejana" (*Bestiario*), took as its starting point an anagrammatic play upon the name of that story's protagonist. In "Satarsa" the starting point is a hybrid of a palindrome and an anagram. That anagram, "atar a la rata" (literally, "to tie the rat") is used as a "way in" to the story: pluralizing that phrase and reading it backward, one gets "satarsa," the title (443). In the story, Lozano and Laura are eking out an existence in difficult times by rounding up rats and shipping them in a van to the coast, whence they are exported to Denmark, supposedly to be used in scientific experiments. This means of survival has taken a horrific toll on the couple's daughter, who has had one of her hands bitten off by the rats. It is clear that the family's difficulties stem from a society beset by severe economic hardship and moreover that it is a society under attack by "rats" of another sort: the military powers-that-be. As conditions continue to deteriorate, Lozano and some friends decide they must step up their rat-catching activities in the hope of raising sufficient funds to enable them to escape the country. We are brought to a scene where, emboldened by a mixture of overeducated rhetoric and simple vengefulness, Lozano and friends confront the army of rats headed by "Satarsa," only to find themselves trapped by the "rats" of the other army. Though not entirely successful as a story, "Satarsa" has the merit of being original and inventive; in its small way, in the figure of Lozano it also brings together those frequently unhappy bedfellows, the thinker and the doer, the intellectual and the activist.

As far as political writing was concerned, there were one or two more radical departures both from discursive writing and from Cortázar's established literary forms. In 1975 he published *Fantomas contra los vampiros multinacionales: Una utopía realizable* (Fantomas versus the multinational vampires: A realizable utopia). This comes with a glossy, eye-catching cover, and some of its contents are in comic-strip form. It uses the popular hero of early

French comics, Fantomas, and also incorporates roles for Cortázar and other prominent intellectuals, such as Octavio Paz, Alberto Moravia, and Susan Sontag. Cortázar developed this idea after he had been sent a copy of a Mexican comic in which Fantomas was the hero and Cortázar made an appearance; he took this material and adapted and expanded it for his own ends in his *Fantomas.*

The action of *Fantomas* begins as the narrator (Cortázar) is leaving Brussels after attending a session of the Russell Tribunal. In the real world, this tribunal had been established by the distinguished British philosopher and activist Bertrand Russell, and its initial brief had been to investigate U.S. conduct in Vietnam. It had met first in Rome, in 1974, and in Brussels a year later, this time to deal with Latin America. The tribunal's varied membership included several Hispanics: two writers, Cortázar and Gabriel García Márquez, a Chilean professor of international law and former ambassador, and Juan Bosch, sometime president of the Dominican Republic; other members represented many nationalities and came from the fields of politics, science, law, and theology. Their report is included in an appendix to *Fantomas;* in addition, parts of it are quoted in the main body of the book. That report identifies a distressing number of human rights violations in several countries and highlights the manner in which multinationals, especially companies controlled by the United States, are exploiting natural resources, controlling the means of production, importation, and exportation, and keeping corrupt regimes in power; it notes that the United States is training Latin American troops and condemns it in particular for its role in Chile. Cortázar was aware that the tribunal's findings were not receiving much publicity, largely due to corporate control of the media. By adopting the popular form of *Fantomas* he hoped to spread the word, and he was successful in that since his book was widely distributed and sold from street kiosks, which are a common source of reading material for Latin Americans. Cortázar contributed the royalties that came from those sales in support of the work of the tribunal.

Though the cover of *Fantomas* raises expectations of comic-book simplicity, it is in fact a multilayered and quite complex structure. After some initial buffoonery, the narrator boards his train to Paris, armed with a comic book hastily purchased at a station kiosk; this he peruses during the journey, while intercalating observations about his fellow passengers and their attitudes to his choice of reading. In other words, *Fantomas* presents itself as a comic and then incorporates a further comic (*La inteligencia en llamas* [Intelligence in flames]) in which, as one might expect, Fantomas is the protagonist. At the same time *Fantomas* the book draws attention to its own diverse textual forms. The dividing lines between the author's reality, the text in the reader's hands, and the one in the author's soon become blurred. For example, Cortázar talks with Fantomas, even on one occasion tells him to read the appendix to *Fantomas,* and characters from the real world enter the comic-within-the-comic. As each does, so his name is asterisked and a corresponding footnote explains who he is. One wonders, reading such a slippery text as *Fantomas,* whether these identifications really are intended as an aid to the uninformed person in the street, in other words, whether they are truly a reflection of Cortázar's effort to reach out to a wider public or whether they have an ironic purpose.

In *La inteligencia en llamas* Fantomas sets out to discover who is responsible for a worldwide spate of destruction of books and libraries. This quest turns out to be something of a red herring, and the real problem is shown to be a wider and very intractable one: the controlling powers of multinationals and especially of the United States. The comic-book format in fact plays only a passing role in *Fantomas,* which turns into a fluid collocation of the author's thoughts stemming from the tribunal's meeting, of certain passages from that tribunal's report, of the somewhat farcical comings and goings of Fantomas, of fictitious telephone conversations (especially with Susan Sontag), of press cuttings, and of images of international icons such as the IBM logo and Capitol Hill. The treatment of Susan Sontag is especially interesting; she appears, perhaps, as the token woman, and the narrator's attitude toward her displays a typical Cortazarian ambivalence, in which awe and a touch of chauvinism both play a part. It is interesting to compare her portrayal with the superficial representations of other female figures who appear in *Fantomas:* the girl whose ankles the narrator eyes in the train and the curvaceous, stock comic images of the women who attend Fantomas.

The underlying concern with the role of multinationals has, of course, been made clear in the fuller title of the book: *Fantomas contra los vampiros multinacionales;* another, slightly more subtle symbol of that concern can be found in the narrator's passing observation that on the cover of the comic book he buys before he boards the train there is a small Pepsi-Cola logo. The title has a further extension—*una utopía realizable* (a realizable utopia)—that signals the book's upbeat conclusion, in which the voices of protest come together and a child is portrayed playing happily but seriously, symbolizing hope for the future in much the same way as did the infant Manuel in "his" book.

The literariness of *Fantomas* is also seen in the way Cortázar opens its initial "chapter" with a parody of the sort of plot summary one finds in much earlier novelists: "Of how the narrator of our fascinating story left his hotel in Brussels, of the things he saw in the street, and of what happened to him at the station" (7). This device is itself made the subject of fun at the start of the following section: "Of how our narrator managed to catch the train *in extremis* (and how from now on there will be no more chapter headings, because there are going to be many fine images to break up and lighten the reading of this fascinating story)" (12). To take another example, on one page an image of a knife piercing an eye is likely to steer the knowing reader's thoughts to Buñuel, and then one turns to the next page to find Cortázar making it clear that that association was indeed anticipated. In all, one can conclude that the political message of *Fantomas* is inescapable and that the book is highly original in conception, but is quite text-heavy, and its playfulness and complexity do imply a certain level of reader sophistication.

Any such refinements disappear in *La raíz del ombú* (1981). Although far less well known than *Fantomas,* it is cast in a slightly similar mold, but is more accessible to unsophisticated readers. The large format of this book (about 35cm x 55cm), combined with its attractive cover, make it look like a book for children. It has a large number of color illustrations, giving the overall impression of a picture book to which text has been added. And so it was: Alberto Cedrón (the brother of Juan, with whom Cortázar collaborated in the production of a recording of tangos, *Trottoirs de Buenos Aires*) had brought Cortázar a number of his illustrations, asking the writer if he could help in bringing them together into some coherent pattern.

Cortázar begins his text by saying that a prologue is unnecessary and then launching into one. He dedicates *La raíz del ombú* to the memory of one Jorge Cortázar, an Argentine *cinéaste,* who committed suicide while in police custody in Paris in 1980, two years after the completion of the book. In the mind of Julio Cortázar, so sensitive to such forms of coincidence, this is yet another instance of reality imitating fiction. Cortázar goes on to explain that *La raíz del ombú* arises from his belief that comics are a means of reaching out to a wide reading public, especially at a time when reading habits are changing, concentration is short-lived, and visual images are carrying the day, not least those of the cinema and television. This particular illustrated book (perhaps not quite a comic, in the sense that its illustrations are not as stylized as are those of *Fantomas*) is the product of the convergence of two artists, the verbal and the visual, linked by a common set of aims that are humorous, artistic, and denunciatory. Cortázar writes: "No member of society, no human being in Latin America is free of blame—whether through silence or inaction—for the crime of *lèse-humanité* that is being committed now, and at every moment, in Argentina, in Chile and Uruguay, to name only the southern trinity engaged in genocide."[24] The political motivation, then, is quite explicitly proclaimed, and the subsequent text leaves one in no doubt as to its message. The image of the ombu tree has its roots in Alberto Cedrón's childhood memories, for there was apparently such a tree in the place where the Cedrón brothers lived as children in Buenos Aires. As an adult, Alberto read Leopoldo Marechal's *Adán Buenosayres* (a book of which Cortázar happened to have written a controversial review during the forties), and in that book Cedrón had been surprised to encounter a representation of the very same ombu, in the suburb of Saavedra. Later, Cedrón's first wife rekindled his memories when she sent him an old issue of *Billiken* (a widely read children's magazine of the time, to which Cortázar refers in other works of his, for example, "Los venenos"). "Alberto" is the narrator of *La raíz del ombú*.

Lost with his car in the Argentine countryside, a traveler stops at a small farmhouse, where he meets Alberto, who offers him shelter for the night. They sit together sipping mate; Alberto begins to reminisce about his family's past, and as he does so, visual images of persecution filter into the book. Alberto tells how his grandfather fled Italy in the SS *Mafalda* (in fact the name of a little girl who stars in a well-known modern Hispanic cartoon series), but the boat caught fire and sank. Surviving this disaster, Alberto's grandfather wandered the pampas in search of work. Eventually he found work as a stevedore in Buenos Aires, where he settled.[25]

Years later, a military disturbance drives the young Alberto to hide under the ombu tree. This tree also serves as a place where children play and from which they can observe the activities of richer neighbors: the children imagine the older ladies of the rich families as ostentatiously devout women who at home beat their servants, while the younger ones are like vampires who come out to do their evil work at night. The era of Peronism brings a sense that people can participate more in the political process, but opportunists take advantage to seize power; these are dubbed "hombres-larvas" (larvamen). Whether civil or military, they know how to close ranks in defense of their privileges. Later, repression increases, and so does resistance activity.

Here the account pauses as Alberto and his visitor decide to retire for the night; but at this point the visitor removes a mask and reveals that he is one of the "hombres-larvas" himself. Shots then ring out, and neighboring fishermen rush to rescue Alberto, overcoming the "baddie." The conclusion is obvious: it is up to the people to act in their own defense. But its obviousness does not stop Cortázar from spelling out exactly that at the end of *La raíz del ombú:* the future is in the hands of the people. In this book Cortázar has given us a crude, potted history of modern Argentina. *La raíz del ombú* is transparently didactic, proving that, for all his frequent insistence on the need to respect the aesthetic dimension, the message here holds sway.

We have seen in this chapter that Cortázar's creative political literature is not always successful and that it is occasionally heavy-handed. Its high spots are stories like "Recortes de prensa" and "Graffiti." So it is, at least, for the texts that have come to be regarded by critics as his most politically charged. However, if one allows a wider view of what may constitute a manifestation of power and authority, then it is evident that an underlying preoccupation with controlling and frequently sinister forces is evident throughout Cortázar's literature. In that broader sense, much of his work can be said to have a political edge.

The effectiveness of "Graffiti" depends to a large extent on anonymity, the anonymity of the correspondents who do not dare to identify themselves and above all the anonymity of the forces of oppression. From *El examen* through stories such as "Casa tomada," "Las babas del diablo," "Los buenos servicios," "Instrucciones para John Howell," "Reunión con un círculo rojo," "Segunda vez," and "Graffiti" to works such as the absurdist play *Nada a Pehuajó,* one senses the role of anonymous controlling powers. Sometimes they are manifest in the form of faceless characters (the backstage triumvirate in "Instrucciones," for example, or the man at the chessboard in *Nada a Pehuajó*), but as often as not they are completely hidden from view, or perceptible only in terms of an arcane awareness of the role of fate. The anonymity of such forces seems to be a crucial element underpinning Cortázar's portrayal of individual fear and disquiet or sense of powerlessness, just as it is crucial to the author's most successful denunciations of political manipulation and abuse, as discussed above. As he neared the end of his life, in the interview with Prego, Cortázar commented on precisely this aspect of his work, speaking of "a sort of latent pervasiveness, a floating atmosphere, in which one cannot know who people are or who is directly responsible. A sort of superstructure."[26] The use of such features, as an alternative to identifying human (but sinister) characters, no doubt avoids the risk that the reader might in some way sympathize with such characters. More significantly, it also reflects the strategy of some of literature's most impressive political works, such as Kafka's *The Trial* and Orwell's *1984* (both of which are mentioned by Cortázar in the interview). It may possibly have given Cortázar some "figural" consolation to realize that his own life was coming to an end, as it happened, in 1984.

CHAPTER 7

The Final Round (and Much More)

Miscellaneous Creative Works

In a videotaped interview given late in his life Cortázar spoke of his "hatred of all that smacks of labeling or classification" (*Espejo de escritores*). It is therefore fitting and not suprising that quite a number of his publications cannot be easily pigeonholed according to customary generic categories. The uncomfortable way in which the indomitably eccentric texts of *Historias de cronopios y famas* were incorporated into the posthumous collection of Cortázar's short stories may be taken as a symptom of the problems one encounters when trying to categorize his works. Some of the most unclassifiable and most indescribable flaunt precisely those qualities: Cortázar was determined to poke his finger in the eye of convention and habit. In the present chapter I discuss many of these works, several of which have been dubbed "miscellanies" or "almanacs."

Historias de cronopios y famas (discussed in chapter 4) can be regarded as the first book really to challenge conventional ideas of genre. Together with *Rayuela,* it introduced a decade, the sixties, during which Cortázar was at his most iconoclastic; it was a decade that saw such unruly inventions as *Les Discours du Pince-Gueule, La vuelta al día en ochenta mundos,* and *Último round,* all of which are discussed below. Each of these works is a "picture book."

Painting, sculpture, and photography all play an increasingly visible role in works written after *Rayuela.* In a few cases Cortázar wrote texts for which illustrations were then made; in contrast, he wrote many more that derived from the contemplation of preexisting visual images. Generally speaking, of text that accompanies works of art one tends to expect description, exegesis, historical contextualization. What is striking in Cortázar's many pieces to accompany works of art is that there is virtually no description, no analysis of the works concerned, virtually no talk *about* the art. On those very rare occasions when his titles seem to encourage the assumption that he is going to launch into conventional art-historical analysis, he in fact introduces a bizarre twist, sometimes mocking both conventional analysis and the work that ostensibly is under scrutiny. Thus, in *Historias de cronopios y famas,* Titian's *Sacred and Profane Love* is said to be a "detestable" piece of work done by an incompetent, if not a pervert (*Cuentos completos,* 2:411). Faced with works of art, Cortázar is not given to attempts at formal description or to lyrical effusions. Instead, art serves as a springboard from which he launches in any number of directions, pursuing his own tastes and interests. The results of his contemplation, of his cohabitation (even quite literally) with artworks, are sometimes poetic, sometimes grounded very firmly in the mundane. Sometimes he gives us a verbal product that in some way is analogous to the visual one that served as inspiration. In no way did Cortázar underestimate or fail to give credit to the influence of visual art on his own work: on the contrary, he emphasized that artists helped him go in directions that otherwise he would never have explored (*Territorios*, 8). In a similarly grateful vein, when asked, as he was quite often, how far the surrealists had influenced him, he would readily acknowledge their part but add that the influence came primarily through painters rather than writers.

Les Discours du Pince-Gueule

Chronologically, the first book that brings together art and written text is *Les Discours du Pince-Gueule*. Not only was this the first such combination essayed by Cortázar, it was also the first of what would become many collaborative ventures with his friend Julio Silva. Moreover, in this case Julio Cortázar wrote, exceptionally, in French. *Les Discours* appeared in 1966, in a limited edition published in Paris. For the title, Cortázar created a neologism: he made the *pince-nez* slip down from the nose to the mouth (for which *gueule* is a vulgar slang word), and no doubt he also had in the back of his mind the term *pince-sans-rire*, meaning a person with a dry humor. In this way the title warns the reader against swallowing the Cartesian promise implied by the word *discours*. In Cortázar's little book the discourse is anything but reasoned. On the contrary, its inspiration probably comes from Edward Lear or Lewis Carroll; certainly the portmanteau word *pince-gueule* would have pleased Humpty Dumpty. Silva's whimsical lithographs only confirm the impression.

A few words in the opening piece of *Les Discours*, "On dessine une petite étoile" (A star is drawn), set a tone of unreality: "Here we are, having already fallen into the trap of another sleep in which one dreams that one has awakened in order to start writing" (1). Someone ought to tell the writer, says Cortázar, that he is part of the action. Drawing the star is the opening gesture, enough to allow the writing to take on a life of its own. A few pages after the ball has been set rolling in this way, a petrifying arrow shot into a cumulus cloud turns it into marble so that it destroys a town below (it will be shot again in a year's time, in *La vuelta al día en ochenta mundos*); a family engages in a breakfast conversation that might have come out of a work by Ionesco; a soup made with undervests is applied to a record of Karajan performing Sibelius; an exhausted mountaineer falls off the north face of Annapurna, unable to hold on any longer because the little boy who is following the account of the climb is such a slow reader; a car breaks down because it needs a cigarette. A section called "Valse viennoise à l'Opern Café" (A Viennese waltz at the Opern Café) consists of the free-flowing association of the visual impressions and the thoughts of someone who, one assumes, is sitting in the café near the Vienna State Opera; cars with evocative names lead to thoughts of cats, of rituals in Egypt, of a bloodbath in Korea that turns out to be on the big screen, and so on. In all, *Les Discours* has twelve such pieces, the last of which tells us that the *Pince-Gueule* the narrator has at home is a creature given to raising itself on its hindlegs and visiting a daily speech upon him. The narrator has realized that paying attention to the *Pince-Gueule* for twenty minutes is not enough to keep it satisfied; he is also expected to provide an immediate summary of the speech. This is impossible to do, because the speeches have no discernible logical structure: they tend to begin onomatopoe-ically, and they progress by sound associations and derivations. The failure of the narrator to provide adequate summaries makes the *Pince-Gueule* so angry that he sometimes goes to the wastepaper basket to sulk, looking vaguely like a sphinx. Because of his inability to provide the summary the narrator grows tense, and the whole thing culminates in mutual insults and tears. But then silence reigns once more, and the two of them are left eyeing each other from a respectable distance.

It is worth noting that Silva's lithographs for *Les Discours* were done to accompany the text, after it had been written. A decade later, in *Silvalandia,* the text followed the pictures. In this last case the centrality of Silva's contribution and the continuing influence of Lewis Carroll are both signaled by the book's title. Carroll's mark is also felt in the opening words, which invite the reader to look at the cover in a mirror, to cross the threshold into a new world of fantasy and fun. Each section of this book's thirty-odd pages comprises a color picture of fantastic creatures of a sort one finds in storybooks for children, accompanied by texts of uncertain humorous quality; perhaps their greater value is in demon-strating the reaches of Cortázar's imagination.

This process of image-then-text applied to virtually all the remaining col-laborative projects that Cortázar undertook with artists: he usually wrote as a response to their preexisting works of art. Approaching the task in this manner, with the art as his starting point, Cortázar was responding to what he called a "a wish to walk alongside friends who are painters, creators of images, and pho-tographers" (*Territorios,* 107). Indeed, by the seventies he was saying that he was writing because of the existence of their art, and pointing out that critics had paid a great deal of attention to literary influences upon him but not enough to a long list of artistic and musical ones.

La vuelta al día en ochenta mundos

The Silva-Cortázar collaboration had already taken a new turn just after *Les Discours du Pince-Gueule*. In the mid-sixties an enterprising editor for a Mexican publisher had asked Cortázar if he had a new book ready for publication, and since the answer was no, Silva suggested to Cortázar that he consider putting together a miscellany of pieces. What resulted turned out to be a significant development in Cortázar's output. The title of the finished product, *La vuelta al día en ochenta mundos* (Around the day in eighty worlds), pays obvious homage to Jules Verne, a fact soon confirmed by the appearance in its initial pages of illustrations of Passepartout and Phileas Fogg, followed by a photo of Verne himself. Other illustrations from Verne's books are scattered through the two volumes of *La vuelta al día en ochenta mundos,* but the book encompasses many other things besides. Among its other images, which range from medieval to modern, there are photos and drawings of cats, several insects, various contraptions (including plans for the "Rayuel-o-matic," a fantastic invention thought up and designed by Francisco Porrúa, who was the editorial director of the famous Buenos Aires publishing house Sudamericana). There are extravagant drawings by Julio Silva, reproductions of Delvaux (one of the painters Cortázar most admired), photos of murderers, writers, musicians, boxers, the Vietnam War, and even Queen Victoria. *La vuelta al día en ochenta mundos* is a highly personal book that reflects Cortázar's formative influences and contemporary interests.

There is a sense in which every creative work is autobiographical. In that light, what becomes interesting is how far writers hide behind their characters, what devices they employ to project an image of themselves. Cortázar was there by implication in his early works, but the masks became more and more transparent as his career progressed. Here in *La vuelta al día en ochenta mundos* we have the public man, writing openly as himself. Also significant is the fact that this is a very visual book; it is agreeable and surprising to leaf through (although in later editions, when it was broken into two volumes of smaller dimensions, that pleasure was considerably lessened).

It is in the nature of almanacs that one cannot summarize their contents. Instead, in the comments that follow I shall draw attention to some of the key components of *La vuelta al día en ochenta mundos*. Such as it is, the rationale for this book really appears at its end, in "Casilla de camaleón" (Chameleon's box). There, addressing himself to the unidentified lady reader who has been implied from the start of the book (a *"lector hembra"*?), Cortázar warns that she should not expect a great deal of coherence from his tour around the day. He goes on to tell of how, listening to another writer who was telling him how vital it was to have a clear-cut ideological message, his attention had wandered back

154

to the moment in the forties when he had shown the manuscript of his book on Keats to an indignant representative of the British Council in Buenos Aires. This anecdote sets the tone for what is to come: Cortázar's critique of rigidity and systematization. He now introduces the idea of the coleopteran, backed visually by a caricatured image of a stag beetle with a birdlike proboscis. Critics, reporters, researchers, he says, all have ideological or aesthetic agendas when dealing with (his) literature. Cortázar has his own ideas, too, but "it is unusual for him to have them systematically, for him to have become coleopterized to the point where he suppresses contradiction as the philosopher-coleopterans and the politician-coleopterans do, sacrificing or ignoring everything that has its origin beyond the span of their chitinous wings" (211).[1] The counterpart of the coleopteran is (in Cortázar's scheme of things) the chameleon, which is flexible and open to whatever presents itself. That kind of openness is what readers can expect to find in *La vuelta al día en ochenta mundos* (and for that matter in any book by a real "poet"), and they may love it or loathe it. Cortázar points out that the phrase "eighty worlds" is not to be taken literally: he is against the "bureaucrats of the spirit" who are inclined to think in terms of exact numbers and orderly progressions. A *cronopio* sees and thinks according to whichever "world" he happens to be in at the time, and so he may be self-contradictory. Spongelike, capable of osmosis, of changing sensibilities, the writer should be an "anarchist" standing against any imposed order. Cortázar then brings us back to John Keats, quoting from the Englishman's correspondence, from a letter in which Keats emphasized the dominance of the present moment and said that if a sparrow alighted on his windowsill, he would share its existence and peck along with it. The idea of the chameleon poet is also attributable to Keats, who said that such a poet delighted in things that exasperated philosophers. Cortázar goes on to predict that there will be criticism of the ludic spirit of *La vuelta al día en ochenta mundos*. He refers to the "commissars" (among whom he lists Plato) who for whatever reason seek to categorize, limit, or direct and who in fact oversimplify and petrify. The terms in which he expresses his admiration for Keats are revealing: he emphasizes the Englishman's "humanity," the absence of the "narcissistic confessionalism" found in the work of some other romantics, in short, his ethical integrity.[2] One is reminded of the fact that Cortázar also liked to call upon Hamlet's injunction "To thine own self be true." Read today, Cortázar seems overinsistent here, his arguments less necessary than they once were. There is little doubt that he was responding to the political pressures he was feeling at that time, now that he had become a public figure, and there is equally little doubt that in its day *La vuelta al día en ochenta mundos* was sufficiently revolutionary as a literary enterprise. Thirty years later it still reads as an innovative book.

Other Cortázar hobbyhorses also get an airing in *La vuelta al día en ochenta mundos.* The lack of naturalness among Argentine writers he construes as proof of underdevelopment (13): Argentine writers cannot put pen to paper without first donning a starched collar; they erect a "a wall of shame" around them and assume a hieratic attitude (34). They are given to using many words and saying very little (95). He acknowledges that, in reaction to this tendency, some new writers have taken to using the vernacular, but they have abused colloquial language, and the result is "writing worthy of a pizzeria." Cortázar says that historically writers in the River Plate region who have resisted the grandiloquence and high seriousness of the tradition have in general been marginalized, although they have displayed exactly the kind of qualities that are desirable in a writer: irony, understatement, and variety, such as are to be found in a Cervantes, a Sterne, a Macedonio, or a Marechal. Above all, Argentine writers tend to be humorless. Cortázar regards himself as fortunate in being a writer who does not feel obliged to be serious (14), despite the laments heard among the worthies of Buenos Aires when his *Historias de cronopios y famas* first made an appearance (34).

By way of proof of his liberty, Cortázar includes surplus material from *62: Modelo para armar*—a conversation between Calac and Polanco about what name to give a cat. Another amusing passage in *La vuelta al día en ochenta mundos* is supposedly written by a chicken. The piece mentioned above about the "Rayuel-o-matic" describes a machine with drawers that feed the chapters of the novel to readers in the right order; it has a special button dedicated to stopping the reading once the reader is trapped in the final loop; there is a luxury model that comes with its own bed, and rumor has it that there is also a built-in toaster. As part of his campaign against national seriousness, Cortázar advocates hanging a poster of Buster Keaton in every Argentine school and showing Keaton and Chaplin films on ceremonial holidays. Schoolteachers are also advised to recite "The Walrus and the Carpenter" to their classes. Further disparaging comments on the habits of Argentina's writers, readers, and educators are offered in "No hay peor sordo que el que" (There's no one more deaf than the person who).

In "Julios en acción" the people implied are Jules Verne, Jules Lafforgue, Julio Silva, and Julio Cortázar (with the assimilation, by happy coincidence, of *Juliet,* wife of a scientist whose report in a *July* issue of *Le Monde* is discussed in the piece). One of the things the four "Julios" are said to have in common is "a clear sense of the absurd that puts them in a better position, enables them to see more clearly than any certainty born of Kantian stock"; and Cortázar adds that "from an early age cronopios have a very constructive idea of the absurd" (18).

The author's musical enthusiasms are reflected in texts about Gardel, Thelonius Monk, and Louis Armstrong. In "Louis, enormísimo cronopio" (Louis, a tremendous cronopio) Armstrong is credited with being the first true cronopio, even though the piece under that title was written in response to a concert the musician gave in Paris in 1952, that is to say, about ten years before the "official" birth of the cronopios. "Para llegar a Lezama Lima" (An approach to Lezama Lima) is an appreciation of one of Cuba's greatest writers, who at that time was not well known outside the island. "El noble arte" is about boxing, describing how the sport first engaged the author's interest and giving details of a match that came to form the basis for his story "Torito" in *Final del juego.*

"Para una antropología de bolsillo" (Toward a pocket anthropology) is a fable about shallowness. Mere seeing (*ver*) is contrasted with looking (*mirar*); there are people in whose eyes everything becomes bland, as if they were fighting shy of what is difficult, unsettling, even painful. As I noted earlier (see pages 55–56), Cortázar quite often draws a contrast between these two Spanish verbs, assigning positive values such as honesty, candor, and intimacy to *mirar.* The imitative titles of "Del sentimiento de no estar del todo" (Concerning the sense of not quite being there) and "Del sentimiento de lo fantástico" (Concerning the sense of the fantastic) hint at their common relevance to Cortázar's poetics; both these important texts are dealt with in chapter 5. These are some of the texts that, together with a few poems and stories, some political material, and yet more besides make up the kaleidoscopic *La vuelta al día en ochenta mundos.*

Último round

Último round, a second miscellany, dating from two years later, had an even more original format, at least in its first edition. It was a two-tier book, its pages divided in such a manner that the top two-thirds constituted the "upper floor" and the lower third the "ground floor." Once again, the idea was Julio Silva's. The effect of dividing and binding separately these two floors is an obvious one: one has the freedom to bring about many different juxtapositions of material, and so the experience of reading is diversified.

The upstairs section contains the texts that Cortázar considered most important, and for its visual effects it relies heavily on photography, beginning with a photo of the author's face distorted by concentric circles. The upstairs images, however, are generally less fantastic than those of the ground floor (or those of *La vuelta al día en ochenta mundos*). One noteworthy feature of the ground-floor illustrations is the series of very simple but highly effective satirical cartoons by Jean-Michel Folon. Throughout *Último round* the sociopolitical content is appreciably stronger than it was in *La vuelta al día en ochenta mundos.*

The upper section contains a good deal of poetry and one or two short stories, including "Silvia." Two pieces that relate directly to Cortázar's writing are "Del cuento breve y sus alrededores" (On the short story and its environs), and "La muñeca rota" (The broken doll), which, as we saw in chapter 6, is helpful in understanding *62: Modelo para armar.* "Tu más profunda piel" (Your deepest skin) and the poem "Naufragios" (Shipwrecks) are frankly erotic; they are attempts to do what Cortázar advocates in "/que sepa abrir la puerta para ir a jugar." The latter, as the unusual form of its title exemplifies, is constructed as a series of sentences (or groups of sentences) that have truncated beginnings; as a result, the reader is obliged to guess the foregoing portions or live with the omissions. The text headed "/que sepa abrir la puerta para ir a jugar" (/should know how to open the door and go and play) is a convoluted exploration of the nature of eroticism in literature. Cortázar maintains that when dealing with the erotic, writers in Spanish have tended to resort to euphemisms or degenerate into pornography. What he advocates instead is the "deflowering" of the language without "raping and strangling" it; in other words, he favors a natural and unselfconscious representation of the role of eroticism in human behavior, which is something that he says is particularly hard for prose writers to achieve. He emphasizes that he is not advocating writing erotic literature as such, but only that things erotic, when they do crop up, should be portrayed in an honest and open manner, in language that is neither "hairy" nor "prudish." Cortázar's obsession with erotic liberation in the sense implied here is symptomatic of his wider commitment to struggling against the limitations and affectations of language (Oliveira's "bitches of words"); more than that, it stems from his profound and general commitment to honesty. "/que sepa abrir la puerta para ir a jugar" is framed by two quotations in French. The first, from Georges Bataille, states that eroticism can only be seen properly if the person doing the seeing is also the person seen; the second, from Jean Pierre Faye, points out that language masks one's vision, so that only by taking control of language can one see. The sequence of photos that accompanies "/que sepa abrir la puerta para ir a jugar" shifts from suggestive architectural shapes through pictures of a seductively attired female rump to a reproduction of one of Salvador Dalí's sexual fantasies.

Quite different is "Turismo aconsejable" (Advice for tourists), an extraordinarily descriptive piece of writing to have come from Cortázar's pen. It ironically contrasts self-accommodating tourism with the horrors of everyday life in Calcutta, which is referred to more than once as "picturesque." For further variety, "Descripción de un combate" (Account of a fight) is another account of a boxing match, couched in the style of a news report, and in "Noticias del mes de mayo" (May news) Cortázar reacts to a compilation of slogans and graffiti from the student uprisings of May 1968 in Paris.

On the ground floor a similar variety is apparent, Polanco puts in another brief appearance, and there is more poetry. On the political front "Mal de muchos . . ." (whose title is recognizable as the beginning of a Spanish proverb but refers more literally to "A widespread disease") reproduces an article from *Le Nouvel Obser-*

vateur about ways in which the United States infringes on the sovereignty of other countries. "Homenaje a una torre de fuego" (Homage to a tower of fire), which was originally written for the Uruguayan publication *Marcha,* is another tribute to the student uprisings of May 1968, a homage to Che Guevara, and a comment on the relevance of both to the future of Latin America. By way of contrast, the title of "El tesoro de la juventud" (The young person's treasury) is borrowed from a children's book that was widely read in Argentina, and the piece that Cortázar writes under that same title, with its accompanying drawings of various anti-quated modes of transport, is primarily an entertainment, a fairy-tale reverse history of transport technology that reaches its culminating point with the arrival of the pedestrian and the swimmer. In another erotic piece, "Ciclismo en Grignan" (Cycling in Grignan), the narrator finds himself in the town famous for being the home of Madame de Sévigné. He is sitting in a café and looking at three pubescent girls, one of whom is astride a bike; as she moves against the saddle an erotic fantasy develops in the mind of the voyeur. Then, back in Paris, someone lends him a copy of Georges Bataille's *Histoire de l'oeil,* and he fully appreciates a scene in it describing a girl astride a bike. There is also another important piece, "Cristal con una rosa dentro," that helps elucidate *62: Modelo para armar* (see my comments on page 114). Also to be found among the texts on the ground floor are "La protección inútil" (Useless protection), "Se dibuja una estrellita" (A star is drawn), "No, no y no," and "Desayuno" (Breakfast), all of which are translations of material that Cortázar had published in French a year or two earlier as part of *Les Discours du Pince-Gueule.*

After the first edition, *Último round* was repackaged into two volumes, a fate that had already befallen *La vuelta al día en ochenta mundos.* In the process the two-tier format of *Último round* was abandoned (engaging and innovative as an idea, but in practice very inconvenient to manipulate) and the texts were reshuffled, so that the volumes of the later editions do not correspond to the floors of the original. The newspaper-style layout of the covers was retained. Sadly, the paper was of poorer quality and consequently so too was the reproduction of the visual images. As far as I have been able to tell, only one short piece of text was sacrificed during the reorganization: a short quotation, in English, of some comments made by Miles Davis about John Coltrane's improvisational technique ("ground floor," 177, in the first edition).

Territorios

When an Italian publisher, Franco Maria Ricci, invited Cortázar to supply a text to accompany a luxurious volume of reproductions of some illustrations by the Austrian artist and visionary Aloys Zötl, Cortázar did so in the form of an extended informal address to Ricci. In the course of that address Cortázar let his thoughts range freely, led by Zötl's images; he talked about the circumstances in which he was writing, reminisced about his past, made a few political points, included cultural references drawn from a wide historical and geographical range, and ultimately said more about himself than about Zötl. The text duly appeared, translated into Italian, in *Il bestiario di Aloys Zötl* (1972). That same text would later find its way into *Territorios,* which was published in 1978.[3]

Territorios has a prologue titled "Explicaciones más bien confusas" (Somewhat confusing explanations) in which Calac and Polanco, the clowns from Cortázar's *62: Modelo para armar,* accuse the author of recycling material, of being up to his old tricks, and even of not asking for permission to reproduce the visual material included. The back cover is also humorous: it consists of an old photograph of Buffalo Bill and the Indian chiefs Sitting Bull and Crew Eagle, together with other people, two of whom have had their heads replaced by those of Julio Silva and Julio Cortázar, those legendary frontiersmen of the artistic. In other respects *Territorios* is largely a serious, contemplative, and poetic work (despite the fact that its author warns readers to watch out for stray toads). This book is defined and structured by its visual components: each "territory" is marked off by the work of an artist, and each such territory incorporates text provided by Cortázar. Some of the artists represented in *Territorios,* such as Antonio Saura and Jacobo Borges, are quite widely known, whereas others are best known because they were Cortázar's friends. (Here it is appropriate to note what may be considered a general weakness of the "miscellanies," their tendency to drop the names of Cortázar's personal acquaintances as if those people—and their work—were as familiar to the reader as to the writer. Tiresomely, it is sometimes as if he were addressing a privileged circle of the initiated; those outside that circle cannot always expect the names to ring bells. Until the reader is well into Cortázar's world and acquainted with his circle of friends, the texts can risk foundering in what seems like egocentrism or provincialism.)

Most of the artists included in *Territorios* are painters and sculptors, but there are a few photographers such as Sara Facio, Alicia D'Amico, and Frédéric Barzilay, and there is one stage performer, a striptease artist called Rita Renoir. The charge leveled by Calac and Polanco that several pieces included here have also made appearances elsewhere is perfectly justifiable; however, the intrusion of Calac and Polanco is, of course, Cortázar's form of acknowledgment that it is so. An example of a reappearing text is the short story that accompanies Borges's picture "Reunión con un círculo rojo" (Encounter with a red circle), which was included in a catalogue for an exhibition of the painter's work and also in *Alguien que anda por ahí.* The text for the Facio and D'Amico photographs is also in *Humanario,* and some poems in the Hugo Demarco section also appear in *Último round,* together with "País llamado Alechinsky" (A land called Alechinsky) and "Diálogo de las formas" (Dialogue of shapes). These repetitions do not mean that *Territorios* is lacking in interest. On the contrary, it is an aesthetically pleasing book, and many of its texts are inventive and revealing, such as "Las grandes transparencias" (Large-scale transparencies) and those that accompany the territory of Antonio Saura. The art reproductions in *Territorios* are mostly black and white, and the overall design is once again the work of Cortázar's close friend Julio Silva. The text that accompanies the territory of Silva himself is another that has migrated from a previous book: "Julios en acción" (Julios in action) had already appeared in Cortázar's first collage book, *La vuelta al día en ochenta mundos.*

Un elogio del tres

Another close friend with whom Cortázar worked was Luis Tomasello, whose art is also represented in *Territorios.* Their collaboration gave rise to the very brief *Un elogio del tres* (1980; In praise of three), of which only one hundred numbered copies were made; they were issued unbound and boxed, with the text in Spanish, French, and German. Tomasello's designs are exceedingly simple, consisting of groups of elongated rectangles in primary colors. As the text progresses, the colors, groupings, and configurations of the rectangles change. One gives way to three, and the final configuration places three rectangles in close approximation to one another, so that the eye links them, completing a suggested Y figure; in other words, three bars have been arranged in such a way as to suggest a total of three three-sided figures (triangles). This at least, is how one may interpret that configuration in the light of Cortázar's text. The poem is preceded by a quotation: "Con el número dos nace la pena" (The number two is the source of suffering). Its opening lines serve as a program for the poem as a whole: "Aquí del uno al dos / del dos al tres" (Here from one to two / from two to three). Another formal characteristic worth noting is that there are two stanzas in the poem that are striking because their structure (each has two lines of three words) mimics the theme of the text. Moreover, one of those lines ("fueron origen fueron") manages to achieve a similar end by using *three* words in all, *two* identical ones and *two* different ones.

The message of the poem is that "la humanidad nace del tres" (humankind is born of three) when "del dos al tres irrumpe el hombre" (man breaks away from two into three). Here the number two is associated with the Fall, with sin and guilt, and with duality. Out of the duality of Eden there comes joy. The true

161

angels are the rebels who construct a world of three "que es música y triángulo y escándalo" (which is music and triangle and outrage). They break free to dance their infinite triads in contrast to the "flawed statuesque perfection" of the echoless dialogue of two. All this would seem to be a cryptic, cabalistic piece of eccentricity, were it not recognizable as a succinct reexpression of so much that Cortázar has said elsewhere in his creative work. Consistently he has opposed opposition, opposed a dualistic worldview; he has resisted convention, advocating a joyous freedom.[4]

Monsieur Lautrec

Toulouse-Lautrec provided the inspiration for a collaboration with the cartoonist Hermenegildo Sabat, with whom Cortázar published *Monsieur Lautrec,* also in 1980. Here about twenty-five color plates are interleaved with small black-and-white cartoons, some of them quite crude, from which Lautrec emerges as a rather ridiculous and somewhat perverse voyeur. The visual material is followed by Cortázar's brief text, which is engagingly straightforward, though not related in any obvious way to the visual material that precedes it. Cortázar's inspirational starting point is a painting in the museum devoted exclusively to Toulouse-Lautrec that is located in the southern French town of Albi. The painting concerned is called *Le Salon de la rue des Moulins;* it portrays a woman seated on a sofa in the brothel where Lautrec spent much of his time. Unusually, Cortázar describes the canvas in some detail. He notes that the woman in it was called Mireille and that she was one of Lautrec's favorites, so much so that the painter came to an arrangement with the madam of the establishment, paying for Mireille to have whole days free to spend with him. In Lautrec's correspondence there is evidence that Mireille left for Buenos Aires, where French ladies of pleasure were highly valued. She was never to return. She became part of the exchange of flesh between the two countries, Argentina's contribution to France being in the form of baby beef. Lautrec had tried to dissuade Mireille from embarking on what he saw as a road to ruin, but she had been undeterred. Although Lautrec himself never traveled further abroad than England, Cortázar allows himself to speculate on what his experience might have been had he followed Mireille to Argentina.

Carlos Gardel, the most famous of tango performers, was born in the city of Toulouse, a town whose name offers a link with that of the painter; whether consciously or not, it seems likely that Cortázar had this constellation of factors in the back of his mind when writing about Lautrec, even though he offers no evidence that that was the case. In any event, it is the tango that provides the basis for the link he established between the painter and Argentina. A creolized "Mireya" appears in the lyrics of a famous tango, and Cortázar chooses to imagine that it refers to the very Mireille who left Lautrec behind. Cortázar first uses this device to compare the expectations and realities of life in both places; initially we seem to be reading a surprisingly engaging piece of social history. The text is called a "gotan" (a word derived from the transposition of the syllables of "tango," as happens in *lunfardo,* the slang of Buenos Aires), and as the text progresses, further homage is paid to tango, with several long quotations of lyrics. From all of this there emerges a nostalgic account of the relationship between the two cultures, of the privileged status accorded to things French in Argentina, and finally some thoughts on the present-day relationship between the two.

Eyed by suspicious Parisians who are not used to men whistling, Cortázar wanders down the Boulevard de Sébastopol whistling tangos that remind him—and he puts this in language worthy of a tango—of a country he can no longer visit, "walled-in at one end of the skein, within one of the huge mirrors that has been the scene of the toing and froing of my heart" (there are no page numbers). He observes that times have changed; now the Argentines settled in Paris are no longer carefree seekers of highlife. This is the understated way in which Cortázar makes his political point about exile, and he is careful to bring Lautrec back into the picture before ending on a rueful note.[5]

Photographic Works

Cortázar also wrote for several books of photographic images. *Humanario* (1976) is a collection of photographs of mental patients in Buenos Aires, taken by Sara Facio and Alicia d'Amico. (These well-known photographers also published a collection of their photos of famous writers, including Cortázar among them.) *Buenos Aires, Buenos Aires* (1968) was also a collaboration with Facio and d'Amico, and 1981 saw a book devoted to Paris, the photographer in this case being Alecio d'Andrade (*París: Ritmos de una ciudad*). *Prosa del observatorio* (1972) has photos taken by Cortázar himself and subsequently enhanced by Antonio Gálvez, and *Alto el Perú* (1984) has text accompanying photos taken by Manja Offerhaus, a friend since the days when both worked as translators for UNESCO. I shall confine my comments to the last two books.

Only fifty-eight pages long, *Alto el Perú* begins with Cortázar meditating on writing, on the incapacity of words to stand in place of complex visual perceptions. He then slides into an "interpretation" of the Offerhaus photos, which he has before him, in Paris. The two realities, Paris and the altiplano, become interlaced: he sees the names of Purcell and Stan Getz, reads the title of a piece of music at the same time as he sees the image of a pig rooting around in a town, an image of corncobs, an image of the package a woman is holding, containing something he cannot identify, although he is sure that it has nothing to do with Purcell's sonatas. Revealing how sensitive to sociopolitical issues he has become in his later years, he wonders, "How can one pass from the pig to Purcell without at least asking oneself deep down whether one has the right to do so?" (39). And so the text of this book becomes a meditation not on writing but on poverty, on the relationship of the artist's conscience to poverty. One part that is especially memorable stems from a fine photo of a young mother in a train, who has fallen asleep, bare-breasted, while feeding her infant.

Prosa del observatorio is one of Cortázar's most difficult texts, a very daunting one for the uninitiated reader. It offers no contextual orientation until its closing pages, and its arcane opening is calculated to project the reader into a realm that is free of the usual parameters of time and space. In a kind of parody of the traditional "Once upon a time" formula, eschewing the verbal forms that might allow a familiar and reassuring frame of reference, Cortázar summons "esa hora orificio" (7; that orifice hour), a time that frees one from a world in which things have their appointed time and place. Other images converge "without warning, without unnecessary signs of transition"—a hotel room, a pair of lovers taking a siesta, a light shining under a door, a café in the *Quartier Latin*, and so forth—as one approaches a world where things are not as expected, encountering "a breach in continuity" (9). Experienced readers will recognize in all this a Cortázar trope: the evocation of the onset of an *état second*, the moment of release into another dimension that may occur, for example, as one (or at least, as Cortázar) is having a shower, walking down the street, listening to music, or riding the *métro*. It is a prelude to creativity and fresh perception.

Next to make their way into the picture are two disparate elements around which the narrative is constructed, on the one hand the Atlantic eel described in scientific studies of its life cycle, and on the other the marble structures of the observatory built in Jaipur by an eighteenth-century Indian sultan, Jai Singh, described verbally and through Cortázar's photos. Contrary to all logic, these images rub shoulders, as if in a dream, with others of Paris at night. Like the fish, who do not know why they are migrating, the reader must go with the flow.

The marble edifices of the observatory are both fantastic and scientific enterprises. Cortázar's photos perambulate through them, inviting us to see them as works of art. In the other narrative, the verbal one, he introduces us to the findings of two French scientists who are authorities on the habits of eels. Solidly respectable though their work is, its aims are not Cortázar's, who views the scientific approach as blinkered and who, though talking about eels, is really concerned with mankind, with "something that comes from music, from amorous engagement and the changing seasons, something that analogy is feeling for in the sponge, in breathing and heartbeats, that is stammering about the way toward a new understanding, in a vocabulary that can't be tabulated" (49).

He is searching for an understanding that is more comprehensive than the scientific. Although he does not totally reject scientific method, he does seem to attribute some teleological underpinnings to it: "Que Dama Ciencia en su jardín pasee, cante y borde, bella es su figura, y necesaria su rueca teleguiada" (55; Let Lady Science walk, sing, and embroider in her garden, for beautiful is her countenance and necessary her teleguided distaff). Lady Science is later characterized as a pediatrician for adults, who swaddles them, limits their vision and constrains their sexual inclinations, saves them from being dreamers, and teaches them to see things in terms of numbers. For all his acerbic irony Cortázar is merely advocating a more open approach to knowledge. He foresees no conclusion, only a continuing utopian quest.

The band of migrating eels suggests a Moebius strip, endlessly curling back upon itself, with no "right" and "wrong" side. There is a political point implied here, too: there is to be a "revolution" from inside out and from outside in. As the text draws to its close, Hölderlin and Marx are said to complement and need each other. Man is "víspera de sí mismo" (69; on the verge of himself); Cortázar's new man will be one who "is not content with the everyday self, with being classified as a worker or thinker . . . who does not settle for the revised present that some party or bibliography promises is the future." "Through openness," he writes, "we shall put an end to man's imprisonment" (70–71). Stepping back a moment, Cortázar assures us that his is a "cold delirium" (73), that he is indeed a romantic, but a hardheaded one.

And what has Jai Singh's observatory to do with all this? He was a stargazer in both senses. According to Cortázar, though rightly described in the guidebooks as a collection of structures dedicated to astronomical observation, the observatory also bears witness to the dreams of a man who questioned givens, resisted the forces of fate and tradition, saw himself as part of the picture; his astronomy was an astronomy of the image, "a science of the total image" (77), his approach almost mystic.

Finally, a few comments about the style of *Prosa del observatorio*. The title is richly ambiguous. This prose is often highly poetic, and hardly prosaic in the way it slides from one stylistic register to another. It exploits scientific, critical, poetic, and political discourse; it is another Moebius strip in which words, not fish, flow. Another ambiguity surrounds the innocent-looking word "del"; because of it, the title could be paraphrased in a number of ways: as "Prose about the observatory," "Prose from the observatory" (i.e., inspired by, arising from, or even written in), "Observatory prose" (alluding to the use of the images as narrative), or "The prose of the observatory" (ironically suggesting its evocative, poetic quality). There is also possibly some exploitation of the two meanings of "observe": watch, contemplate on the one hand, and heed, respect on the other.

Un tal Lucas

This book, published in 1979, is in very marked contrast. Thematically, it is a kind of self-exposé, the amusements, foibles, and worries revealed in it being those of Cortázar himself. As to style, *Un tal Lucas* (*A Certain Lucas*) is a hybrid born of *Historias de cronopios y famas* and the miscellanies. The book is made up entirely of short, independent prose passages, which cohere only by virtue of their shared relevance to the central personage: Lucas/Cortázar. There are three parts, the first and the last consisting of pieces whose titles refer directly to Lucas, while the second is more free-ranging; this second part is on the whole darker, more sinister. In general, in *Un tal Lucas* Cortázar is bearing his soul, but above all he is deploying his armory of humor.

In "Lucas, sus clases de español" (Lucas and his Spanish classes), Lucas is told by the director of the Berlitz School where he teaches to avoid Argentine Spanish and to keep to useful, Castilian language. Lucas therefore gives his class a passage about a bullfight, taken from Spain's major newspaper, *El País*. However, one soon sees that this passage is written in a preposterous style and full of abstruse vocabulary that is barely comprehensible to all but the cognoscenti; while the students are trying fruitlessly to work out its meaning with the aid of their dictionaries, Lucas stares out of the window. By the time the director returns, most of the students have left in frustration, but there remains one earnest fellow who mistakenly thinks he might have spotted an allusion to a famous Spanish poet. On hearing this, the director congratulates Lucas for encouraging appreciation of the Spanish masters, but advises him to begin with something more modern and everyday, like a passage about a bullfight.

"Texturologías" ("Texturologies") is a parody of the posturing of critics, whose political agendas and personal rivalries so color their comments. Predictably, as one follows the critical exchanges, the text that is supposed to be under discussion is submerged, though it makes a triumphally ridiculous return at the end. The American critic is attacked by the Russian, who is attacked by the English critic, who is attacked by the French. This last is one Gérard Depardiable (an amalgam of the name of a real critical guru, Gérard Genette, and a demonized version of that of Gérard Depardieu, the film star). Depardiable writes in a journal called *Quel Sel* (a name that obviously pokes fun at *Tel Quel,* a real-life vehicle for some of the most obscurantist of critics). For its part, the title "Texturologías" hints at Roland Barthes's *Mythologies,* and the book that the critics are ostensibly commenting upon is a collection of poetry called "Jarabe de pato" (Duck syrup), which loosely suggests the Marx brothers' *Duck Soup.* Perhaps, too, there is a point being made about cultural dependence, because the Mexican critic is very much in thrall to the French one.

166

"Observaciones ferroviarias" ("Railway Observations") and "Familias" consist of absurd conversations starring Señora Cinamomo, who also makes appearances in other Cortázar books.[6] "Nadando en la piscina de gofio" ("Swimming in a Pool of Chickpea Mush") is an entertaining fantasy about the consequences of swimming in a murky pool of porridge made with chickpea flour (Argentine children in Cortázar's day would buy packets of the flour, sweetened with sugar). On a more personal front, "Lucas, sus pudores" ("Lucas Ashamed") describes the acute embarrassment that Lucas feels when he is in the bathroom and the noise of his bodily functions betrays him by interrupting the intellectual discussions of those in an adjacent living room. All things considered, Lucas is a person who is rather given to mishaps. For example, in "Lucas, sus compras" ("Lucas Goes Shopping") he finds that he has run out of matches, goes out to buy some, gets caught up in all manner of situations involving other people's problems, and finally, lost on the wrong side of town, is approached by an old lady asking for a match.

But not all is humor in *A Certain Lucas*. "Un pequeño paraíso" ("A Tiny Paradise") is a political fable about a (possibly African) country whose corrupt leaders milk the populace dry but deceive them into thinking they are happy with their lot. "Nos podría pasar, me crea" ("It Could Happen to Us, Believe You Me") is about the control of information. "Lucas, sus discusiones partidarias" (Lucas and partisan discussions) is about pressures on him to write accessibly. Armed with a poem, Lucas tries to defend his (Cortázar's) by now well-known views, and the opposing political hacks conclude that he is mad and propose that he be defenestrated (could this be a reference to Oliveira on his ledge?). Several pieces in *Un tal Lucas* are exercises in experimental writing or in some way thematize the subject of writing. For example, in "Diálogo de ruptura" ("Breaking-up Dialogue") every sentence is broken off, but this is only a formal way of pointing to the fact that the dialogue is between a couple who are breaking up. "Maneras de estar preso" ("Ways of Being Captive") and "La dirección de la mirada" (The Way to Look) are both metafictional, the latter being dedicated, for good measure, to John Barth. "Lucas, sus sonetos" (Lucas and His Sonnets) is a lighthearted account of how the "Zipper Sonnet" came to be written. This, of course, is a palindromic poem, one that can run down or up; Cortázar includes a Portuguese translation of it, done by the Brazilian poet Haroldo de Campos. There follows a tongue-in-cheek critique of the sonnet. The piece ends on an ironic note, with Lucas dreaming of a future Zipper Sonnet whose two readings would be perfectly contradictory of one another, but would suggest a third way of reading; however, he admits that the only evidence of progress so far toward this goal is a full ashtray, a cluster of empty glasses, and an overflowing wastepaper basket.

To conclude this selective summary of *Un tal Lucas,* I will mention two related pieces titled "Lucas, sus hospitales" ("Lucas and Hospitals"). The first, "Lucas, sus hospitales I," is a playful piece of nonsense. When he finds himself a patient in a luxury clinic, where the customer is always right (unless he happens to have liver disease and is demanding a bottle of gin), Lucas takes advantage to ask if he can have a flower in his room; then he asks for some water to keep it in; then a special table so that it can be admired at the foot of his bed; then some armchairs so that his visitors can look at it in comfort; then a tablecloth and a couple of bottles of whisky (and bottles of sodawater and some nice cut-glass goblets, plus some ice). Thinking that the flower is getting lost among all these things, Lucas now requests an armoire so that his clothing can be put away and the flower can take its rightful place on top. When the exhausted nurses have done all this and finally departed, Lucas gets out of bed and throws the flower out of the window on the grounds that he doesn't really like that sort of flower anyway. The tone of the other hospital piece, "Lucas, sus hospitales II," is in great contrast to this. Now it is not Lucas but his companion Sandra (no doubt a stand-in for Carol Dunlop) who is in hospital; the piece emphasizes the feeling of panic and desperation that overcomes him as he tries to be supportive. The shift in tone between these two hospital pieces, the fact that both imply the illnesses that would mean the end for Cortázar and his companion, symptomize the underlying seriousness of this book. Despite its general playfulness, *Un tal Lucas* also conveys a sense of nostalgia and an awareness of the approach of death. In fact, it turned out to be the last truly funny book to come from Cortázar.

Los autonautas de la cosmopista

When Cortázar was sixty-nine years old, he and Carol Dunlop conceived a bizarre expedition down the French *autoroute* running from Paris to Marseille. They drove down the motorway in their aging Volkswagen camper and wrote about the experience in a style that parodies the chronicles of history's great explorers. A few self-imposed rules applied to these successors of Magellan and Marco Polo: they were to stop at every designated parking area, whatever its size and regardless of whether it offered any facilities, lunching in the first they came across each day and spending the night in the second. Since there were sixty-five such stopping places on the southbound route, the journey took just over a month. They agreed that they should not allow themselves to leave the motorway at any time during the trip, except to enter the parking areas, but they were permitted to take advantage of any facilities they came across in them. Since the capacity of the vehicle was not sufficient for the two adventurers to be able to stock provisions for the whole trip, and bearing in mind the risk of falling victims to scurvy if they were not properly nourished, it was agreed that two friendly couples would bring them supplies at ten-day intervals. In practice, one or two other friends came to visit them during the trip, providing some relief from the tedium, but in general few people were aware of Julio and Carol's adventure until it was over. At that point, several people asked them what underlying purpose they had had in undertaking the journey, to which they replied that there had been none.

The "expedition" is chronicled in a book called *Los autonautas de la cosmopista* (The autonauts of the cosmoroute). This book opens with a dedication to an eccentric Englishman who in the eighteenth century marched backwards from London to Edinburgh, singing Anabaptist hymns. There is also a reprint of a polite letter to the French minister of transport, in which Cortázar reminds him that some time previously he had given permission for said ministry to use his story "La autopista del sur" in one of its official publications. Cortázar goes on to ask if, in a similar spirit of cooperation, they would grant a waiver of a regulation specifying that no one should spend more than two consecutive days on an *autoroute*. That letter went unanswered, whereupon the undaunted and intrepid explorers concluded that silence signified assent.

The book is illustrated with drawings done by their "cartographer," Carol Dunlop's teenage son, some time after the trip was over, and by a large number of photographs taken by the two explorers during it. A few of these photographs are of passing interest. The texts, written to a demanding daily schedule, range over the usual subjects—music, politics, literature—and many others besides, including descriptions of the places and people encountered along the way, food consumed, as well as a daily log of progress. Some of the stopping places were as little as five minutes apart. At the end of the expedition, as they leave the motorway, there is a description of the emotions that are commonplace among people who have traveled together over a lengthy period in isolation from the wider world: disorientation mingled with sadness.

In all, one takes a certain vicarious pleasure in reading about two such happy people sharing an experience that is more meaningful to them than to anyone else. One of the entries begins: "Bored with parking places? To us they seem ever more varied, like microcosms" (252). The problem, however, is that the reader cannot really share their enamored perspective on it all. *Los autonautas* has some nostalgic value for former owners of Volkswagen campers, but it is most significant as testimony to the continuing eccentric playfulness of Cortázar and his new wife, to whom he was so devoted. In a moving postscript, he tells the reader how he was obliged to put the finishing touches on the book by himself; not long after their return to Paris, Carol had finally succumbed to leukemia.[7]

Poetry

Finally, there is the poetry. After the sonnets of Julio Denis, so heavily influenced by Mallarmé, after the heavily poetic *Los reyes* with which Cortázar began to publish under his real name, poetry as such slipped out of the picture. Poetic qualities were appreciable at certain points in the stories, and Cortázar spoke often of the poetic as a general characteristic of creative writing, as if intent on denying distinctions between genres. In the late sixties, conventionally recognizable poetic works reappear in the unconventional context of the miscellanies, and there they are presented in a way that undercuts the traditional editorial packaging of poetry. This was done partly because Cortázar believed that the declining interest in poetry among readers of the new age was attributable to the traditional style in which it had been published.

All along, Cortázar had continued to write poetry, and he was always an avid reader of poetry, but he had not thought of publishing much of his own, among other reasons because he felt that it was too personal. Two Spanish friends, José Agustín Goytisolo and Joaquín Marco, finally persuaded Cortázar to let them publish what, in 1971, became *Pameos y meopas*. This collection spans poems written between the mid-forties and the late sixties. Its title, a play on the word "poemas" (poems), coupled with the jokey prologue that Cortázar wrote for this anthology, strike one as self-deprecating, almost embarrassed. In that prologue Cortázar tells us that the passing of his youth also marked the passing of a sense of respect for poetry that had been inculcated in him by bourgeois humanism. As time had gone by, such values had inevitably given way to new ones: "Nowadays I believe that the best poetry does not necessarily come along in the genre's traditional vehicles, among other reasons because genres no longer exist (9)."[8] The new vehicles included forms such as popular song and graffiti. Alongside literary figures such as Octavio Paz and Carlos Drummond de Andrade, the new poets Cortázar had in mind included people like Bob Dylan and Atahualpa Yupanqui. The new generation had a different vision of mankind and of history, a new way of expressing itself, one that those ensconced in their rocking chairs might find hard to countenance. Here, then, writing his prologue on the threshold of the seventies, Cortázar is insisting on the post-Cuban, post-1968 sociopolitical dimension of his worldview and signaling to the reader that the poems in the anthology are going to reflect the changes that have been wrought in him over the years.

The poems on *Pameos y meopas* are grouped into six sections and are not ordered according to strict chronology of composition. Some were written in Europe, some in Argentina, some in Africa, India, and Cuba. In a section headed "Larga distancia" (Long distance), consisting of poems written in Paris in the early fifties, when the author had recently taken up residence in that city, there is a strong sense of nostalgia, of longing for the absent loved one, for the country left behind. The poems are generally brief, penetrable, and appealing. In "After Such Pleasures" (many of the poems have titles in English) the "I" of the poet seems to express regret at having indulged in an amorous adventure that relegates a (possibly only metaphorical) lover in the other place to the past; but there is also a bittersweet longing for that lost past, and the innocence that went with it: "olvidada pureza, cómo quisiera rescatar / ese dolor de Buenos Aires" (forgotten purity, how I wish I could recapture / that pain of Buenos Aires) (18). In "El niño bueno" (The good child) the poet is a lover and yet still a child toeing the conventional line; he is too inhibited to defy the watching gendarmes and nannies in the park, jump into a fountain, and present his lover with a goldfish. One is reminded of those short stories in which adolescents try to break away from apron strings, or well-bred middle-class Argentines make transitions into bohemia ("El otro cielo" is the prime example).

Other poems betray the influence of the Spanish poet Pedro Salinas (who is credited in the introduction as a formative influence, along with Keats, Hölderlin, Leopardi, Darío, and, of course, Mallarmé). In general, the lover is seen as an ally in the quest for something new and extreme. In "Encargo" (Charge) the poet writes:

Te pido la cruel ceremonia del tajo,
Lo que nadie te pide: las espinas
Hasta el hueso. Arráncame esta cara infame,
Oblígame a gritar al fin mi verdadero nombre.

I ask of you the cruel ceremony of the cut,
that which no one asks of you: thorns
even to the bone. Tear from me this infamous face,
make me cry out at last my true name.
(25)

In a section titled "Razones de cólera" (Reasons for anger) there are several poems that are directed against complacency, in particular among Argentines. In "1950, Año del Libertador, etc." (1950, Year of the Liberator, etc.), building on a line from a tango lyric, Cortázar calls on Argentines to bewail the self-satisfaction, the mediocrity, the unchallenging predictability of their daily lives. In "Aire del Sur" (Air of the south) he paints a picture of a pampas dweller cowed before the wind, stoically drinking mate, resigned to the whims of fate. That person's existence is described as grayish brown, and his only vision of the stars is said to come via a reflection in a well. "Las tejedoras" (Weaving women) (34), a poem

171

that I have mentioned previously, is perhaps the most important one Cortázar ever wrote; it evokes sinister images of ubiquitous women, "pálidas babosas escondidas del sol" (pale slugs hidden from the sun), covered in fluff ("pelusas," a frequent image in Cortázar), inexorably weaving the stultifying fabric of life. They are the "hacendosas mujeres de los hogares nacionales" (the industrious women of our nation's households). In that poem "our voice," a symbol of individual existence, constitutes the skein from which love, the spider, is weaving the colorless fabric of death. The poem ends with a transfer to another of Cortázar's obsessive images, that of the autonomous, threatening hand. The weavers rise in silence, their hands take over, invading their whole bodies, they become manual equivalents of centipedes silently carrying out their work against "an intolerable silence of tangos and discourse." This poem, which reappears in other books, seems to encapsulate many of Cortázar's themes: his ambivalence toward women (figures of fear and power, but also of love), his sense that the expectations and comforts of normal life are seductive but militate against change, against the discovery of a truer self, his sense of superior controlling forces at work, and all this in relation to an Argentina that is superficial and complacent.

Some other poems of the fifties are more translucent, less given to arcane imagery. "Por tarjeta" (By postcard) alludes to a young man who has abandoned his known habits and his maternal home, "Sarao" (Soirée), to received bourgeois social values. The poems in the section "Preludios y sonetos" (Preludes and sonnets), as its title implies, are structurally tighter and written in clear homage to traditional forms and to poets of bygone days. There are nods in the direction of the Golden Age poets Garcilaso de la Vega and Góngora, and in the direction of the modern Spanish poet Pedro Salinas. There is also an obvious allusion to the musical properties of poetry. As for the sonnet itself, this is a form which Cortázar enjoyed using throughout his career, a fact that he acknowledges in "Lucas, sus sonetos" (*Un tal Lucas,* 187).

Several poems draw on mythology, as did the author's prose during the fifties and sixties. Some are responses to visits to places such as Italy and India. In general, one may say that Cortázar's poetry is characterized by a strong sense of euphony, that it exploits striking imagery and metaphor (rather than simile), that it is heavily symbolic, sometimes very erudite, and can be cryptic. Yet there is perhaps evidence in "El poeta," a poem dating from sometime between 1944 and 1957, that Cortázar was even then aware of the risks of his detached aestheticism, or at least that he felt a need to defend his independence:

Yo no estoy lejos de la calle
Porque abra arriba mi balcón,
ni lejos del cantar mi voz

porque en el coro usual no cante.
I am not far from the street
just because my balcony looks down onto it,
nor is my voice far from the song
simply because I do not sing in the usual chorus.

(49)

As the years pass, a careful, somewhat sanitized aesthetic style gives way to a more carefree and linguistically iconoclastic one. Increasingly, Cortázar delights in juxtaposing the mundane and colloquial with the high-flown, but always one senses and shares the pleasure he finds in sound and form. His poetry is not always easy, however.

With his death approaching, Cortázar completed and delivered another anthology to his publisher, *Salvo el crepúsculo* (Save twilight). The title is taken from a poem by Bashō: "Este camino / ya nadie lo recorre / salvo el crepúsculo" (This way / is no longer trodden by anyone / save twilight) (179). Fragments from many other poets are included in Cortázar's book, which brings together most of the poems of *Pameos y meopas* with others written in later years and intercalates prose passages in which the Cortázar of the early eighties reflects on his life, past and present, and on the poetry itself. Early in the book he quotes some words of Marguerite Yourcenar's, which may be understood as alluding to the unusual work that Cortázar has produced, but also serve as his epitaph for himself as a writer: "No doubt he had a fever. But perhaps fever allows one to see and understand what one would otherwise not see and not understand" (15).

In the opening pages of *Salvo el crepúsculo* Cortázar explains that his is to be an unmethodical discourse, that there is no real chronology, and that the reader (like readers of *Rayuela*) can dip into the collection as he or she wishes. The comparison with *Rayuela* is mine, not Cortázar's, and I believe that it extends beyond the invitation to the reader to trace his own path through the book. For Cortázar is providing a context, adducing historical, biographical, social, and cultural factors that redefine the poetry, in a sense prescribe how it should be read. He asserts that he is suspicious of the autobiographical and of anthologies, describing these as two of Cerberus's heads, but adds that the third, caution, is the one that must be overcome. Slowly making his way into the book, shuffling and reshuffling material, he begins to enjoy himself and at least feels reassured that it is not too serious an undertaking. Calac and Polanco, Cortázar's regular sparring partners, again reappear as a means of self-criticism.

Among the new poems that are included are some of the tango lyrics that Cortázar wrote for music by Edgardo Cantón (which were recorded on a disk called *Les Trottoirs de Buenos Aires*). "Veredas de Buenos Aires" (The sidewalks of Buenos Aires) (72) is autobiographical, speaking of a child drawing hop-scotch patterns on pavements that later saw him wandering around trying to catch the attention of girls; in time it fell to him to travel far away, but the affection for the sidewalks remained with him, the memory of them like "the faithful caress of [his] homeland."

In one of the prose commentaries, Cortázar says that he can safely date his work simply by looking at the vocabulary used, whereas his moods and themes have hardly changed; in those he is still "romántico/sensiblero/cursi (todo esto sin exagerar, che)" (117; romantic/sentimental/vulgar [there's no exaggeration in all this, you know]). The greater the distance between the verbal construct and the social construct, the more time has passed. Nowadays (the early eighties) he is not exactly seeking out the concrete in the manner of New York poets, but things concrete are seeking him out. Nostalgia for times past, however, leads him to close the relevant section of *Salvo el crepúsculo* with a Petrarcan sonnet from the forties, a time when abstraction and form were enough to satisfy him.

This book, really another collage rather than an anthology of poetry, has no visual component beyond the changing typeface and the varying disposition of text on its pages, but it does vary greatly in style. The poems are offered unamended, though occasionally with glosses. As usual, a word is put in for practitioners of the playful, such as Macedonio Fernández and Alfred Jarry. P. G. Wodehouse is quoted at one point. But so too are extracts from some quite cerebral and meta-physical poets. There are many poems in which love is the main theme, including several dedicated to "Cris" (no doubt the Uruguayan writer Cristina Peri Rossi, a dear friend of Cortázar, but of a different sexual persuasion). Elsewhere, erotic poetry is represented, for example by "Viaje infinito" (Endless journey) (136).

The point is reached where Polanco grumbles that electronic games are more fun than Cortázar's book. When the author tries to defend his approach, Polanco retorts that he could do a better cut-and-paste job himself, whereupon Calac points out that while that may be so, Polanco's version would not get into print. Cortázar seems to be aware, then, that it is his privileged position as a famous writer that is allowing him to indulge himself. Making a familiar case, he says that when all is said and done, he has only been the first to cast the dice, that he is the first reader of a sequence that is only one of many possible sequences.

The long sectional poem arising from his 1959 visit to Greece (169–177) is in a combination of English, French, and Spanish, as its trilingually configured title indicates:

<pre>
      CE
GRE CIA 59
     ECE
</pre>

The prose passage that precedes this poem describes Cortázar's early fascination with the classical world and its mythology and the influence upon him of one of his teachers, Arturo Marasso. He suggests that the trilingualism of the poem reflects his rejection of the idealized view of the classical world; that certainly is one's impression as the poem proceeds to create a picture of a Greece under assault by tourists and the associated trappings. Similar sentiments are expressed in "Las ruinas de Knossos" (The ruins of Knossos) (342). In the light of these poems, one may recall a comment in the story "La isla a mediodía," made by the radio officer to Marini as the latter dreams about visiting his utopian island: "Get a move on if you want to go there, the hordes will be there any moment, Genghis Cook's ready to pounce" (*Cuentos completos,* 2:565). That story must have been written in the wake of the poems. But for Cortázar the disenchantment was not simply with the effects of tourism; his whole worldview was changing. In the trilingual poem three jets fly over the islands, carrying out a reconnaissance mission that concludes that there are no longer any gods.

Dipping once more into the world of the forties and fifties, the author recounts how he returned by boat from his first visit to Europe and felt that he had to leave Buenos Aires for good. The prose piece "La madre" (The mother) (329–30) on one level evokes the conflicting sentiments of a son who feels that he has no option but to strike out on his own and assert his difference, but on another level it speaks of the alienated patriot, implied in the words of Apollinaire that are quoted in *Rayuela* at the start of the section "Del lado de acá" (the "Argentine" one), to the effect that one has to travel afar, but always loving one's home. Ruefully, Cortázar closes the book with these words: "Desde luego, como Orfeo, tantas veces habría de mirar hacia atrás y pagar el precio. Lo sigo pagando hoy; sigo y seguiré mirándote, Eurídice Argentina" (Of course, like Orpheus, I was to look back many times and pay the price. I am still paying it to this day; I still, I will always, look at you, Argentina, Eurydice) (345). Cortázar could, by his own admission, be rather sentimental.

Although nostalgia is the dominant tone of *Salvo el crepúsculo,* some of its poems dating from the later years, as one might expect, deal with sociopolitical concerns and the defense of freedom of artistic imagination. In all, *Salvo el crepúsculo* is, to use the author's own description, "a home-made maelstrom in which the past and the present slip through the funnel and bump into each other" (343). It is a work that makes engaging reading for those familiar with the author's work, but one likely to puzzle those who are not.

CHAPTER 8

Down, but Not Out

Posthumous Publications

El examen

At the time of his death, Cortázar had been preparing for publication a novel that he had finished three and a half decades previously: *El examen.* He had completed it in 1950, on the eve of his departure for Europe, and it was published in 1986, two years after he died. More than a decade since its publication it remains a surprisingly underexplored work. Certainly the vogue for Cortázar criticism waned somewhat in the eighties, and whatever intrinsic value *El examen* has clearly pales in the light of works published previously, but it remains an interesting novel because in embryonic form it contains a number of the elements, both thematic and formal, that are observable in works that Cortázar composed later. Moreover, seen in a biographical and historical light, *El examen* can be viewed as a product of an era that was unsettling for the author personally and for his country.

The referents of the novel's title are at least three: an examination that some of the characters in it are due to take in their college, an examination—albeit not a very orderly one—of the meaning of life, and an examination of Argentina in general, and of Buenos Aires in particular. That the setting is Buenos Aires is beyond doubt, for it is proved by numerous references to streets, cafés, and other public places and by the attitudes and language of that city's inhabitants. That the novel speaks of the era of Perón is equally certain, for beyond the dates of composition of *El examen* we have inescapable evidence within it: behavior, events, and an atmosphere that occasionally make explicit references to the sociopolitical climate but are more often allusive (yet no less clearly relevant).

Here, masked behind the characters of the novel, especially behind Juan and Andrés (both character names that Cortázar used to hide behind in other novels) is the man who had just resigned his teaching post at the Universidad de Cuyo and wished to escape before any more harassment was visited upon him. Here is the Cortázar who was on the verge of spending the rest of his life in voluntary exile and embarking on a difficult relationship with his home country, a relationship involving both affection and rejection. By the mid-sixties, after fifteen years as an exile, Cortázar was confessing that his return visits had been like a nightmare in which attraction and repulsion both had a role; he said that, on returning to Argentina, he felt like a ghost among the living, or, worse still, like a living being among ghosts.[1] It is probably fair to say that Cortázar loved and hated Argentina as it has loved and hated him.

By the early fifties, when *El examen* was offered—unsuccessfully—for publication, the poems of Julio Denis had passed unnoticed, the stories "Casa tomada," "Lejana," and "Bestiario" had been published in respectable outlets, but *Los reyes,* the poetic drama that had appeared in 1949, had been greeted with an almost total silence. In short, Cortázar was not very well known at the time, and what was known of his literature scarcely suggested that a work like *El examen* would come from him. By the mid-eighties, the many who had read Cortázar's earlier publications were bound to find reading this posthumous novel problematic, partly because any reading was influenced by all the things that had intervened since the days when it had been written, not only the political and biographical but also, as Borges might have pointed out, the many other publications by Cortázar that had appeared between 1950 and 1986. In that sense, then, *El examen* could not be read innocently: it *was* a novel of the eighties.

As I hinted earlier, taken at face value, the title of *El examen* leads the reader up a cul-de-sac. The novel's focus is on a group of young student friends whom we accompany in their intellectual and physical perambulations through Buenos Aires in the hours leading up to an exam, but they never do take that exam. However, there can be little doubt that what is really involved is an examination of an ontological kind, a probing into the meaning of existence; in that sense, the dénouement signals that some of the characters have passed a test. Halfway through the book Andrés, one of the main characters, seems to provide the vital key to it all when he speaks of delaying to the end the only real duty one has and quotes the words "To thine own self be true" (138).

In *Rayuela* Cortázar presented us with the couples Traveler and Talita and Oliveira and Gekrepten. Here in *El examen* he does something similar: Andrés and Stella, Juan and Clara, members of the inevitable *barra* (gang of friends), together with another main character, who is a newsreporter but who is identified only as "el cronista" (the chronicler), while away the hours leading up to a final exam. Although the setting is quite palpably Buenos Aires, it is an apocalyptic Buenos Aires that is enveloped in mist and suffers from subsidence, a city whose metro system is inhabited by dogs (an underworld with its Cerberus?), a city in which there is a mysterious outbreak of fungus. Crowds gather there, to view a bone displayed in a mausoleum in the Plaza de Mayo, its main square, and there are many signs of unrest among the people and of assertion of power by the authorities.[2] If the author's early story "Casa tomada" portrayed a house taken over, then this early novel seems to picture a city in a similar plight; in both cases neither reader nor protagonists understand the whys and wherefores of the takeover. As in the story, in the novel there are disturbing developments or signs that the characters take in their stride and do not appear to heed; for example, a rat crosses their path, and pieces of fluff persistently attach themselves to their bodies or clothing.

Initially, the behavior of the characters in *El examen* strikes the reader as self-indulgent, even performative; these are bright, self-absorbed, well-read, and somewhat arrogant intellectuals who engage in a display of witticisms and literary allusions and play games with language. For all their talk, however, it is conspicuous that they hardly ever discuss what is happening around them. "El cronista" (a writer figure who is surely a predecessor of Persio, Morelli, and "el que te dije") stands out somewhat, sometimes inclined to trivialize or deflate discussions that have any substance, consequently appearing to be cynical. It is noticeable that, when the novel reaches its climax, the chronicler drinks himself to sleep, thus sidestepping (and perhaps mocking) the seriousness of the ending. Clara and Andrés emerge as the most sensitive of the group; they share a bond whose nature and origins are never fully articulated, though it is clearly a deeper bond than exists between Clara and her companion, Juan. Stella, unlike the others, is no intellectual, but good-natured and somewhat *cursi* (vulgar), a precursor of Gekrepten in *Rayuela*. Stella's relationship with the thoughtful Andrés is only credible when she is understood as representing bland acceptance of the status quo, a passive attitude to which part of Andrés is drawn, though one that he finally renounces.

The closing episode of the novel describes Stella returning home and carrying out banal routines in the confident expectation that Andrés will return home as usual (one thinks of Gekrepten's cookies in a closing chapter of *Rayuela*). Stella's expectations are false, however; she is wholly impervious to the momentous event in which Andrés has just been involved: "[Andrés] vio el movimiento de Abel, lo sintió que se le venía encima. Bajó el seguro de la pistola y la levantó. 'Desde aquí miraba los barcos,' alcanzó a pensar, y lo demás fue silencio, tan enorme que lo golpeó como un estallido" (289; Andrés saw Abel move, sensed that he was coming down toward him. He raised the safety catch on the gun and took aim. 'I/he used to watch the boats from here,' came the thought, and the rest was silence, so profound that it struck him like an explosion). That Andrés should be confronting death, something of which he has had a premonition, comes as no great surprise, but the ambiguity of this passage raises an important question: quite who is killing whom? The reader may understand that the hitherto gentle Andrés has turned a gun either on himself or on Abel, or even that Abel has done the shooting. In order to make some sense of these ambiguities we must first explore the identity of Abel, a character who is accorded a brief physical description early in the novel but who thereafter seems to exist largely in the minds of some of the other characters, like a presence lurking in the background. It is left to the reader to work out quite why the others are so preoccupied by Abel and what his relationship with them might be. At times, Abel seems to be a lost or alienated friend; at others an alter ego for Andrés. He is perhaps an embryonic *paredro*. It is the latter reading that helps us understand the vagueness of the shooting scene at the end of the novel: as Andrés dies, so does another self, Abel. Indeed, this reading approaches the explanation given by Cortázar himself in a letter to Ana Hernández del Castillo, one of very few critics who enjoyed access to *El examen* long before it was published: "When Andrés aims the gun, he doesn't kill Abel. He kills himself, and of course Abel is eliminated at the same time, since he had no separate identity."[3]

This view of the death of Andrés is compatible with a reading of *El examen* that takes as its point of departure Cortázar's reference, in his preface to the novel, to its pervasive "melancolía porteña," to a melancholy that is characteristic of Buenos Aires. Andrés, faced with a dead man in a bookshop, sees a portent of his own death ("he was thinking of the dead man but was watching himself in the process of decomposition") (177), indeed he lives throughout the novel haunted by an awareness of death. (In passing, note that a premonition of death, coupled with a need to do away with the old self, is characteristic of later texts such as "La isla a mediodía.")[4]

A different slant on the Abel figure is proposed by another major Argentine writer, Luisa Valenzuela. Bearing in mind Cortázar's propensity for anagrams, she points out that "Abel" can be rearranged to give "El B A" and suggests that the character therefore stands for Buenos Aires itself.[5] Far-fetched though this idea may at first seem, it receives some support from a comment in *El examen* that is made by Juan, who volunteers: "Yo creo que Abel es como la ciudad, algo que *a bel et bien disparu*" (280; I think Abel is like the city, something that has well and truly disappeared). Finally, in the closing pages of *El examen,* as Andrés approaches his own form of escape from his other self, he persuades Clara and Juan that they too must escape the threat of Buenos Aires and the stifling existence associated with it, for "quedarse es Abel" (277; staying behind is Abel).

Various comments suggest that Abel represents bland conformism of the kind associated with Stella; for example, Juan, calling on Baudelaire for support, tells us that "Cain, the rebellious one, must see to the well-bred, unctuous, superbland Abel" (190). So if Andrés kills Abel, he is playing the role of Cain; but Cain, like the Minotaur in *Los reyes,* is another monstrous figure made good by Cortázar's subversion.

By escaping, Clara and Juan have a chance of preserving their youthful iconoclasm and spontaneity instead of ceding to social pressures, though Andrés seems to understand better than they do that this is the case. The city atmosphere that Juan and Clara leave behind them is one of decay and authoritarianism, evidenced by the fungal infestation and recurrent encounters with fugitive or wounded people. Cultural institutions have become ossified; hence, in part, the reverence for the bone in the Plaza de Mayo. A strange establishment called the "Casa" is offering readings aloud of literary works in various languages, performed with a concertlike formality to passive audiences.

In a preface to the 1986 edition of *El examen,* written as he approached his own death, Cortázar explains that he wrote the novel "in a Buenos Aires where imagination did not have to supply a great deal in order to achieve the results the reader will see" (13). The book had in fact proved to be unpublishable in the early fifties, perhaps due to censorship in one or another of its forms. It is reported that there was an unsuccessful attempt to publish it in Mexico as well as in Argentina.[6]

Indeed, with hindsight it is difficult to avoid seeing this novel as an expression of disquiet at the atmosphere created by early Peronism, with its mass movements and its pressures on intellectuals; political sensibilities may well have played a part in keeping the novel back. In the 1986 preface Cortázar informs us that in its day the manuscript circulated only among a few friends and that some of them, as he later discovered, "believed that in certain episodes they had seen a premonition of events that graced our annals in 1952 and 1953" (13). One of his friends, Saúl Yurkievich, certainly regards *El examen* as prophetic. He says that the Perón era is clearly signaled by references that are occasionally direct but for the most part allusive (but unambiguous). These range from the president's photo being on display in every public place through the 1950 dedication to the honor of General San Martín to the ritual marches and mass meetings, the demonstrations, the invasion of the center by the proletarian masses, and the fetishistic worship of the maestro at the concert.[7] We might add to this list the fact that the confluence of people to see the bone in the mausoleum makes one think of the homage later paid to Evita on her death.

Yet, however prophetically relevant these features are to the Perón era, it is nonetheless prudent to remember that many of them are typical of authoritarian and populist regimes in general. Indeed, they are in many ways relevant not just to Perón but to the military regimes of the seventies and early eighties. That said, it is clear that the Cortázar of the late forties and early fifties, the liberal intellectual, reacted, as did many at that time, against the demagogy, the vulgar catering to the masses, the sycophancy, and the totalitarianism they saw around them.

Yurkievich says, and Cortázar himself acknowledged, that the intellectuals of the day sensed the affinity between the military-supported, nationalistic, and popular Peronism on the one hand, and fascism on the other, yet they did not understand that the Peronist movement bore the seeds of legitimate popular participation in the political process. Moreover, Cortázar had been alienated by personal experience, having resigned his teaching post at the Universidad de Cuyo in protest at the advances being made by nationalists at the expense of university autonomy. According to Yurkievich, Cortázar shared the scorn expressed by Juan for the vulgarity of the proletariat, and yet, again like Juan, had been displeased with his own background. I believe, however, that it is quite clear that Cortázar expresses—and examines—his own views and feelings through several of the characters of *El examen,* not only through Juan. (To what extent is this Juan the Juan who opens *62: Modelo para armar?* Is this Andrés the Andrés of *Libro de Manuel?*)

In relation to Cortázar's alleged sense of disgust at the vulgarity of the masses let us remember that a decade later the less sophisticated among the passengers on the *Malcolm* in his first-published novel, *Los premios,* are portrayed with amused irony, rather than with scorn and that one of them who is clearly a caricature at the outset, Atilio Presutti, acquires a certain heroic stature by the end of that novel. Presutti's nickname, "El Pelusa," means "fluff," and so he is linked to the ubiquitous fluff that flies about in *El examen.* "El Pelusa" represents the *cabecitas negras,* the humble and uneducated people who had supported Perón and had been felt by the upper classes to be taking over Buenos Aires in the late forties and early fifties. Cortázar says exactly this in interviews with Evelyn Picón-Garfield, declaring that he and others like him had been wrong to feel that way about people like Atilio Presutti. In *Los premios* Cortázar had started out portraying "El Pelusa" ironically, only to find that as the plot progressed Atilio would reveal admirable, even heroic, qualities.[8]

Perhaps even in the early fifties Cortázar was beginning to move away from being an aesthete in the direction of a greater rapprochement with his characters, toward a clearer humanism. By his own account, the change in him came with his translation to Paris, and the key text that marked the change, as we saw earlier, was "El perseguidor." At the time he finished *El examen,* then, Cortázar was on the verge of being transported to Europe and transformed in attitude. Thus, as he approaches his own crossing of the water to begin his long life in exile, in *El examen* he has Clara and Juan ferried across a canal to something new, and he has Andrés cross to the other side that is death. If this novel can be read as political allegory, it is even more clearly concerned with metaphysical matters: crossing the river suggests the achievement of a freedom that is more than political, it is a symbolic act replete with mythological connotations. The suggestion of an association with Hades also confirms that, even in those days, Cortázar viewed death as liberation, as a passing to the other side of being, a view that he would more openly espouse later, when he became influenced by Buddhist ideas.

Scenes and symbols of passage, as we have already seen at several points, become commonplace in Cortázar's work: one thinks of the frequent highlighting of forms of transport, for example, the fixation on trams in *62: Modelo para armar,* or the galleries in "El otro cielo" that lead from a conventional lifestyle in Buenos Aires to a Bohemian one in Paris, and of course the famous bridge episode in *Rayuela.* Rather as in that novel, the crucial act of transition for Juan and Clara in *El examen* is accompanied by the sort of humor that also came to be recognized as a Cortázar trademark. Witness the sudden appearance on the scene of one Calimano, an oafish *porteño* parody of Charon, the boatman of Hades, who is engaged for the purpose of ferrying the couple across the canal, as if in ironic fulfillment of an observation made by Andrés, made much earlier in the novel, that "mythology ends up coinciding with crude reality" (28). Calimano's name is very suggestive, possibly connoting mist (*calima*) and brother/friend (*mano,* in some varieties of colloquial Spanish), or even a coat of whitewash (*mano de cal*). More probably, his is a name calculated to evoke an association with Caliban, the brutish Shakespearean figure from *The Tempest.*[9] A hint by Cortázar in the direction of Shakespeare's Caliban sits quite comfortably with another Shakespearean note that is struck at the point where Andrés and Abel make their final exit. There, as we saw, the narrator echoes Hamlet's dying words "The rest is silence" (289).

The characters of *El examen* wander through the novel exchanging ideas and as often as not providing reasons for mistrusting those same ideas. Theirs is a world full of literary references, one of playfulness but of deep ontological concern. The novel is loosely plotted, sometimes frustratingly so; very little seems to happen for almost two hundred pages. One occasionally feels the need for more clarity than it delivers. To Luis García Martín, in a review of *El examen* that was published in 1987, it seemed to be "too discursive, a loose compilation of conversations, a novel whose language and style [were] drowned on occasion by an unsuccessful, and not always necessary, experimentalism"; its images tried to mimic those of surrealism and it was, in short, a book that was unlikely to enhance the author's reputation.[10] All of which does not alter the fact that many of these features come as no surprise to the hardened Cortázar reader. In any case, the imprecisions are to some degree an inevitable concomitant of one of Cortázar's main points: that one senses, dimly perceives, what cannot readily be known, still less rationally expressed in words.

As in later texts, here Cortázar often leaves his reader with a foot in the air, with a half-articulated idea, an unfinished sentence, a question in the process of formation. Although narrated by an omniscient third person, much of the text of *El examen* consists of fragmented perceptions or thoughts, so that the reader must forge links and work out which correspond to which characters; clearly this approach tries to satisfy some of the prescriptions that Cortázar would make explicit through the musings of Morelli in *Rayuela* and then put into practice in *62: Modelo para armar*. In chapter 109 of *Rayuela* we read:

> Leyendo el libro se tenía por momentos la impresión de que Morelli había esperado que la acumulación de fragmentos cristalizara bruscamente en una realidad total. Sin tener que inventar los puentes, o coser los diferentes pedazos del tapiz, que de golpe hubiera ciudad, hubiera tapiz, hubiera hombres y mujeres en la perspectiva absoluta de su devenir, y que Morelli, el autor, fuese el primer espectador maravillado de ese mundo que ingresaba en la coherencia (Reading the book, one occasionally had the impression that Morelli had waited for the fragments that had accumulated to crystallize all of a sudden into an complete reality. That without having to build bridges or sew the various pieces together to make a tapestry, there would suddenly be a city, a tapestry, men and women who were seen to be developing clearly, and that Morelli, the author, would be the first amazed witness of this world as it acquired coherence).

El examen does overstrain the reader's tolerance. The self-indulgence of Cortázar's characters is, when all is said and done, his own self-indulgence, a reflection both of his personal discomfiture as a marginalized intellectual at the time of composing *El examen* and also of the self-referential impulse that comes out more clearly in other novels.

Other features that find echoes elsewhere include the concert episode, which, with its fear and mass hysteria, its blind conductor, and its insect imagery, anticipates the story "Las Ménades." There is also evidence of a radical suspicion of language allied to an attraction to music, "el sonido, sustancia necesaria, carne para la idea inalcanzable" (233; sound, that necessary substance, that flesh for the unattainable idea). There is a foretaste of *glíglico,* the nonsense language of *Rayuela:* "¡Te incubadoro! ¡Te pirimayo! ¡Te florimundio!" (248). And not all is gloom and doom: like so many later works, this novel has its liberating moments of humor, such as those detailing Juan's absurdly protective obsession with a cauliflower or the episode in which Clara's very respectable father becomes caught up in a brawl over a communal comb that hangs from a chain in the gentlemen's bathroom. In all, there are many ways in which *El examen* clearly foreshadows political, ontological, aesthetic, and biographical features that one associates with the later Cortázar and his work.

Politics apart—and it is worth repeating that the political is only one dimension of *El examen* and probably not the most important one at that—one wonders what the reaction of readers might have been had this novel been published in the early fifties, with the poems of Julio Denis little known and only a few stories and *Los reyes* already in print. The fact is that, for all its many imperfections, *El examen* would have represented a massive advance. Quite possibly it would not have been understood at all at that time and not recognized as the significant step it undoubtedly was. The fact that to this day, despite the benefit of all our knowledge of Cortázar's mature works, *El examen* remains a little-studied novel reflects both its shortcomings and the difficulty in coming to grips with it. Would the present-day reader be able to make such observations as those I have offered above were it not for benefit of hindsight?

Mention must be made, in relation to *El examen,* of another posthumous publication, the *Diario de Andrés Fava* (1995), which, according to the publisher, had originally been composed as part of *El examen,* but then excised by Cortázar and kept by him for possible future publication. Writing this diary, says its author (I use "author" with deliberate ambiguity), is like getting things off one's chest, "a wiping of one's nose that puts mental snot on paper." Andrés/Cortázar records his thoughts and feelings in fragments that arise from any number of stimuli: a childhood memory, a moment of ecstatic contemplation while waiting for a bus, a response to reading a book or hearing a piece of music. A few of these musings are interesting, but reading them does little to foster any sense of greater unity or clarity of purpose in the parent novel. Indeed, direct references to the events and characters of *El examen* are quite rare, limited to an appearance, now spectral, now carnivalesque, of Abel (a figure who sometimes seems reminiscent of the one in Watteau's painting *L'Indifférent*), to the occasional exchange of ideas with Juan, the odd reference to Clara and Stella, and above all thoughts on death accompanied by a pervasive fog. As if to remind us of the impossibility of explaining things rationally, Andrés makes a passing reference to the "poor old Chronicler [who is] so hopeful that there are explanations" (119), and he quotes this passage from Céline's *Voyage au bout de la nuit:* "Perhaps all that the exhaustion that comes with living boils down to is having to go through so much in an effort to be reasonable for twenty or forty years or more and not just be truly oneself, in other words, disgusting, awful, absurd" (116). A few passages from the diary shed some light on the enigmatic death scene in *El examen:* in a section headed "Estoicismo sobre papel" (Stoicism on paper) Andrés writes: "I should like the act of death not to come from outside and not to be too noisy. . . . If killing oneself is a window, then to make an exit without slamming the door." Emphasizing the low key once again, he offers an analogy with writing: "The final full stop is tiny and easy to miss on the written page; you notice it because of the contrast, when the blank paper starts just afterward" (115). In a similar manner, at another point he speaks of writing "the novel of nothingness. Everything must conspire to make the reader gather that the awful subject of the work is that there is none. Reveal the most secret (even though today it is making a public appearance) of human suspicions: that one is inherently, intrinsically useless. Insinuate that the religion of work (in its highest forms: art, poetry) is also *a game.* Lay into hypocrisy" (110). Once again, such self-referential comments—the writer addressing the act of creative writing during the course of such writing—clearly foreshadow those of Morelli in *Rayuela.* In much the same vein, at another point that seems to symbolize the identification of Cortázar with Andrés, we are told that Stella, the character who has seemed most rooted in everyday reality, does not exist (119). Finally, that the author of the diary is "really" Cortázar is confirmed by a passage (104–5) that gives a blueprint for what would become a story of his, "Continuidad de los parques" (Continuity of parks).

It is easy to find further evidence that here, in Andrés's diary, Cortázar is baring his soul, voicing many of the concerns that would preoccupy him for much of his life, and groping for the ways he would later use to express them (for example, the inclusion of metatextual commentary and references to everyday experiences, particularly reading experiences, that occurred during the process of composition). Clearly, however, by omitting *Diario de Andrés Fava* from *El examen* Cortázar avoided adding more static weight to a novel that already suffers from an overload. *Diario* is not by any means without interest, but its interest is greatest for specialists who are delving into the archaeology of Cortázar's world; had he lived longer, perhaps he would have continued to keep the diary in a drawer.

Divertimento

Quite a lot of what has been said above in relation to *El examen* may be applied, *mutatis mutandis,* to *Divertimento.* This short novel was published in 1986 but dates back to the time of publication of *Los reyes,* having been completed in early 1949. The opening words of the novel locate us in the time of a narrator who is tirelessly filling his leisure time with words that are remembrances of things past, sparked off, in his case, not by madeleines but by separating out segments of an orange. Conjured up once again are two central couples, comprising a painter and a poet and their sisters, plus a fifth character who is a little like the *cronista* of *El examen,* though he is clearly identified with the narrator. Like predecessors of the members of the Snake Club in *Rayuela,* these characters meet in an inner sanctum, which they refer to as the "Vive como puedas" (Live as you may), and there they display their wit and culture. Jorge, the poet, like a good surrealist dictates elegant automatic poems to his sister, Marta, "oiling the bicycle wheels," as she aptly puts it (13). She draws the narrator's attention to the fields visible through the window, a Poussin to her eyes, a Rousseau to his. These few initial references will suffice to give a taste of the strong cultural seasoning that Cortázar is once again applying. The literary and visual combine, as always, with the musical, as the title itself suggests. It is in Italian, not Spanish; it suggests artificial, not to say superficial, lighthearted artistic entertainment; it connotes Mozart at his most playful.

Cortázar deploys the usual elements, for example, references to jazz, art, and boxing, animal imagery, humor, and games with words. Three images dominate *Divertimento.* One is the avantgarde painting that Renato is struggling to finish, which is in two parts, portraying two men violently confronting each other, though their identities are not clear. The second image is (yet again) the skein, which also has two facets: there is a literal skein that is being worked on by two women and a metaphorical skein that is the work of the author/narrator. Each has knots in it like a *quipu.* The two women unraveling the skein, Laura and Moña, live in a world of frustrating, claustrophobic banality; their home, with its stamp-collecting uncle, is rather reminiscent of the one in "Casa tomada." The third image is a reflected one, conveyed by the name of another character who is called Narcissus; he is a person who is in the background much of the time (shades of Abel and Persio) and who sometimes gathers the other characters together for seances. In one such seance, a woman called (euphemistically) Eufemia is summoned, a woman with, again, a skein whose knots she is trying to unravel. That other weaver, the narrator, is nicknamed "Insect" by the other characters (probably a humorous allusion to Cortázar's own long-leggedness).[11] As far as he is concerned, untying the knots in the narrative thread seems to entail discovering how the various elements of the novel might coalesce in meaningful ways. In other words, in this respect *Divertimento* seems to be heralding Persio's thoughts and the search for *figuras* that is so important a part of *62: Modelo para armar.* But in *Divertimento* the patterns never quite coalesce, and one is left with the sense of having witnessed only a showy performance with much inventive and associative play and with a great number of cultural references. There is a cat that slinks its way in here, too, named after a conservatory of music in Argentina, though we learn that it came perilously close to being called Paul Claudel. The dominant cultural references, except where jazz is concerned, are very European, very typical of Cortázar, and symptomatic of a certain Argentina.

The narrative of *Divertimento* is built around the images I have referred to and through free associations based on words and cultural links. As in *El examen,* many pages go by before there is any real action, and when it does come, it does not convey the portentousness of the other novel. *Divertimento* apparently heralds violence and death, but at the end only the cat has died off, and even that is due to natural causes. Renato's canvas, which seemed also to portend something significant, is destroyed as the novel nears its conclusion.[12] If there is a key statement for the understanding of this novel, then perhaps it is this one, which fundamentally seems to speak of signs existing in a world of their own: "The funny thing in all this is that at bottom Renato doesn't believe a word. What he's interested in is symbols, just in case you think he's a fatalist or he believes he's ruled by supernatural forces" (91). If so, then Cortázar's novel, though no great work, is a little ahead of its time, evincing some characteristics of the *nouveau roman*. It transpires that the superficiality that Cortázar treats with some scorn at the beginning of his novel has in fact been its substance. Renato, when all is said and done, has only been trying to portray a nightmare, a figment of the imagination; Narciso has similarly invoked the imaginary; and so has the author in his fiction.

Theater

Apart from *Los reyes,* Cortázar's dramatic writing comprises four short plays that were gathered together and published well after his death as *Adiós, Róbinson, y otras piezas breves* (Goodbye, Robinson, and other short plays). One of the plays included therein had first been published by itself in the year of his death; this was *Nada a Pehuajó* (Nothing to Pehuajó).

Pieza en tres escenas (Play in three scenes) and *Tiempo de barrilete* (Kite time) are grouped as "two word games." The first of these dates from the time of *Los reyes* but apparently has little in common with it. The title is of a kind one might find given to an abstract painting, and it is clearly intended to signal the artificiality of the play that follows. *Pieza* lurches from the symbolic to the absurd to the metafictional. This potpourri is foreshadowed in the long list of inspirational influences provided in the book's dedication: Leonora Carrington, Igor Stravinsky, Federico García Lorca, George S. Kaufman, Benjamin Péret, and Jean Cocteau. The initial setting is a town square, one of whose buildings includes a window that is framed as if to suggest a painting. During the course of the play, various characters constitute the subject matter of this "painting" by posing in the window. The first scene is played in the town square, the second inside the house. At various points characters make the transition between the two. In the square, Nélida longs for her lover. Inside the house is Nuria; she is another weaver, described by her companion Remo as "a tireless spider," and for her own part offers the observation that Penelope knew what she was doing when she chose her work. Remo comes out of the house to meet Nélida and together they repair to a gothic castle, but later he will slide back inside and once again become part of the "picture" beside Nuria. The parents of Nélida also make the transition, in their case from outside to in, but once there, they are uncomfortable; it is a place with a huge net (on which Nuria works) and an invisible bird (an image that Cortázar sometimes uses to represent an unsympathetic godlike power), and there are phonograph records strewn on the floor.

Humorous elements in this play include a group of sailors who sometimes wax poetic and play with a beach ball, a rather erudite park attendant, and an Ionesco-like exchange of banalities between Nuria and the parents of Nélida that entices the latter into the house. On the self-referential front, the characters sometimes question their own lines or the staging; for example, as Nélida and Remo make off to their "remote" castle, he explains that it doesn't look far away, but that is only because it is part of a stage set.

It must be clear from the above comments that some typical Cortázar things are being rehearsed—multiple levels of reality, the oneiric, transitions, routines. The style of the play is very varied, and except for a few stiffly worded passages it has little in common with the poetry and grandiloquence of the contemporaneous *Los reyes*. Unfortunately, *Pieza en tres escenas* is overcharged with arcane symbolism, its characters reduced to mannered devices. It is a play that cries out for visual support, depending heavily on staging and movement, yet it is hard to imagine that it could ever have been successfully staged in the late forties; perhaps, with the benefit of today's technological panoply it would be possible to provide the nonverbal flesh that this "word game" needs.

By contrast, *Tiempo de barrilete* relies very little on the visual, placing almost all of the burden of meaning on dialogue, usually between two people. In this it is somewhat like *Los reyes;* however, the dialogue in *Tiempo* moves freely between stylistic registers, never giving in to pompousness. *Tiempo* opens (almost inevitably) with the figure of a woman sewing; this is Leticia, a fugitive from her parents, who has found happiness (as her name presumably indicates) by taking refuge in a house on a prosperous *criollo* estate where she now lives with David. David is an architect, who has been called in by the owner to do some remodeling work and, like Leticia, has stayed on, though he is not sure why. He is also a man worried by death (as was the Andrés of *El examen*) and beset by existential disquiet (somewhat like Oliveira in *Rayuela*). Leticia was once in love with the daughter of the owner of the house, Isolina, but Leticia's love has been replaced by fear of her; David also longs hopelessly for Isolina. In the second scene we move to a wood, where Isolina is in conversation with her brother, Aníbal; one deduces that they are abnormally close and that Aníbal resents David's intrusion. It also becomes clear that Isolina is manipulative and cruel by nature. The wood (the only environment in which we see Isolina and Aníbal) is not quite edenic: it is inhabited by "mancuspias" whose bite can apparently be fatal. (Cortázar borrowed the invented word "mancuspia" from a friend; it is better known for its appearance in his story "Cefalea" in *Final del juego*.)

During the initial conversation between David and Leticia there are two amusing and apparently anachronistic interruptions: a character called the Boy Next Door comes in to ask where in the country the mandioc root is cultivated, and one called the Gentleman issues a proclamation that henceforth all sunflowers must be blue. Since during this first scene there are also two references to summary decapitation, one is reminded of the treatment meted out by the Queen of Hearts in *Through the Looking Glass*. Indeed, the owner of the estate, Señor Robledo, does seem to have something of her capriciousness; it transpires that he is given to issuing decrees such as the one involving the sunflowers, not to mention his inclination to brush away imaginary invaders from his shoulders. But he is also a Prospero who controls the creatures in his realm.

In the fourth scene David, armed with a sandalwood stick that seems to offer protective properties, ventures into the Arcadian wood, reciting verse. Isolina meets him, saying that she knows that the first line he has just recited is by Cortázar and that she can see that there is a twisted piece of plagiarism involved in the second; once again, as in the previous play, ironic self-awareness on the part of the writer is being displayed. As the play ends, Isolina first embraces the Boy Next Door, the "puppet" for whom she has lusted all along, Aníbal departs into the woods, and Isolina, after doing a pirouette, half obscured from view by the partially lowered curtain, falls dead, bitten by a mancuspia. In the final scene David mourns somewhat fatuously over her body while she looks on, ghostlike, from her perch in a tree. He vows that he will eventually have her, but she has the final word, saying that that will never happen. She will continue to be "Isolina," the little island.

At bottom, *Tiempo de barrilete* seems to be about power and free will and about willingness to be adventurous. There is some thematic overlap with *Pieza en tres escenas* and with "Casa tomada," and it is noticeable that formally the play is structured around two couples, as is so often the case in Cortázar's works.

Various myths seem to be implied in a play that, like the one that preceded it, is excessively dense and cryptic. *Tiempo de barrilete* appears to come from the same era as *Pieza en tres escenas* and to have been completed during Cortázar's voyage on a boat called the *Anna C.* back to Argentina at the end of his very first visit to Europe. It will be recalled that *Los premios* was written several years later under similar conditions, as an escape into privacy from the society of other passengers.[13] The title of *Tiempo de barrilete* refers to the time when Isolina and Aníbal would play with kites, contrasted with the time when they turned to hoops; in accordance with an unwritten rule each activity would be understood to preclude the other.

Nada a Pehuajó is by far the most accomplished piece of Cortázar's writing for the theater, and it would surely be the easiest to stage. It consists of a single, long act, the action taking place in a restaurant with a reception desk running along the wall to the left, suggesting a hotel. Nine tables are set on a floor that is marked out in black-and-white squares like a chessboard, and at one of them toward the back of the set sits a mysterious Man in White, who throughout the play remains silent but who periodically moves condiments and pieces of cutlery about the table in front of him as if he were playing chess; when he does so, characters seem to behave in ways that respond to his movements of these pieces. The Clerk is another of several nameless characters; for the most part he stands at the reception desk, doing paperwork. A third such character is the Customer, an "insignificant-looking little man whose clothes are clean but rather threadbare" (95).

The *maître* and the waiters fuss over the first person to enter the restaurant, a regular called Señor López, who proves to be a glutton. Other characters, who soon come in to occupy other tables, are a caricatured American Tourist and an Architect, accompanied by an overawed lady companion. Two farcical episodes ensue. First a chicken refuses to be cooked until it sees that it is being upstaged by a plate of mushrooms. Then the Defense Counsel enters, upon which the Customer jumps to his feet, approaches the Clerk at the desk, and soon becomes embroiled in absurd bureaucracy when making an unsuccessful attempt to dispatch certain items to a place called Pehuajó. Other characters now enter: The Judge, who sits at a table, weighing carrots on scales, and close behind him the Woman in Green. They are followed by a young couple, Gina and Franco. Franco offers a few observations that serve as a red light to any spectator who might think that this play is merely absurd: it is a day, he says, that makes one feel as if one were floating on the edge of things, *as if one were dreaming or in a theater.* When Gina replies that it is unsettling not to understand why it is so, he answers that there is no need always to look for reasons and that we cannot expect to understand everything that has an influence over us. This exchange is fundamental to the understanding of the play. Its absurdities and the strangeness of the behavior of its characters are all part of a manipulative construction symbolized by the actions of the Man in White. The characters are like pawns who move in accordance with the dictates of superior powers. Some of them appear to be regulars not of the restaurant as such, but as enactors of a ritual, the puppets of a play-within-the-play, and in that play the Customer and Gina and Franco are but innocents. So it is that some of the enactors of the ritual can group together to act as a parodic Greek chorus and warn the Judge against the paths of sin: "¡Usía, aténgase al severo régimen / que siguen las columnas / las columnas de la sociedad!" (132; Milord, cleave to the rigors of the regime / observed by the pillars / the pillars of society). When they do so, the Judge is on the verge of succumbing to the temptation of some ice cream offered him by a woman who talks about serpents and apples. At the height of the pressures upon the Judge, the Defense Counsel rises and launches into a pompous and verbose discourse, which is promptly cut short by the Man in White moving one of his "chess" pieces. The Judge takes the safe path, toeing the line of convention. In the Judge's past, however, and on his conscience, there is a condemned man called Carlos Fleta, with whom the intimidated Customer seems to be identified. (There is a formal reflection of this link in the fact that the Customer has been trying to send goods—*fletar* in Spanish.) At the end of the play the collusion between the triad of the *Maître,* the Man in White, and the Woman in Green becomes evident. As the action nears its conclusion, the Man in White declares checkmate, as if to indicate that the ritual has run its course. One is left with the Judge wondering if it hasn't all been just a nasty dream and with a cynical comment on that thought made by the *Maître,* who says that calling it a nightmare is too convenient an escape route. Recalling Gino's early comments, we may surmise that the dream, the theatrical experience, has implications for real life. In this the conclusion of *Nada a Pehuajó* is comparable to that of the story "Instrucciones para John Howell." Very funny though it often is, clearly this play has both political and existential implications; there are several layers of authority at work, manipulating and controlling in ways and in pursuit of ends that are unexplained. At the bottom of the hierarchy of power is the Everyman figure of the Customer. Yet the young couple have offered some resistance to this hierarchy, and that implies some hope.

The last work included in *Adiós, Róbinson, y otras piezas breves* is the title play, which was written for radio. Cortázar, who had translated *Robinson Crusoe* many years previously, takes Robinson and Friday back to Juan Fernández. Centuries after Robinson's shipwreck on the island, he and Friday circle above it in a plane and see that it now has skyscrapers, marinas, and oil rigs. Friday, who despite his education "smells" change in the air, has changed too. He has developed an involuntary giggle that escapes from him each time he addresses Robinson as "Master"; but he has been to analysts of both the Freudian and Jungian persuasion and has it on the authority of Jacques Lacan that it is only a matter of a nervous habit and that it will probably go away. It does. By the end of the play, and without asking for permission, he is calling Robinson by his name.

At the broadest level, then, this play is about technological and social change. Arriving at the airport, Robinson is met by a lady who is to be his official government guide and he is shepherded through the VIP channel. Friday, meanwhile, goes the way of ordinary folk and soon befriends a taxi driver called Banana, who is a member of the same tribe, recognizable by their abnormally long thumbs. Friday is soon integrated into the merry life of the common people (women, in particular, are said to like men with long thumbs). Robinson, however, is condemned to a tightly programmed touristic visit, an anonymous international hotel, and distance from the native experience. The lady official (he makes a pass at her, only to discover that she is the wife of a police chief) explains that there is not much sympathy for the former colonial power, but she also admits later that her own view of Juan Fernández is a falsified and distanced one, like his; it is "a series of clear-cut images seen through car windows. A museum, when you think about it, or a slide show" (166). As the action progresses, it transpires that not only official policy but also a cultural divide keep Robinson from contact with the natives. He begins to doubt the value of the "civilization" that he so proudly inculcated in the once naked and barbaric Friday. Friday, ironically demonstrating his acquired culture by profluent use of expressions in Italian and German, explains to Robinson that the island of Juan Fernández, though believed to be named after an explorer, bears one of the most commonplace names in Spanish, equivalent to John Smith in English, Jean Dupont in French, or Hans Schmidt in German. In other words, it stands for the common man. Metaphorically, Robinson is still alone on his island, unable to communicate with the ordinary people, who are marching toward a different future. Words apart, Cortázar makes the same point more subtly by having Duke Ellington's "Solitude" sound as a recurrent leitmotif throughout the play. Its closing pages are somewhat heavy-handed, and the ending is naïvely utopian. *Adiós, Róbinson* is a play with a political edge, but in the course of it Cortázar is also engaging in some self-analysis when referring to the difficulty a cultured man has in communicating with ordinary people. There are a few parallels between this play and earlier texts. In "La isla a mediodía" a utopian island-based existence is located on the other side of a glass barrier, viewed initially from a plane, associated with the sensual, and contrasted with technological advance; and in several stories, such as "Apocalipsis de Solentiname" (involving another island), the false framing of reality and the problems of communication are thematized.

Negro el diez

"Negro el diez" (Black ten) was Cortázar's last work. He completed it while confined to a hospital, in collaboration with his friend Luis Tomasello, on whose drawings it is based, and a small number of signed copies were made and distributed to friends at that time. On the tenth anniversary of Cortázar's death, Aurora Bernárdez, who with Tomasello had been at the author's bedside when he died, had 150 copies of a facsimile edition of Cortázar's manuscript made privately. Subsequently, permission was given to reproduce the poem in certain newspapers and journals, but it is still not widely available.[14]

This second collaboration with Tomasello invites comparison with the first, *Un elogio del tres*. Both appeared in special limited editions, both draw on the symbolism of numbers, and both are loosely based on the Christian myth of creation. As we saw when discussing *Un elogio del tres* (chapter 7), an initial unity—one—leads to an Eden of dualism and sin—two—and on to a world of three that is associated with happiness, freedom, and celebration. None of that optimism is evident in *Negro el diez,* which is probably the most somber piece Cortázar ever wrote. Comments on the poem, it must be said, are somewhat compromised by the fact that one is dealing with a facsimile of a manuscript that includes a number of changes, deletions, and annotations made by its author.

Cortázar leads us from nothingness through chaos to life and eventually to death, from one to ten (one plus zero). Nothingness and chaos are black, a cock crows the dawn of life, and light breaks through only to be absorbed by coal and basalt, agents of the blackness that relentlessly asserts its primacy. This is a worldview worthy of certain works by Goya, to whom Cortázar makes reference in the poem. Blackness is the "pez abisal de los orígenes" (the primordial pitch [or possibly "fish," for there is ambiguity here] of the abyss), it is the "Estigia contra el sol" (Styx opposing the sun), it symbolizes the end of change and the onset of silence. In its nocturnal realm it reduces the spectrum to shades of purple (a color associated with solemnity and mourning). Here Cortázar employs some of the most impressive imagery in his poem; he writes: "Su palacio nocturno: el sueño, el párpado / sedosa guillotina del diurno pavorreal" (Its nocturnal palace: sleep, the eyelid / a silken guillotine for the diurnal peacock). Blackness is a trampoline from which other things spring, defining themselves in contrast to it, yet all such things, emotions, adventures, signs of life, will ultimately be petrified by it. Black is the horse in the nightmare, the sacrificial ax, and the ink of the written word and the artistic design. It is number ten on the roulette wheel of life, life's wheel of fortune. Predictably, the poem is in ten sections. The last of these, the poem's capstone, consisting of only one line, is this: "Tu sombra espera tras de toda luz" (Your shadow awaits behind all light).[15]

A Postlude

Julio Cortázar's death was immediately followed by a flurry of tributes, not least from distinguished writers, all over the world. Initially, the praise was loudest outside Argentina, in places such as Mexico, Spain, and France. Among writers from Latin America who spoke warmly of Cortázar, Carlos Fuentes, who at one time or another had called him both the Che Guevara of literature and the Simón Bolívar of the novel, emphasized that, despite his many years in France, he was essentially an Argentine. According to Fuentes, together with that of Octavio Paz, Cortázar's was the liveliest aesthetic mind of a whole generation of writers. Gabriel García Márquez described him as the most impressive human being he had ever known. Sergio Ramírez, a novelist and member of the first Sandinista government in Nicaragua, said that he had never met a famous person who was as unpretentious. As for Borges, in his characteristically oblique manner, but clearly alluding to factors that had made Cortázar a controversial figure in Argentina, he wrote that his own understanding was that, apart from questions of ethics, whatever opinions one had were "superficial and ephemeral." And Cortázar was a man driven by ethics, as Borges implies.[1]

The title of a tribute by García Márquez was "El argentino que se hizo querer de todos" (The Argentine who made everyone love him), a title that fairly reflects the closeness to the writer that was felt by many thousands of ordinary readers all over the world, so much so that when Cortázar died, it seemed to them that they had lost a friend.[2] However, in Cortázar's homeland the homage was at first decidedly muted; many could not forgive him his exile, his criticisms of Argentina, his politics, his insistence on individual freedom. It took a decade before Argentina began really to recognize him: it was as if, on the tenth anniversary of his death, the newspapers were publishing the tributes that had been due a decade earlier. It was then, too, that Tristán Bauer's documentary film was released. Also to mark that anniversary, Fuentes and García Márquez devised another tribute, endowing a Cortázar chair at the University of Guadalajara in Mexico and bringing a former president of Argentina, Raúl Alfonsín, for its inauguration. This was a particularly appropriate gesture, since during Cortázar's final visit to his homeland, with Alfonsín in office, he had been denied official recognition.

At about the same time Mario Vargas Llosa, Cortázar's codefendant in the debates of the sixties about what constituted an appropriate role for Latin American writers, contributed an interesting prologue to the *Cuentos completos*. Whereas Cortázar had evolved from being a largely apolitical person toward active participation on the side of the political Left, belying the more common human tendency to grow more conservative with age, Vargas Llosa had taken the opposite course, starting as a Marxist and becoming a champion of the political Right. But Vargas Llosa makes it clear in that prologue that what he had come to regard as Cortázar's political mistakes he also saw as having been sincerely and ingenuously committed, and for that reason he had never lost his respect and affection for Cortázar, despite their political differences. Most would agree in recognizing Cortázar's sincerity, and many people have thought him ingenuous in matters of politics. As one commentator put it: "Cortázar may have made mistakes and erred on the side of ingenuousness in matters of politics, but no one can doubt the sincerity of what he said."[3] He was a fundamentally honest man in his public life, as in his literature, and he sometimes paid a price for it. Cortázar was the man who gave the world *Rayuela,* as if in anticipation of the hippie era. Yet there was something that was awkward and modish, however sincere, about the tall, gangly figure who in his late fifties was rubbing shoulders with young protesters in Paris.

Although there is a clear evolution in Cortázar's literature from an era dominated by aesthetics, mythology, and fantasy toward more psychological and writerly explorations and the difficult and sometimes successful treatment of sociopolitical issues, at the heart of his writing there is a remarkable unity. That unity is based on an ethics of writing that prescribes that literature explore both itself and metaphysical matters. In many ways, Cortázar was a man obsessed: obsessed by certain images, by certain fears, by perceptual possibilities, by language, but above all by the need for restless exploration. He was fond of quoting Gide's "Il ne faut jamais profiter de l'élan acquis" (One should never take advantage of the impulse one has already acquired). He was a revolutionary in the widest and fullest sense of the word. Cortázar, as we know, hated all forms of compartmentalization. Fittingly, then, without submitting to any of the isms that critics would like to foist upon him (for how can one constantly renew and search if one is pinned down?), Cortázar and his works respond to some degree to all of the labels they have used: he is romantic, surrealist, existentialist, neofantastic, avant-gardist, and, yes, even a bit postmodern.

How much punch is there now left in his works? The standard view, with which one can scarcely disagree, has been that Cortázar is an exceptional shortstory writer, probably the greatest ever to have come out of Latin America, and the author of one exceptional novel. When Cortázar himself was asked late in life what he thought about his work, he echoed that opinion: to the desert island he would take *Rayuela* (his most complete personal testimony), but he would be thinking of the stories (*Espejo de escritores*). He considered himself more of a short-story writer than a novelist (*A fondo*).

Some other Cortázar works are foundering rapidly as the realities of the times in which they were written grow ever more remote and seem less and less consequential. *La vuelta al día en ochenta mundos* and *Último round* remain interesting for the adventurousness of their conception, although the material in them always was a trifle esoteric, much of it meaningful only to those who had accompanied Cortázar through his earlier works and his political ups and downs. Among such unconventional (and probably, even these days, relatively unpublishable) works, two stand out for their quality: *Territorios* and especially *Prosa del observatorio*. And I venture to suggest that the poetry, which Cortázar held so dear, but in a sense also held back, and which has been rather ignored by critics, deserves greater recognition. For the rest, the picture is very uneven: his creative writing often is aesthetically satisfying, moving, beautiful, and hilarious, but it can occasionally smack of trendiness and seem mannered and self-indulgent, and sometimes understanding it depends too heavily on one's having past experience as a Cortázar reader. As for his work as an essayist and literary critic, there is, especially in the early work, a passionate, intensely personal, even idiosyncratic quality; one has the feeling that he is revealing as much about himself as about the subject he is addressing.

Cortázar is like an actor who, whatever the role he is playing, cannot help being himself; in this connection one remembers another of his favorite quotations, Shakespeare's "To thine own self be true." All of Cortázar's works can be called egocentric, not in a bad sense, but in the sense that they respond to a deep-seated impulse to explore the self. As the title of a recent book puts it, Cortázar's is an "aesthetics of searching."[4] Ringing the narrative changes, his works strive restlessly toward something that is more authentic, that is "other." Understanding Cortázar depends on understanding that this process is ongoing, that his writing is an endless refocusing of that search. What gives value to Cortázar's literature is not only the themes, but also the ingenuity with which he revisits his obsessions and explores the reaches of his artistic imagination.

Habré tenido el privilegio agridulce de asistir a la decadencia de una cosmovisión y el alumbramiento de otra muy diferente; y si mis últimos años están y estarán dedicados a ese hombre nuevo que queremos crear, nada podrá impedirme volver la mirada hacia una región de sombras queridas, pasearme con Aquiles en el Hades, murmurando esos nombres que ya tantos jóvenes olvidan porque tienen que olvidarlos, Hölderlin,

Keats, Leopardi, Mallarmé, Darío, Salinas, sombras entre tantas sombras en la vida de un argentino que todo quiso leer, todo quiso abrazar.

—Cómo escribe—dijo Calac.

—Madre querida—dijo Polanco.

I shall have had the bittersweet pleasure of witnessing the decline of one worldview and the rise of another that is quite different; even though my last years have been and will be devoted to that new man we are trying to create, nothing can stop me from casting my eyes back to a region of dear shadows, strolling with Achilles in Hades while murmuring the names that so many young people today are forgetting, because they must forget them: Hölderlin, Keats, Leopardi, Mallarmé, Darío, Salinas, shadows among so many others in the life of an Argentine who wanted to read it all, embrace it all.

—My, how he writes!—said Calac.

—Lord, help us!—said Polanco.

Julio Cortázar, in his prologue to *Pameos y meopas,* 1971

Notes

All page numbers refer to Cortázar's original works.

Chapter 1: Sparring Session

1. Aronne Amestoy, *Mandala,* 9.
2. Poniatowska, "Vuelta," 29–30.
3. Castro-Klarén, "Lector," 11.
4. Prego, *Palabras,* 30.
5. Some details of his time in Chivilcoy can be read in Alberto Perrone, "Un profesor en Chivilcoy," and in Cócaro et al., *El joven Cortázar.*
6. González Bermejo, *Conversaciones,* 27.
7. These early works are included in the posthumous publication by Alfaguara of Cortázar's complete stories, in two volumes, *Cuentos completos* (Madrid, 1994). Although in later chapters of this present book I refer on many occasions to the titles of the various volumes in which most stories made their first appearance, all page references that have to do with stories refer to their appearance in *Cuentos completos.*
8. Many of Cortázar's short stories have been translated, but they have not always been grouped in translation under titles that reflect their original groupings in Spanish. Some of those in *Bestiario,* for example, appear in *Blow-up and other Stories* and in *End of the Game and Other Stories.* For further details, see the list of translations into English included in the bibliography.
9. Collazos, *Revolución.*
10. Ibid., 73.
11. Guibert, "Escritor."
12. Rama, "Venezuela."
13. The translated volume that appeared under the English title *Around the Day in Eighty Worlds* is in fact a compilation of some selections from *La vuelta al día en ochenta mundos* and some from *Último round.*
14. In this connection mention should be made of the failed journal called *Libre,* which Cortázar and others thought would provide a forum for discussion of Latin American issues, especially by people in exile. There were disagreements about policy and finance, about who should be allowed a voice, and about Cuba's potential role in the project. The Padilla Affair is the subject of an article in *Libre* by Carlos Fuentes ("Documen-

tos: El caso Padilla") and of a book by Lourdes Casal (*El caso Padilla: Literatura y revolución en Cuba*).

15. The fullest bibliography of Cortázar's works and his critics, covering the period up to his death, is that of Mundo Lo. Another useful one, of about the same time, is contained in a special issue of *Explicación de textos literarios* (1988–89).

Chapter 2: The Weigh-In

1. González Bermejo, *Conversaciones,* 33.

2. Harss, *Los nuestros,* 264.

3. One of the most celebrated and significant episodes in *Rayuela* features *piolines* (a dialectal word for "cord" or "thread"). Also, the theme of incest is by no means confined to *Los reyes.*

4. Dolphin images still decorate the painted walls of the palace of Knossos, the setting for the story.

5. González-Echevarría, "*Los reyes:* Cortázar's Mythology of Writing," in Alazraki and Ivask, *Island,* 63–72.

6. González-Echevarría, "Mythology," 66–67.

7. García Canclini, *Antropología,* 20.

8. See Taylor, "*Los reyes,*" 555–56.

9. Curutchet, *Crítica,* 15–16.

10. Harss, *Los nuestros,* 265.

Chapter 3: Winning by a Knockout

1. The exception among the themes is politics, which is the subject of chapter 7.

2. González Bermejo, *Conversaciones,* 53.

3. There are one or two instances of the use of a first-person narrator in stories written earlier, but they were not published until much later.

4. That creative process is outlined in chapter 4.

5. The role of rivers in Cortázar's work would merit a study by itself. There is some evidence that he had a phobia regarding water.

6. González Bermejo, *Conversaciones,* 141.

7. "Estación de la mano" dates from the days prior to *Bestiario,* but it was first published in *La vuelta al día en ochenta mundos* (1967). It is one of the first stories that Cortázar wrote in the first person.

8. González Bermejo, *Conversaciones,* 130.

9. Ibid., 11–13.

10. Prego, *Palabras,* 66–68.

11. Picón-Garfield, *Cortázar,* 20.

12. Cortázar spoke a little about this episode and about homosexuality in his other

works in his interview with Picón-Garfield, *Cortázar,* 121–22. Recent fashions in criticism have led some critics to pounce on any such references.

13. In an interview with Elena Poniatowska, "La vuelta a Julio Cortázar en (cerca de) ochenta preguntas," 30, Cortázar says that when he was young and living in Banfield, he and his mother used to play a game that consisted of studying the clouds and inventing stories.

14. Cortázar has taken the quotation and the name Annabel Lee from Poe.

15. González Bermejo, *Conversaciones,* 48.

16. Picón-Garfield, *Cortázar,* 81.

17. Prologue to Cristina Peri Rossi's *La tarde del dinosaurio,* 16–17.

18. Picón-Garfield, *Cortázar,* 77–81.

19. Ibid., 108. This may be related to the gladiatorial contest in "Todos los fuegos el fuego."

20. Prego, *Palabras,* 73.

21. Picón-Garfield, *Cortázar,* 44, 108–9.

22. Harss, *Los nuestros,* 293.

23. Picón-Garfield, *Cortázar,* 115.

24. Prego, *Palabras,* 125.

25. "Looking" (the verb *mirar* is the key term) is to become a standard sign in Cortázar, a sign of frankness and of genuine communication (see pages 55–56).

26. Prego, *Palabras,* 58.

27. González Bermejo, *Conversaciones,* 54.

28. It is so, at least, in the first printing of *Alguien que anda por ahí* (Alfaguara, 1977), and it is clear from his comments in interview that that is as the author intended. Unfortunately, in the *Cuentos completos* the effect has been wasted by transferring the explicit reference to Jacobo Borges to the foot of the opening page.

29. Borges's painting has the alternative title "Rueda de locos" (Circle of madmen).

30. Karine Berriot, *Enchanteur,* 261–62, speculates that this story has to do with Cortázar's love for Carol Dunlop—he was living with her by the time it was written—and their cat Flanelle, with which she shared a quiet complicity. Berriot's book also has a reproduction of a photo of Cortázar, camera in hand, looking out of a window at the cat, which is on its hind legs, paws against the glass, looking at him.

31. Prego, *Palabras,* 74–75.

32. Diana's moment of revelation in "Fin de etapa" (*Deshoras*) also begins, more loosely, at noon.

33. Harss, *Los nuestros,* 266; González Bermejo, *Conversaciones,* 64–65.

34. That comment brings to mind Borges's statement of a very similar kind in "El Aleph": "Now I come to the ineffable core of my tale" (*El Aleph* [Madrid: Alianza, 1971], 168). That story dates from the forties.

35. Picón-Garfield, *Cortázar,* 97.

36. González Bermejo, *Conversaciones,* 101. There is a long discussion of music in the González Bermejo interview (100–110).

Chapter 4: Break

1. Ernesto Sábato's short existentialist novel *El túnel* was published in 1948; in that same year, Cortázar published a review of Sartre's *La nausée,* which his future wife, Aurora Bernárdez, had translated.

2. *Obra crítica,* 1:103.

3. Ibid., 1:132–33.

4. Ibid., 2:17–23.

5. Ibid., 2:225.

6. Ibid., 2:240.

7. Ibid., 2:265–85.

8. Ibid., 2:268.

9. Ibid., 2:272.

10. Ibid., 2:278.

11. Another major essay of the early period is called "La urna griega en la poesía de John Keats" (The Grecian Urn in the Poetry of John Keats), first published in 1946 and reprinted in volume 2 of the *Obra crítica.* Keats's precise words are these: "If a Sparrow come before my window I take part in its existence and pick about the Gravel." Cortázar's long book on the English poet, *Imagen de John Keats,* was published posthumously. On the Englishman's influence on Cortázar see Hernández del Castillo, *Keats.*

12. *Obra crítica,* 2:278.

13. Ibid., 2:279–80.

14. In *Otras inquisiciones* (Buenos Aires: Emecé, 1960, 67) Borges speaks of the use of language as the "the unruly obligation of every writer."

15. *Obra crítica,* 2:281–82.

16. Ibid., 2:285.

17. Ibid., 2:365–85.

18. Ibid., 2:373.

19. Ibid., 2:374.

20. Ibid., 2:375.

21. Ibid., 2:381.

22. Ibid., 2:385. Essentially, these are the views expressed in the Paris debate and in *Literatura en la revolución y revolución en la literatura.* Cortázar's "Situación del intelectual latinoamericano" (the open letter to Roberto Fernández Retamar, dated 1967) and "Realidad y literatura" (1981) make for an interesting comparison. Both are reproduced in volume 3 of *Obra crítica.*

23. Cortázar is unsure about the origin of this quotation, and so am I. I suspect that it may be quoted by R. D. Laing.

24. The time of composition (mid-sixties) is significant: Cortázar was in the thick of controversy.

25. González Bermejo, *Conversaciones,* 29.

26. Prego, *Palabras,* 61.

27. Perdomo, Preface to *Lector activo.*

Chapter 5: Winning on Points

1. See the comments of Antonio Pagés Larraya in the Buenos Aires periodical *Ficción,* September–December, 1961. A full account of social types and their portrayal through varieties of language is offered by Gladys Oñega, *Los premios.*

2. Benedetti, "Sobre Julio Cortázar," 14.

3. Cortázar relates that while revising the proofs of a translation of this novel he reread the Persio passages in order and by themselves, realizing in the process that they could be viewed as a separate and coherent entity in their own right. See González Bermejo, *Conversaciones,* 91.

4. For more allusions see Sverdloff, "Mitología."

5. Picón-Garfield, *Cortázar,* 17. Mario Goloboff, in his biography published in 1998, 17, notes that when Cortázar was a timid schoolchild in Banfield, one of his champions was a fellow pupil called Atilio Presuti [*sic*], who became a truck driver in adult life.

6. González Bermejo, *Conversaciones,* 92.

7. Andrés Amorós in the edition published by Cátedra, Madrid, 1984, 16.

8. González Bermejo, *Conversaciones,* 69.

9. The *Cuaderno* is also appended to the most complete and authoritative edition of *Rayuela,* edited by Julio Ortega and published in the Colección Archivos, in several countries, in 1991.

10. Some of Oliveira's comments in chapter 90 of *Rayuela* are relevant too.

11. Picón-Garfield, *Cortázar,* 117.

12. Interestingly, in *Los autonautas de la cosmopista,* one of the last books to come from Cortázar's pen, his wife Carol Dunlop contributes a section headed "Extractos del manual de los lobos" (Extracts from the manual on wolves). "El lobo" (The Wolf) was her affectionate way of referring to Julio. Among the entries to the manual there is one that reads, "Should it be necessary, accuse him gently of being *machista,* and gradually he'll stop being it."

13. Schneider, "Cortázar," 24.

14. See, for example, Picón-Garfield, 1975, chapter 2. On pages 91–93 of his biography of Cortázar, Mario Goloboff says that Maga is in fact based on a woman whom Cortázar knew in real life. During the long boat crossing for his very first visit to Europe in 1950, Cortázar had crossed paths with a younger Jewish emigrée whose family had escaped Nazi Germany and settled in Argentina. She and Cortázar later met again, quite by chance, in a Paris cinema queue, enjoyed each other's company, but made no attempt to set up a further meeting, as if to leave it in the hands of fate. Fate duly obliged by providing another such chance encounter, whereupon they became closer; their friendship was to survive until his death. (Some years after Cortázar's death a cultural journal began publication under the title *La Maga,* one of its issues being in homage to Cortázar on the tenth anniversary of his death [see bibliography]. The journal ceased publication in 1998.)

15. Harss, *Los nuestros,* 219–20, 229–30.

16. Picón-Garfield, *Cortázar,* 117.

17. Ibid., 115.

18. *The Complete Works of Lewis Carroll* (New York: Random House, 1937) 155.

19. García Canclini, *Antropología,* 19.

20. Sara Castro-Klarén, "Ontological Fabulation," in Alazraki and Ivask, *Final Island,* 140–50.

21. González Bermejo, *Conversaciones,* 13.

22. Prego, *Palabras,* 93.

23. González Bermejo, *Conversaciones,* 93–94.

24. Prego, *Palabras,* 94–95.

25. Picón-Garfield, *Cortázar,* 109.

26. Lucille Kerr, "Betwixt Reading and Repetition (apropos of Cortázar's *62:A Model Kit),*" in Alonso, *Julio Cortázar: New Readings,* 102, 103.

27. Interestingly, the portrait, by Tilly Kettle, still hangs in the Courtauld Institute in London; the flower is clearly identifiable and the subject of comment in the note beside the picture.

28. Octavio Paz and Julián Ríos. Cortázar says in an interview with Alain Sicard that "it's true that it's a very, very pessimistic novel, and I'm not a pessimist by nature . . . at the time I wrote it I was going through a stage in my life where one sad thing followed another . . . it's a novel one finishes with a great sense of sadness and frustration because the destinies are not fulfilled." See the special issue of *Drailles,* 14–15. The interview took place in 1979.

29. Prego, *Palabras,* 97.

30. Incledon, "Clave," 265, has unearthed a possible link between Polidor, the son of Katmos, and the latter's grandson, Acteon.

Chapter 6: The Brawl Outside

1. *La Nación,* 2 July 1995, 6.

2. González Bermejo, *Conversaciones,* 12.

3. Prego, *Palabras,* 127–28.

4. Here it is appropriate to recall the religious dimension in "El perseguidor," which was discussed in chapter 4.

5. Aníbal González, in "Revolución y alegoría en 'Reunión' de Julio Cortázar" (included in Burgos, *Los ochenta mundos*), has argued that the author is also playing with the numbers three and four, with possible religious and mystical intent. If so—though González does not suggest this—then perhaps Cortázar is taking another leaf out of Borges, specifically from "La muerte y la brújula."

6. Within the fiction of the Boom period, *62: A Model Kit* has a place that is comparable to the one occupied by José Donoso's *El obsceno pájaro de la noche* (*The Obscene Bird of Night*); by this I mean that it is fiction in its most "pure" form, construct as meaning. After these novels, from the late sixties on, Spanish American fiction veers away from such rarefied climes in the direction of things that are simpler, more linear, and more popular. The beginnings of this process of change can be readily seen in the novels

of younger writers such as Manuel Puig (in his *Boquitas pintadas* [*Heartbreak Tango*], for example) and in certain works by others who were already well known, such as Vargas Llosa's *La tía Julia y el escribidor* (1977; *Aunt Julia and the Scriptwriter*).

7. The relevant passage of the letter appears on page 55 of Hernández's "Cortázar: El libro de Andrés + Lonstein = Manuel." The Andrés Fava of *El examen* is discussed in chapter 9 of the present book.

8. For more on Lonstein, and on the general question of the relationship between play and the erotic, see Jonathan Tittler's "A Manual for Manuel: Homo Lewdens" in his *Narrative Irony.*

9. Thanatophobia is a marked characteristic of the Andrés of *El examen.*

10. Picón-Garfield, *Cortázar,* 69–70.

11. Margery Safir, "An Erotics of Liberation," in Alazraki and Ivarsk, *Final Island,* 84–95.

12. Picón-Garfield, *Cortázar,* 72–73, 102–3.

13. Also worth mentioning is the comparability of the sodomy episode with the notorious closing scene of Bertolucci's film *Last Tango in Paris,* which was released a year later. Despite the fact that Bertolucci's title seems to suggest some connection with the Argentine writer working in Paris, there was apparently no collusion between the two men, who did not know each other.

14. Cortázar told Picón-Garfield, *Cortázar,* 29–30, that he did not know who the dead man was. He had written the closing pages in a trance-like state, a common experience for him when nearing the end of a work. He also said that some time after having written it he had reread the final page and thought that he had noticed some similarities with a widely publicized photograph of Che Guevara's dead body. Any such similarity was, however, quite unconsciously introduced; to have done so deliberately would have been "cheap."

15. Boldy, *Novels,* 161.

16. The full text of the telex to Cortázar is quoted by Goloboff, *Biografía,* 230–31.

17. González Bermejo, *Conversaciones,* 125.

18. Reported in *Crisis* (Buenos Aires), no. 41 (1986): 41.

19. Prego, *Palabras,* 138–39.

20. Ibid., 138.

21. *Magazine Littéraire,* special issue nos. 151–52, (September 1979): 9.

22. In the Maeght catalog for Barcelona the story is reproduced from typewriter script on coarse paper (a very fitting medium, given the style of the painter). It also appears typeset in a Catalan translation by the poet Pere Gimferrer, on the back of a large, folded reproduction of *Et Amicorum,* one of Tàpies's most famous works. (Edicions 62, n.d.). In the corresponding Paris catalog (Maeght, 1978) the text appears in a French translation by Laure Bataillon, who translated many of Cortázar's works; it is interleaved with several reproductions, *Et Amicorum* among them. In its various printings the spelling of the story's title has varied (sometimes "Graffiti," sometimes "Grafitti").

23. In this connection see Peter Standish, "Magus, Masque and the Machinations of Authority: Cortázar at Play," in Peavler and Standish, *Structures,* 1996.

24. Significantly, this book was published in Venezuela. No page references are given here, since there are no page numbers.

25. There was also a brief reference to Mafalda (and to Charlie Brown) in *Fantomas* (14).

26. Prego, *Palabras,* 134.

Chapter 7: The Final Round (and Much More)

1. Coleoptera is the order of insects that comprises beetles. Chitin is a substance that contributes to the rigidity of their exoskeletons, their "shells." Cortázar also invokes the image of the coleopteran in other works, for example in the story "Las Ménades."

2. Cortázar's voluminous (and of course subjective) account of Keats was published posthumously as *Imagen de John Keats* (1996).

3. The work of Zötl (1831–1887) attracted little attention in his own time, but it was praised by André Breton. Zötl's meticulous images are sometimes reminiscent of those of Henri Rousseau.

4. Karine Berriot, *Enchanteur,* 205–6, quoting a letter from Cortázar to Tomasello, shows that here again Cortázar was writing in *response* to art (that is, the art was not produced to accompany his preexisting text). The letter also provides further evidence of how Cortázar would contemplate artworks for a long time until a text took on life: "I looked and looked at your compositions for ages . . . and when I sensed the rhythm and saw that it went from *one* to *two,* and from two to three, and that from then on three was in play and that three was kept up, the text gave birth to itself, and the delivery was absolutely painless." Also of interest is the fact that Cortázar talks about his awareness of how the layout of the text might convey meaning: he says that he sees the text as a series of blocks (in the finished product, each little block in fact has a page of its own) and draws attention to the fact that he has used only capital letters, omitted accents, and used spaces instead of punctuation marks. For example, the line "NAQUIT LA SUEUR   NAQUIT LA MORT" is proposed. (Once again, a two-and-three pattern is achieved.) It is worth remembering the symbolic value of three as a rejection of the binary system. Also, note the following sentence from *62: Modelo para armar:* "Éramos tres, cifra galvánica por excelencia" (240; We were three, the galvanizing number par excellence).

5. The end of 1998 saw the première in Nancy (France) of *Un Tango pour Monsieur Lautrec,* an opera by Jorge Zulueta with libretto by Jacobo Muñoz, based on the initial idea of Cortázar's text in *Monsieur Lautrec.* Each act was presided over by a reproduction of the painting in question, and the drama dealt with the relationship between painter and prostitute in France and the latter's life once an Argentine cattle rancher had bought her and taken her to Buenos Aires. The Argentine author Alicia Dujovne Ortiz wrote a novel, *Mireya,* that was inspired by Cortázar's idea and also published in 1998.

6. Cinamomo is a variety of tree from which rosary beads are made.

7. Royalties for *Los autonautas* were donated to the Sandinista movement in Nicaragua.

8. References are to the only edition of *Pameos y meopas,* published by Ocnos (Editorial Llibres de Sinera), Barcelona, 1971.

Chapter 8: Down, but Not Out

1. Bottone, "Testimonio," 86.

2. The Plaza de Mayo, of course, was to acquire a special notoriety two decades later as the place where the mothers of the "disappeared" made their protests.

3. See Hernández del Castillo, *Keats, Poe, and the Shaping of Cortázar's Mythopoesis,* 61. Hernández del Castillo compares Cortázar's novel to Poe's "Narrative of Arthur Gordon Pym."

4. See O'Connor, "Melancolía."

5. Valenzuela, "La geometría del sueño," in Burgos, *Los ochenta mundos de Julio Cortázar,* 26.

6. See Ana María Barrenechea. Barrenechea also says that *El examen* was entered for the Losada Prize and was not even granted a mention. Cortázar said in interview that its language was thought too bad to allow its publication.

7. Yurkievich, *Mundos,* 90–91.

8. Picón-Garfield, *Cortázar,* 17.

9. Caliban had already been made important in Latin American cultural history by José Enrique Rodó, who in 1900 published his *Ariel,* a book in which Caliban is a symbol of functional materialism, as opposed to spiritual and aesthetic values. Much later, the idea was further exploited by the Cuban writer Roberto Fernández Retamar.

10. García Martín, "Prehistoria," 154–55.

11. On page 123 there is an aside in which "Insecto" refers to his unpublished novel *Soliloquio.* This was in fact the title of the very early novel that Cortázar destroyed.

12. The picture includes a background image of a cloud that is etched out like an eye. This obvious evocation of the most notorious image in Buñuel's "Un Chien andalou" speaks of the important role that surrealism plays in this novel. Given its apparent lack of coherence, it may be relevant to bear in mind Buñuel's statement that the only criterion determining the making of his film had been that none of its sequences should have any rational relationship with any other.

13. The Alfaguara editions of Cortázar's works are usually reliable. Unfortunately, in this one of *Adiós, Róbinson, y otras piezas breves* there is a trying number of misprints. Some doubt regarding the date of composition of *Tiempo de barrilete* arises from the fact that in different places it is stated that it was finished in 1950 and 1960. I assume that 1950 is the correct date, based on a reference by Cortázar, on pages 319–20 of *Salvo el crepúsculo,* to his return on that boat from the 1949 visit to Europe.

14. It is reproduced in the issue of *El Cronista* dated 25 March 1994 and in the article by Jorgelina Loubet, "Negro el diez."

15. *Cuaderno de Zihuantanejo: El libro, los sueños* is another, very minor, posthumous publication (1997). The text appears to date from August of 1980 and consists of a

notebook chronicling some of the author's dreams and thoughts during a short period he spent in Zihuantanejo, Mexico.

A Postlude

1. There is an account of the international reaction to the news of Cortázar's death in an article by Joaquín Roy, "El impacto de la muerte de Julio Cortázar en la prensa argentina y española," in the special issue of *Inti* (1986): 22–23.

2. *Casa de las Américas* (1984): 25, 145–46. It was also published in *El País*.

3. Ruffinelli, *Término,* 257–58.

4. Ortiz, *Estética.*

Bibliography

Works by Julio Cortázar, by date of publication

Los reyes. Buenos Aires: Gulab y Aldabahor, 1949.

Bestiario. Buenos Aires: Sudamericana, 1951.

Final del juego. Buenos Aires: Sudamericana, 1956. An expanded edition appeared in 1964.

Las armas secretas. Buenos Aires: Sudamericana, 1959.

Los premios. Buenos Aires: Sudamericana, 1960.

Historias de cronopios y famas. Buenos Aires: Minotauro, 1962.

Rayuela. Buenos Aires: Sudamericana, 1963.

Todos los fuegos el fuego. Buenos Aires: Sudamericana, 1966.

Les Discours du Pince-Gueule. Paris: Michel Cassé, 1966. Text in French, with lithographs by Julio Silva.

La vuelta al día en ochenta mundos. 2 vols. Mexico, DF: Siglo Veintiuno, 1967.

Buenos Aires, Buenos Aires. Buenos Aires: Sudamericana, 1968. Text accompanies photos by Alicia d'Amico and Sara Facio.

62: modelo para armar. Buenos Aires: Sudamericana, 1968.

Último round. Mexico, DF: Siglo Veintiuno, 1969.

Viaje alrededor de una mesa. Buenos Aires: Rayuela, 1970.

Pameos y meopas. Barcelona: Ocnos, 1971.

Il bestiario di Aloys Zötl. Parma: Franco Maria Ricci, 1972. Text, in Italian, accompanies Zötl's illustrations.

Prosa del observatorio. Barcelona: Lumen, 1972.

Libro de Manuel. Buenos Aires: Sudamericana, 1973.

Octaedro. Madrid: Alianza, 1974.

Vampiros multinacionales: Una utopía realizable. Mexico, DF: Excelsior, 1975.

Silvalandia. Mexico, DF: Ediciones Culturales, 1975. Illustrated by Julio Silva.

Humanario. Buenos Aires: La Azotea, 1976. Text to accompany photos by Alicia d'Amico and Sara Facio.

Alguien que anda por ahí. Madrid: Alfaguara, 1977.

Territorios. Mexico, DF: Siglo Veintiuno, 1978.

Un tal Lucas. Madrid: Alfaguara, 1979.

Un elogio del tres. Zurich: Sybil Albers, 1980. With illustrations by Luis Tomasello.

Queremos tanto a Glenda. Madrid: Alfaguara, 1980.

Monsieur Lautrec. Madrid: Ameris, 1980. With illustrations by Hermenegildo Sabat.

La raíz del ombú. Caracas: Ediciones Amón, 1981. With illustrations by Alberto Cedrón.

Deshoras. Madrid: Alfaguara, 1982.

Cuaderno de bitácora de "Rayuela." Buenos Aires: Sudamericana, 1983. With Ana María Barrenechea.

Los autonautas de la cosmopista. Barcelona: Muchnik, 1983.

Nicaragua tan violentamente dulce. Managua, Nicaragua: Nueva Nicaragua/Monimbo, 1983.

Nada a Pehuajó; Adiós, Róbinson. Mexico, DF: Katún, 1984.

Argentina: Años de alambradas culturales. Barcelona: Muchnik, 1984.

Alto el Perú. Mexico, DF: Nueva Imagen, 1984. With photos by Manja Offerhaus.

Imagen de John Keats. Madrid: Alfaguara, 1984.

Salvo el crepúsculo. Madrid: Alfaguara, 1984.

París, ritmos de una ciudad. Barcelona: EDHASA, 1984. Text to accompany photographs by Alecio de Andrade.

Divertimento. Madrid: Alfaguara, 1986.

El examen. Madrid: Alfaguara, 1986.

Cuentos completos. 2 vols. Madrid: Alfaguara, 1994. The following collections of short fiction are gathered in the two tomes of *Cuentos completos:* Volume 1: *Bestiario* (1951), *Final del juego* (1956, amplified edition 1964), *Las armas secretas* (1959), *Historias de cronopios y famas* (1962), *Todos los fuegos el fuego* (1966). Volume 2: *Octaedro* (1974), *Alguien que anda por ahí* (1977), *Un tal Lucas* (1979), *Queremos tanto a Glenda* (1980), *Deshoras* (1982).

Obra crítica. Vol. 1. Edited by Saúl Yorkievich, Vol. 2. Edited by Jaime Alazraki, Vol. 3. Edited by Saúl Sosnowski. Madrid: Alfaguara, 1994. The three volumes of the *Obra crítica* contain, respectively: *Teoría del túnel* (a single long essay on the novel, dating from 1947); other, mostly literary, essays written prior to the time of *Rayuela;* and those written thereafter (largely concerned with matters of politics).

Negro el diez. Facsimile edition of 150 copies under supervision of Aurora Bernárdez. [Paris?]: Clot, Bramsen et Georges, 1994. First printed at the time of the author's death in a private edition of 60 copies with illustrations by Luis Tomasello.

Diario de Andrés Fava. Madrid: Alfaguara, 1995.

Adiós, Robinson, y otras piezas breves. Madrid: Alfaguara, 1995.

Cuaderno de Zihuantanejo. Madrid: Santillana, 1997.

Cortázar also wrote the lyrics for a record of tangos (*Les Trottoirs de Buenos Aires*); the music was written by Edgardo Cantón; the performer was Juan Cedrón.

Tristán Bauer's film *Cortázar,* made a decade after the author's death, is a dramatized documentary that successfully combines biographical elements with extracts of interviews and feature programs recorded during Cortázar's lifetime.

There have been a number of stage productions based on Cortázar's works: On *Monsieur Lautrec* (Nancy, France, 1998); on *Rayuela* (Buenos Aires, 1994); on the story "No se culpe a nadie"; and on Cortázar in general (a one man show by José Luis Pellicena, directed by Emilio Hernández, Madrid, 1996).

Works by Julio Cortázar translated into English

Blowup and Other Stories. Trans. Paul Blackburn. New York: Pantheon, 1963. Selected stories from *Bestiario, Final del juego,* and *Las armas secretas.*

The End of the Game and Other Stories. Trans. Paul Blackburn. New York: Pantheon, 1963. Selected stories from *Bestiario, Final del juego,* and *Las armas secretas.*

The Winners. Trans. Elaine Kerrigan. New York: Pantheon, 1965.

Hopscotch. Trans. Gregory Rabassa. New York: Pantheon, 1966.

Cronopios and Famas. Trans. Paul Blackburn. New York: Pantheon, 1969.

62: A Model Kit. Trans. Gregory Rabassa. New York: Avon, 1972.

All the Fires the Fire and Other Stories. Trans. Suzanne Jill Levine. New York: Pantheon, 1973.

A Manual for Manuel. Trans. Gregory Rabassa. New York: Pantheon, 1978.

A Change of Light and Other Stories. Trans. Gregory Rabassa. New York: Knopf, 1980. Selected stories from *Octaedro* and *Alguien que anda por ahí.*

We Love Glenda So Much. Trans. Gregory Rabassa. New York: Knopf, 1983.

A Certain Lucas. Trans. Gregory Rabassa. New York: Knopf, 1984.

Around the Day in Eighty Worlds. Trans. Thomas Christensen. San Francisco: North Point, 1986. Selections from *La vuelta al día en ochenta mundos* and from *Último round.*

Unreasonable Hours. Trans. Alberto Manguel. Toronto: Coach House Press, 1995.

Works Cited

A fondo: Julio Cortázar. Madrid: RTVE, 1977. A two-hour videotaped television interview conducted by Joaquín Soler Serrano. Much of it is interesting, and it gives a good idea of Cortázar's personality.

Alazraki, Jaime, and Ivar Ivask. *The Final Island.* Norman: University of Oklahoma Press, 1976. Cortázar was honored at a small conference of specialists held at the University of Oklahoma, and this is a compilation of proceedings, containing some valuable essays, some less so.

Alonso, Carlos J., ed. *Julio Cortázar: New Readings.* Cambridge: Cambridge University Press, 1998. A quite varied collection of essays, some of which are insightful.

Aronne Amestoy, Lida. *Cortázar: La novela mandala.* Buenos Aires: Fernando García Cambeiro, 1972.

Barrenechea, Ana María. "Con Julio Cortázar: Diálogo a través del espejo." *Co-Textes* 11 (April 1986): 81–90. A special issue devoted to Cortázar.

Benedetti, Mario. "Sobre Julio Cortázar." *Cuadernos de la Revista Casa de las Américas* (Havana) 3 (1967).

Bernárdez, Aurora. "Los inéditos de Julio Cortázar." *La Nación,* 2 July 1995, 6.

Berriot, Karine. *Julio Cortázar: L'Enchanteur.* Paris: Presses de la Renaissance, 1988. Berriot herself calls this a halfway house between criticism and biography. She was a friend of Cortázar and also translated some of his work into French.

Bocaz, Luis. "*Los reyes* y la irresponsabilidad ante lo real." *Atenea* 45, 166 (1968): 47–53.

Boldy, Steven. *The Novels of Julio Cortázar.* Cambridge: Cambridge University Press, 1980. The best study of the four novels that were published during Cortázar's lifetime.

Bottone, Mireya. "Cortázar en el testimonio." *Boletín de Letras Hispánicas* 6 (1966).

Burgos, Fernando, ed. *Los ochenta mundos de Cortázar: Ensayos.* Madrid: EDI-6, 1987. Selected proceedings of a conference that took place at Oklahoma State University in 1986. Contains some useful essays.

Casal, Lourdes. *El caso Padilla: Literatura y revolución en Cuba.* Miami: Universal, 1971.

Castro-Klarén, Sara. "Julio Cortázar, lector: Conversación con Julio Cortázar." *Cuadernos Hispanoamericanos* (Madrid), nos. 364–366 (1980): 11–36.

Cócaro, Nicolás, Cecilia Noriega, and Pío Clementi. *El joven Cortázar.* Buenos Aires: Ediciones del Saber, 1993.

Collazos, Oscar. *Literatura en la revolución y revolución en la literatura.* Mexico, DF: Siglo Veintiuno, 1970. Based on debates concerning the role of Latin American intellectuals. A significant volume for studies of Latin American literature in general.

Coloquio internacional: Lo lúdico y lo fantástico en la obra de Cortázar. 2 vols. Madrid: Fundamentos, 1986. A wide-ranging collection of essays from a conference held at the Université de Poitiers. Useful for its coverage of unusual texts.

Curutchet, Juan Carlos. *Julio Cortázar, o la crítica de la razón pragmática.* Madrid: Editora Nacional, 1972. One of the initial flurry of critical studies on Cortázar. Often perceptive but sometimes too single-minded.

Drailles 9 (1988). Special issue of a journal published in France. Contains some new material, some reprinted.

Dujovne Ortiz, Alicia. *Mireya.* Buenos Aires: Alfaguara, 1998.

Espejo de escritores. Hanover, N.H.: Ediciones del Norte, 1983. Videotaped interview by Saúl Sosnowski, recorded toward the end of the author's life.

Explicación de textos literarios 17, nos. 1–2 (1988–1989). Includes a major bibliography.

Fuentes, Carlos. "Documentos: El caso Padilla." *Libre* 1 (1971): 119–30.

García Canclini, Néstor. *Julio Cortázar: Una antropología poética.* Buenos Aires: Nova, 1968. One of the most interesting of the early books about Cortázar, though it is difficult to find one's way around.

García Márquez, Gabriel. "El argentino que se hizo querer de todos." *Casa de las Américas* 25 (1984): 145–46. In a special issue of the journal, following Cortázar's death.

García Martín, Luis. "*El examen:* La prehistoria de Julio Cortázar." *Cuadernos Hispanoamericanos,* no. 444 (June 1987): 154–55.

Goloboff, Mario. *Julio Cortázar: La biografía.* Buenos Aires: Seix Barral, 1998. The immodest title implies that this is the definitive biography. In fact, it was not entirely well received in Argentina. Goloboff, like Berriot, knew Cortázar. His book is more truly biographical than hers, though it lacks some documentation of interview material. Much of the information in it is available from other sources, but it remains useful.

González Bermejo, Ernesto. *Conversaciones con Cortázar.* Barcelona: EDHASA, 1978. One of three books based on interviews with Cortázar, and very interesting. A reprint, including new prologues and some late photos, was published in 1986, but it does not contain new interview material (Buenos Aires: Contrapunto).

Guevara, Ernesto. *Reminiscences of the Cuban Revolutionary War.* New York: Monthly Review Press, 1968.

Guibert, Rita. "Un escritor y su soledad." *Life en español* 33, 7 (April 1969): 43–55.

Harss, Luis, and Barbara Dohmann. *Into the Mainstream.* New York: Harper and Row, 1966. This book is based on interviews with several prominent or upcoming writers of the sixties, and a chapter is devoted to Cortázar. It is freer and less academic in tone than most. A slightly different Spanish version appears under Harss's name alone as *Los nuestros,* Buenos Aires: Sudamericana, 1967.

Hernández, Ana María. "El libro de Andrés + Lonstein = Manuel," *Nueva Narrativa Hispanoamericana* 5, 1975: 1–2, 35–56.

Hernández del Castillo, Ana María. *Keats, Poe, and the Shaping of Cortázar's Mythopoesis.* Amsterdam: Benjamins, 1981. Dense and provocative at times. An important account of the author's formative influences.

Incledon, John. "Una clave de Cortázar sobre *62: Modelo para armar.*" *Revista Iberoamericana* 41, 90 (1975).

Inti (1986): 22–23. Special issue of a journal devoted to proceedings of a conference held in Germany.

Loubet, Jorgelina. "'Negro el diez,' poema inédito de Julio Cortázar." *Boletín de la Academia Argentina de Letras* 59 (1994): 82–92.

La Maga 5 (1994). Special commemorative issue of an Argentine magazine, published to mark the tenth anniversary of Cortázar's death. Contains literary extracts, biographical information, critical comments, and personal testimonies by fellow writers.

Mundo Lo, Sara de. *Julio Cortázar, His Work and His Critics: A Bibliography.* Urbana, IL: Albatross, 1985. The fullest bibliography, though it covers publications only up to Cortázar's death.

O'Connor, Patrick J. "'Melancolía porteña' and Survivor's Guilt: A Benjaminian Reading of Cortázar's *El examen.*" *Latin American Literary Review,* 23, no. 46 (1995): 5–32.

Oñega, Gladys. "*Los premios.*" *Boletín de Literaturas Hispánicas* 6 (1966): 29–41.

La Opinión. Issues of 26 November and 8 December 1974. Controversy over *Libro de Manuel.*

Ortiz, Carmen. *Julio Cortázar: Una estética de la búsqueda.* Buenos Aires: Almagesto, 1994.

Paz, Octavio, and Julián Ríos. "Modelos para a(r)mar." *El Urogallo* 3, 15 (1972).

Peavler, Terry J., and Peter Standish. *Structures of Power.* Albany: State University of New York Press, 1996.

Perdomo, María Teresa. *El lector activo y la comunicación en Rayuela.* Morelia, Mexico: Universidad Michoacana, 1980.

Peri Rossi, Cristina. *La tarde del dinosaurio.* Barcelona: Plaza y Janés, 1984.

Perrone, Alberto. "Un profesor en Chivilcoy." *La Opinión Cultural* (Buenos Aires), 18 April 1976.

Picón-Garfield, Evelyn. *¿Es Julio Cortázar un surrealista?* Madrid: Gredos, 1975.

213

————. *Cortázar por Cortázar.* Jalapa, Mexico: Universidad Veracruzana, 1977. Based on early interviews with Cortázar. Often useful, though not well signposted and occasionally rather personal in style.

Poniatowska, Elena. "La vuelta a Julio Cortázar en (cerca de) ochenta preguntas." *Plural* (May 1975).

Prego, Omar. *La fascinación de las palabras.* Barcelona: Muchnik, 1985. The best of the three books based on interviews, the others being those of González Bermejo and Picón-Garfield. Prego's were conducted late in Cortázar's life and are therefore the most comprehensive.

Rama, Angel. "Julio Cortázar en la Universidad Central de Venezuela (Diálogo con los estudiantes de la UCV)." *Escritura* 1, no. 1 (January–June 1976).

Ruffinelli, Jorge. *Julio Cortázar: Al término del polvo y el sudor.* Montevideo, Uruguay: Biblioteca de Marcha, 1987.

Schneider, Luis Mario. "Julio Cortázar." *Revista de la Universidad de México* 17, 9 (1963: 24–25.

Sverdloff, Brent. "La mitología clásica en *Los premios* de Julio Cortázar." *Romance Linguistics and Literature Review* 3 (1989): 64–75.

Taylor, Martin C. "*Los reyes* de Julio Cortázar: El Minotauro redimido." *Revista Iberoamericana* 39 (1973).

Tittler, Jonathan. *Narrative Irony in the Contemporary Spanish-American Novel.* Ithaca, N.Y.: Cornell University Press, 1984.

Yurkievich, Saúl. *Julio Cortázar: Mundos y modos.* Madrid: Anaya/Muchnik, 1994.

Index